Jean-Luc Godard is one of the two or three most significant
filmmakers of the contemporary era. An extraordinarily
inventive and challenging filmmaker, his series of movies in
the 1960s remain some of the richest works in the history of
cinema.

There's no one else quite like Godard. Where the flood of
movies globally now runs into many thousands, Godard's
works stand out as original, acerbic, romantic, ironic,
humorous and explorative.
This book includes chapters on all of Godard's output.

•

'Everyone is searching. Everyone is in between'.

Jean-Luc Godard

MEDIA, FEMINISM, CULTURAL STUDIES

THE POLITICAL FILMS OF JEAN-LUC GODARD

POCKET MOVIE GUIDE

THE POLITICAL FILMS OF JEAN-LUC GODARD 1968-1973

POCKET MOVIE GUIDE

Jeremy Mark Robinson

CRESCENT MOON

First published 2025. © Jeremy Mark Robinson 2025.

Set in Helvetica Neue Condensed, 9 on 14pt.
Designed by Radiance Graphics.

The right of Jeremy Mark Robinson to be identified as the author of this book has been asserted generally in accordance with sections 77 and 78 of the Copyright, Designs and Patents Act 1988.

British Library Cataloguing in Publication data available for this title.

ISBN-13 9781861712431 (PBK)

Crescent Moon Publishing
P.O. Box 1312
Maidstone, Kent
ME14 5XU, Great Britain
www.crmoon.com

CONTENTS

ACKNOWLEDGEMENTS

Thanks to Colin MacCabe, Chris Fassnidge and Danny Rivers.

To the authors and publishers quoted.
To the copyright holders of the illustrations.
New Yorker Films. Jerry Ohlinger Archives. Cinema Parallel. La Bibliothéque du Film. Argos Films.

Every effort has been made to contact copyright owners of the illustrations. No copyright infringement is intended. We welcome enquiries about any copyright issues for future editions of this book.

ABBREVIATIONS

G   *Godard On Godard*, ed. T. Milne, 1986

M   *Godard, Images, Sound, Politics,* C. MacCabe,
          1980

Mac   *Godard*, C. MacCabe, 2003

B   *Everything Is Cinema,* R. Brody, 2008

'This life is either nothing, or it has to be everything'.

Jean-Luc Godard

PART ONE

JEAN-LUC GODARD

Cette obscure clarté qui tombe des étoiles.
(This dark brightness that falls from the stars.)

Pierre Corneille, *Le Cid*

1

INTRODUCTION

GODARD CINEMA /
GODARD CINÉMA

Everything can be put into a film. Everything should be put into a film.

Jean-Luc Godard (G, 239)

An original, a one-off, a genius – there's no one else quite like Jean-Luc Godard. You could take a few frames from one of his films and know they were by the Maître and nobody else. Where the flood of movies globally now runs into many thousands, and most are interchangeable, or barely make any impression at all, Godard's works stand out as individual, acerbic, romantic, ironic, humorous and explorative.

Watching Jean-Luc Godard's films again after a gap can be astonishing. He remains one of the most inventive and challenging of filmmakers. His series of films in the 1960s (sixteen features!) are still some of the richest works in the history of cinema – a run of movies with few parallels.

I first saw Jean-Luc Godard's films, appropriately enough, at film school in the early 1980s, where our tutor Chris Fassnidge showed us 16mm prints of *Breathless, Weekend* (on April 8, 1983) and *Masculin/ Féminin* (June 1, 1983), among others. These films make an immediate impact as the work of one of the most distinctive voices in all of film.

Later, I went to double bills of God-Art's movies at the repertory cinemas in London. I remember seeing *Slow Motion* and *Prénom Carmen* in Bloomsbury with Sergio (a guy from São Paolo) and his girlfriend, Sarah Webb, a friend of my sister's (Sarah had much better French than me, having working in Switzerland as an *au pair*. I remember she laughed a lot more at Godard's films than the British audience in the cinema – there seemed to be more jokes and humour in the film than carried through to the subtitles, or to the po-faced London crowd). Godard 'seems so serious, but you always had great fun', recalled actress Anna Karina.

For me, Jean-Luc Godard is one of the two or three most significant filmmakers of the period 1960-2010. The others would be Ingmar Bergman and Akira Kurosawa. Go and look at Orson Welles, and *Citizen Kane* in particular, is advice sometimes handed out to film students. Similarly, you can tell people who want to know about contemporary cinema: just go and look at Godard's films. He does *everything*. And then some. Don't bother with whoever is touted as the latest trendy filmmaker (Quentin Tarantino, Luc Besson, Robert Rodriguez, Christopher Nolan, Kevin Smith, Steven Soderbergh, etc), just go to Godard. Godard has several movies in the top movie lists among critics: *Contempt, Vivre Sa Vie, Pierrot le Fou* and *Breathless.*

1 *Pierrot le Fou* is no. 43 in *Sight & Sound*'s 2012 poll of top movies among critics. *Pierrot le Fou* 'feels like the audacity of a new artistic vision', as David Thomson put it (2012, 380).

While for some film critics watching a Jean-Luc Godard film can be a painful experience – because it's a foreign (i.e., non-American, non-English) film, or because it's an art film (and a European art film), or because it's a *Godard* film (Godard has plenty of detractors) – for me it's hugely enjoyable. Watching a Godard film isn't like doing 'homework',[2] as taking on 'foreign' or subtitled films can be for many. Let's face it, given the choice between watching a big, loud action-adventure film like *Star Wars* or *James Bond* or a soft-centred romantic comedy like *You Got Mail* or *What Women Want,* and watching a Godard film, many audiences will go for Hollywood every time.

I don't agree: a Jean-Luc Godard film like *Pierrot le Fou* or *A Woman Is a Woman* or *Masculin/ Féminin* or *Hail Mary* is very enjoyable: there's constant invention, a lot of humour, and even if you don't 'get it' all, there are beautiful and amazing people like Anna Karina or Jean-Pierre Léaud or Myriem Roussel to watch.

The rapid pace, as Pauline Kael noted (in *Going Steady*), Jean-Luc Godard's restlessness, irritates some viewers (1971, 92), but it's another aspect that's very enjoyable (and helps his movies to stay fresh and not appear dated). By comparison, so many contemporary, Western movies are s-o-o-o-o *s-l-o-w.* I agree with Orson Welles:[3] do we need to see a shot which shows a character walking right to the end of the road? (no! – Some of us have got lives to lead!). This is one of the chief appeals of Hong Kong action cinema and Japanese *animé*: they are *very fast.*

Jean-Luc Godard assumes that his audience can follow his movies, can understand the cultural and historical references, and enjoys the Americanized, cartoony devices he

---

2 But Godard's work can seem demanding: Godard makes the audience part of the collaboration: 'Godard makes his audiences work, and demands their full attention and participation at all times,' pointed out Wheeler Dixon (51).
3 Welles was thinking of Michelangelo Antonioni.

employs (P. Kael, 92-93). But for the viewers who want a serious, European sensibility, that too can irritate.

So, watching a Godard-helmed movie, you might look for a story. No, there isn't really one. So then you might look for characters. Umm, not really – fragments of characterization, possibly. OK, so you search for themes. Yes – but presented in such a casual, jigsaw (or wilfully obscure) manner, you'll have to work to put the pieces together. *D'accord,* you could look for performances. Some, but disconnected with (and in) each other – you get 30 seconds of an interesting performance, but then 4m 15s of not much. So then you hunt out ideas, say, or philosophy, or other bits of cleverness (like quotations/ allusions/ *hommages*, etc).

No wonder, then, that some people, including 100s of highly respected critics, many celebrated filmmakers, and thousands of fans, find Godard's movies as director/ writer boring, stupid, patronizing, narrow-minded, pretentious, ugly, chauvinist, anti-semitic, obscure, and difficult. (Sometimes Godard's films don't make it easy for the viewer in other ways: the repeated cuts to a black screen, the repetition of takes, the captions, the brutal chopping up of music, the alarming use of sound, and so on).

Maybe Godard's films should include a summary of the plot like the crawl in *Star Wars*: a few short paragraphs to tell the punters the plot.

Certainly Jean-Luc Godard's films have polarized critics, and tended to create intense reactions, for and against. But there's no ignoring Godard: he's a giant. Among Godard's supporters among critics were Susan Sontag,[4] Richard Roud,

---

4 For Sontag, Godard was 'one of the great culture heroes of our time' (*Styles of Radical Will*, Farrar, Straus & Giroux, New York, 1966, 150).

Andrew Sarris, Pauline Kael,[5] Vincent Canby, Colin MacCabe, and David Sterritt. (More on Godard's cultural impact below).

Some of Jean-Luc Godard's films have been received badly by critics, and have had bad screenings. The screening of *Le Gai Savoir* in Berlin was 'disastrous', and the audience walked out; when *Un Film comme les autres* was shown at the Lincoln Center in Gotham more than 900 people left, leaving less than 100 to watch the second reel. (And Godard's films have been released out of sequence in the U.S.A., which hasn't helped.[6] It took a while for North[7] America to go Godardian: *Breathless* was shown in 1961, *Vivre Sa Vie* in 1963, but by 1965, the pictures *A Woman Is a Woman, Contempt, A Married Woman, Band of Outsiders* and *Alphaville* had not been released. *La Chinoise* was a hit, however, in the U.S.A.; it opened in Gotham on April 3, 1968).

J.-L. Godard's films are also difficult to market – not only do they not fit into a particular niche or genre (even when they are genre films, such as thrillers), they can't be summed up in a few words. They are anti-high concept. They have unusual stories, and subjects, and don't always feature recognizable stars.

I don't think *absolutely everything* Jean-Luc Godard has produced (or said) has been a work of genius. Watching Godard's output in the cold light of film criticism[8] reveals some failures: *Slow Motion*, for instance, which some critics greatly admire, is very flawed, *Detective* and *The Soldiers* are

5 Pauline Kael attributed the influence of her writings about Godard to being hired on the *New Yorker*, because they had attracted the attention of the editor, William Shawn. However, Kael didn't get *Slow Motion*, and was among some other American critics who found Godard's later work increasingly difficult.

6 According to Jonathan Rosenbaum, the films have been released in this sequence: 1, 4, 6, 3, 8, 2, 9, 7, 10, 11, 12, 5, 14, 13, 15, 17, 16 (1992).

7 Using the term *North* America, which I do all the time now, is Godardian – in *Éloge de L'Amour,* a character complains that 'America' has no name or history. Do you mean South America? Brazil? Canada? What is 'America'?

8 Which can be very, very cold!

patchy, the agit-prop late 1960s/ early 1970s films are very hard-going (and sometimes close to unwatchable), and *King Lear* can appear so bad you wish that Godard had never made it.

It's extraordinary (but not all that surprising) that God-Art, I mean Godard, doesn't rate himself very highly as an *auteur*.

> John Cassavetes, who was more or less my age – now he was a great director. I can't imagine myself as his equal in cinema. For me he represents a certain cinema that's way up above. (2000)

And Jean-Luc Godard told Andrew Sarris in 1994 that he didn't think he'd

> succeeded in making any really good films. There are moments, scenes, whole movements that sing. It has all added up to a cinema of sorts, even though I'm still learning my art. (1994)

Jean-Luc Godard was acutely aware of his own status as a filmmaker in the film community; he knew that he was worshipped by some people. Godard said that some folk, especially men,

> are too overwhelmed by the name... in any relationship with me they [the public] have too much respect and too much admiration, which is ruinous. You can't have a normal relationship, you're constantly being put in an elevated position. (M, 76)[9]

Jean-Luc Godard's films are so recognizable, so familiar, it can seem not only that they are part of your life, as familiar films are of course, but that you have participated in them in

---

9 Godard is being too modest again: this is someone who's made 45 major film and video pieces (15 of which are masterpieces), and who appears – and will appear – in any history of the first 100 years of cinema.

some way. Some critics have felt that they *could* have made this or that Godard film, so they *did* make the film. Godard's pictures do seem to enter the blood-stream, the unconscious, the dream life. Except, of course, that *very* few people could have made those films. There are only a handful of filmmakers on the planet at any one time who would be capable of such brilliance.

❂

Jean-Luc Godard has a truly astonishing output in film, TV, video, visual art, writing, and so on. Apart from the famous feature films, there are a large number of television and video projects. And many of those are hard to track down and obtain (part of the reason is that only a small percentage of films and TV from any particular country gets released or shown outside that territory). Also, some of the TV/ video works are poor quality copies of already low res video (much of it was made for broadcast on French television, and has never been broadcast outside of France).

In Britain, for instance, you just don't have Godard's films and TV and video output being broadcast regularly (actually, even the well-known features are shown only rarely. When was the last time you saw a Godard film on a major television network, not a niche cable/ satellite channel?). To consider Godard's TV work alone, or his video work alone, would require another book.

I reckon the number of people who have seen absolutely everything that Jean-Luc Godard had produced is very small – across the whole globe, and including la France. Filmmakers like Donald Cammell or Andrei Tarkovsky are much easier to take in. You can watch Tarkovsky's seven feature films, the two shorts and the documentary *A Time To Travel*, and that's the whole *œuvre*. But with Godard, as with other prolific filmmakers like Yasujiro Ozu and Ingmar Bergman, there's a huge amount of material to consider. Godard simply never stops. As his biographer put it, 'one of the remarkable features of Godard's career is that he never ever stops making films'.[10]

This book is a spin-off from my 2023 study of Godard. The focus is on the political films from 1968 to 1973, so *One Plus One* and *Tout Va Bien* are included (although almost all of Godard's output is highly political, so one could bring in many of the movies of the 1960s, for example, such as *Weekend* and *Pierrot le Fou*).

MOVIES AS DIRECTOR

The following is a select list of the main features and TV work of Jean-Luc Godard as film and TV director – ignoring short films, notes for films, segments in anthologies, documentaries and others:

> *Breathless* (1960), a.k.a. *À Bout de souffle*
> *The Little Soldier* (1960/ 63), a.k.a. *Le Petit Soldat*
> *A Woman Is a Woman* (1961), a.k.a. *Une femme est une femme*
> *My Life to Live* (1962), a.k.a. *Vivre sa Vie*
> *Contempt* (1963), a.k.a. *Le Mépris*
> *The Soldiers* (1963), a.k.a. *Les Carabiniers*
> *Band of Outsiders* (1964), a.k.a. *Bande à part*
> *A Married Woman* (1964), a.k.a. *Une femme mariée*
> *Crazy Pete* (1965), a.k.a. *Pierrot le Fou*
> *Alphaville: A Strange Adventure of Lemmy Caution* (1965), a.k.a. *Alphaville, une étrange aventure de Lemmy Caution*
> *Made in U.S.A.* (1966)
> *Masculine, Feminine* (1966), a.k.a. *Masculin féminin: 15 faits précis*
> *Two of Three Things I Know About Her* (1967), a.k.a. *2 ou 3 choses que je sais d'elle*
> *Weekend* (1967), a.k.a. *Le Week-end*
> *La Chinoise Or, More Actually, After the Fashion of the Chinese* (1967), a.k.a. *La Chinoise, ou Plutôt à la Chinoise*

10 Colin MacCabe, in Mac, 242.

One Plus One (1968), a.k.a. *Sympathy For the Devil*
A Film Like Any Other (1968), a.k.a. *Un film comme les
autres*
Joy of Learning (1969), a.k.a. *Le gai savoir*
The Wind From the East (1970), a.k.a. *Le vent d'est*
British Sounds (1970), a.k.a. *See You at Mao*
Pravda (1970)
Vladimir and Rosa (1970), a.k.a. *Vladimir et Rosa*
Struggle in Italy (1971), a.k.a. *Lotte in Italia*
All's Well (1972), a.k.a. *Tout va bien*
Number Two (1975), a.k.a. *Numéro deux*
Here and Elsewhere (1976), a.k.a. *Ici et ailleurs*
France/ Tour/ Detour/ Two Children (1977), a.k.a. *France/
tour/ detour/ deux enfants*
How's It Going? (1978), a.k.a. *Comment ça va?*
Scenario For Sauve Qui Peut La Vie (1980), a.k.a.
Scénario de 'Sauve qui peut la vie'
Slow Motion (1980), a.k.a. *Sauve qui peut (la vie)*
Passion (1982)
First Name: Carmen (1983), a.k.a. *Prénom Carmen*
Detective (1985), a.k.a. *Détective*
Hail Mary (1985), a.k.a. *Je vous salue, Marie*
Soft and Hard (1986), a.k.a. *A Soft Conversation Between
Two Friends On a Hard Subject*
Grandeur and Decadence (1986), a.k.a. *Grandeur et
décadence d'un petit commerce de cinéma* (part of
Série noire TV series)
Keep Your Right Up (1987), a.k.a. *Soigne ta droite*
King Lear (1987)
The Darty Report (1989), a.k.a. *Le rapport Darty*
New Wave (1990), a.k.a. *Nouvelle vague*
Germany Year 90 Nine Zero (1991), a.k.a. *Allemagne 90
neuf zéro*
Woe Is Me (1993), a.k.a. *Hélas pour moi*
The Children Plan Russian (1993), a.k.a. *Les enfants
jouent à la Russie*
Hail, Sarajevo (1993), a.k.a. *Je vous salue, Sarajevo*
JLG By JLG (1995), a.k.a. *JLG/ JLG – autoportrait de
décembre*
For Ever Mozart (1996)
Histor(ies) of Cinema (1998), *a.k.a. Histoire(s) du cinéma*
Origins of the 21st Century (2000), a.k.a. *De l'origine du
XXIe siècle*
In Praise of Love (2001), a.k.a. *Éloge de l'amour*
Liberty and Homeland (2002), a.k.a. *Liberté et patrie*
Chosen Moments of Histoire(s) of Cinema (2004), a.k.a.
Moments choisis des histoire(s) du cinéma
Our Music (2004), a.k.a. *Notre musique*

The True False Passport (2006), a.k.a. *Vrai faux passeport*
Socialism (2010), a.k.a. *Film socialisme*
Goodbye To Language (2014), a.k.a. *Adieu au Langage*
Bridges of Sarajevo (2014), a.k.a. *Les Ponts de Sarajevo*
The Image Book (2018), a.k.a. *Le Livre d'Image*

Even missing out many other pieces, this is a totally remarkable body of work.[11]

Maybe Colin MacCabe is right to say that if Jean-Luc Godard had embraced narrative, he might have been among the greatest filmmakers of narrative cinema. But I still think he is, although it's as a film essayist that Godard is the undisputed master (Mac, 322).[12] Godard has admitted that he just can't make normal films: 'I wish I could make a normal picture, normally, but with me, I don't know why, it's not possible' (ibid). Of course, we wouldn't have Godard make films any way other than however he wants to make them.

❂

It's tempting to get into the manifold ways in which Jean-Luc Godard has influenced contemporary cinema. As an editor, for instance, Godard has influenced Bernardo Bertolucci, Rainer Werner Fassbinder,[13] Pier Paolo Pasolini, Wim Wenders, Arthur Penn, Robert Altman, Oliver Stone, Martin Scorsese and Quentin Tarantino.[14] François Truffaut quoted Professor Chiarini: 'There is the cinema *pre*-Godard and *post*-Godard'. Certainly no filmmaker on Earth is Godard's equal as an editor (despite some strong competition – Tsui

11 About his high productivity, Godard said jokily that he was competing with Christian Jacques and Claude Chabrol.
12 'I cannot see how anyone can regard him now as other than one of the most important directors and the crucial visionary for an age in which film has yielded to video and worse', remarked David Thomson (1994).
13 Rainer Fassbinder said what he learnt from Godard 'was a way of reacting quickly to the cinema in terms of my own reality' (in D. Georgakas, 187).
14 D. Fairservice, 2001, 315. Brian De Palma said he was 'very much influenced by Godard's *Masculin/ Féminin*' when he made *Greetings* (1968). 'Godard's a terrific influence, of course', De Palma remarked (J. Gelmis, 61).

Hark, for example).

I think it's probably easiest to name some of the artists who've cited Jean-Luc Godard as an influence: Oliver Stone, Martin Scorsese, Bernardo Bertolucci, Rainer Werner Fassbinder, Donald Cammell, Pier Paolo Pasolini, Wim Wenders, Francis Coppola, Peter Greenaway, and Robert Altman.[15] All of the *cinéma du look* filmmakers (Luc Besson, Jean-Jacques Beineix and Léos Carax, who appeared in Godard's *King Lear*).[16] Godard also influenced later Ingmar Bergman and Luis Buñuel, Miklós Jancsó, Danièle Huillet, Richard Lester, Ken Russell, Derek Jarman, Jean-Marie Straub, and Latin American political filmmakers.[17]

Chinese filmmaker Wong Kar-Wai (*In the Mood For Love, Chungking Express, Ashes of Time*) is clearly influenced by Jean-Luc Godard. Wong's cinema has the freshness and self-confidence of early Godard: there's a sense of urgency, of energy, of shooting in real places with one or two actors, in urban centres which are full of life. Wong shares other aspects with Godard: the headlong, Eisensteinian montage; the kinetic, handheld camerawork; the impatience with traditional storytelling; the young characters; the use of genres (such as crime and *film noir*); and heterosexual romance. Parts of *Chungking Express* (1994), for instance, recall *Breathless, My Life To Live* and *Le Petit Soldat*: the young couple in the modern city. In the films of Wong and Godard there's a sense of contemporary culture, of the

15 David Thomson said that Godard taught him 'so many things', such as 'to be parsimonious with beauty', the importance of montage and collage, that cinema needs ethnologists (novelists, dancers, painters, even critics), not only filmmakers, and how the computer 'now poses such a threat to the validity of life itself' (1994).

16 Godard is one of Léos Carax's key influences. In *Mauvais Sang,* the Godardian influence can be seen in the depiction of young lovers, a favourite Godardian topic, especially in his early 1960s films (but also in later works, such as *Hail Mary*), and in the colour scheme of *Mauvais Sang* (red and grey/ black, which recalls Godard's use of red, blue and yellow in *Le Mépris*).

17 According to Robert Kolker, 1983, 191.

technological, urban environment, of street markets, bars, cafés, brothels, seedy hotels, and bohemian apartments, of life lived at a frenetic pace.

Alain Tanner and John Berger were big admirers of Godard, and they followed his work 'with great interest'. For Berger, Godard was 'the great film critic of our time', but he produced films instead of written works; 'he makes films which are criticism of film' (in D. Georgakas, 301).

Jean-Luc Godard's influence can be spotted in literally hundreds of places in global cinema, although many of the filmmakers who've been influenced by him reach a far bigger audience than Godard's own films. Godard's influence is all over pop music movies like *A Hard Day's Night*, *Help!*, *Performance*, *Catch Us If You Can*, *Easy Rider*, etc. *JFK* and *Natural Born Killers* are very Godardian films (director Oliver Stone is a huge fan), but how would audiences respond if, instead of *Natural Born Killers* or *The Doors*, *Weekend* or *Breathless* were shown in their local cinema? Truth is, when it comes to absorbing Godard's priceless lessons in making cinema, most of the well-known, post-Godardian practitioners have couched their Godardisms within conventional narratives, something that Godard himself has always refused to do.

Pier Paolo Pasolini remarked that Bernardo Bertolucci's 'real master is Godard' (1969, 138). Bertolucci is a passionate Godardian, but his films have been much more mainstream and conventional than Godard's. Bertolucci has used Godard in numerous ways, including obvious ones like the casting of Jean-Pierre Léaud in *Last Tango In Paris* as a New Wave director. For Bertolucci, Godard, like himself, has always made the same film.

> I am making always just one film. The filmmakers I love have made only one film. Godard started with *Breathless* and continued with the same film that proceeds along

with his life. It's one film... It's the same film and it walks along with him. To make film is a way of life. (J. Gelmis, 170-1)

Bertolucci was ever Godardian, despite his ambivalence towards Godard, especially Godard's political turn of the late 1960s (P. Kolker, 1985, 215).

So many filmmakers have tried to put some Jean-Luc Godard on the screen: Pier Paolo Pasolini, Francis Coppola, George Lucas,[18] Oliver Stone, Martin Scorsese, Luc Besson, Jean-Jacques Beineix, Bernardo Bertolucci, Terence Malick, Donald Cammell, Abel Ferrara, Rainer Werner Fassbinder, Wim Wenders, Peter Greenaway, and Robert Altman. But not even cinema giants like Coppola or Pasolini have managed it as successfully as the Maestro himself. As they say, Godard is still the Man.

And Pauline Kael is right that Jean-Luc Godard beats every other filmmaker at their own game: he gets there first, he's faster than anyone else,[19] and filmmakers who take up his ideas and approaches come across as mannerist (1971, 173). He is impossible to follow, because he's burned up the ground. He invents his innovative techniques to deal with his material, and you can't follow that, you can't become 'Godardian'. He also possesses the uncanny ability to predict future trends, so he also appears to be in advance of everybody else.

In short, there's only one Jean-Luc Godard.

18 As well as Akira Kurosawa, George Lucas admired Jean-Luc Godard, as did Francis Coppola and numerous other filmmakers in the 1960s. The influence of Godard's incredible films is direct on films such as *THX-1138* and *American Graffiti*, and Lucas's early shorts. *Alphaville* certainly influenced *THX-1138*.
Godard visited the University of Southern California in the late 1960s (at the invitation of Charles Lippincott), where George Lucas was studying cinema. 'I *loved* the style of Godard's films. The graphics, this sense of humor, the way he portrayed the world – he was very cinematic', enthused Lucas. 19 As David Thomson commented, 'Godard was too brilliant, too rapid: he saw a new way of doing film that is still beyond the generality of directors, and audiences' (1995, 292).

It's significant, I think, that Jean-Luc Godard has said that he thinks of himself as a *French* filmmaker, rather than an *international* filmmaker, that he has been making films primarily for the French audience (though perhaps not only the French in France),[20] rather than for an international audience. It's an important distinction, except that Godard has become a name well-known outside France, of course. We say 'global' now, instead of 'international'.

Visiting the Pompidou Centre in Paris during Christmas, 2008, I found a marvellous collection of Jean-Luc Godard's films, including his 1970s movies with Anne-Marie Miéville. More and more I think that Godard encapsulates better than most Paris and France and French life and French culture and French cinema from the 1960s to the 2000s. He gets everything into his films. *Everything*. His cinema *is* French cinema, as no other French filmmaker is. He is *so* French, and so amusing, and so much fun.

Jean-Luc Godard's films of the 1960s, before European and international co-production became commonplace in film production (really from the late 1970s for Godard), were films made in France for a French audience. That's one reason why they were low budget films – because they had to make most of their money back in France. Some of Godard's contemporaries, of course, went to Hollywood or tended to mount big, European co-productions. Godard could've been a director-for-hire and never stopped working (and he would've been the greatest hired hand of recent times). Godard, however, has always enjoyed his relative independence – the more film producers that are involved, or the more money there is, the less control the filmmaker has. In the 1960s, Godard said that his movies were financed by advances against future sales by distributors, and they had a say in the

---

20 The French Republic has a population of 58 million (in 1997), and a land mass of 210,026 square miles.

production (G, 210). Gaumont has been a valuable source of support Godard. He was their Resident Genius.

As Pauline Kael noted, Jean-Luc Godard 'makes it all seems so effortless – just one movie after another', movies which could be made because they were low budget, because Godard was 'so skilful and so incredibly disciplined', and could find an audience within France to sustain them (1969, 19). That gave Godard an independence almost unknown among his contemporaries. He could seem to do what he wanted. It was certainly a rare position.

Jean-Luc Godard's is a supremely well-read, well-informed and intellectual cinema (reflecting the man himself). It is not uncommon to find references to writers and thinkers such as Goethe, Hölderlin, Hegel, Proust, Joyce, Rimbaud, Freud, Marx, Mao and Brecht in his films. Brechtian 'epic theatre' is clearly an influence on Godard's cinema, with its separation and foregrounding of the elements of the medium, its alienation effects, its self-reflexivity.[21] The Soviet filmmaker Dziga Vertov, who came to name the group of filmmakers Godard formed in the late 1960s with Jean-Pierre Gorin and company, is another influence, with his notions of *kino-glaz* ('cinema-eye') and theory of *kino-pravda* ('cinema-truth'), and, importantly for Godard, the emphasis, as with Sergei Eisenstein, on montage. Politically, Mao Zedong made an impact on Godard (this is the politics of the Mao of the *Little Red Book*, and the Great Proletarian Cultural Revolution of 1966).

Godard is certainly one of the great interviewees in all of film history. Not only can he talk about cinema at length, referencing 100s of films and filmmakers (including citing

---

21 The distancing or estrangement effect of Bertholt Brecht was called the *Verfrem-dungseffekt*. The goal was to make the audience always aware of the mechanisms of the play and staging: 'to allow the spectator to criticize constructively from a social point of view', as Brecht put it. (Quoted in *Brecht On Theatre*, ed. J. Willett, Methuen, London, 1964, 125).

many he knew personally),[22] he can also discuss philosophy, politics, science, sculpture, painting, theatre, you name it.

It's hard to think of any filmmaker, producer, studio executive or critic who could take on Godard in a debate and win.

A long interview with Godard, produced in 2010, is remarkable and highly recommended: he may be in his 80s, but he can still talk wittily about cinema, including his own films (and he's still sucking on a giant cigar).

ACCESS TO GODARD

You'd think, wouldn't you, that the key works by one of the great filmmakers in the history of cinema would be readily available? Not at all with Jean-Luc Godard's films. Ironically, it's Hollywood and the Americans (of the North) who are more concerned with archiving and preservation than the film-mad French.

James Quandt has written of the difficulty of putting together a Jean-Luc Godard film retrospective. Godard's works are in a 'state of near unattainability', and the rights to many pieces are uncertain or disputed (this occurs with so many movies). While the 1960s films (comprising an incredible *sixteen* feature-length movies, plus many shorter films), have become classics, they are often shown in poor conditions, and the Dziga Vertov Group films are virtually un-obtainable (go into your local home entertainment store and try to find *Vent d'Est* or *Pravda*. No, not a chance).

And the later works are difficult to source, too, including the one production everyone agrees is a total masterpiece,

---

22 'Godard has the entire history of cinema in his head... he is a walking reference library of the cinema', remarked Wheeler Dixon (183).

Histoire(s) du Cinéma. If this piece is one of the great works of our time, as every critic attests, it should be easily available. Unfortunately, that isn't the case, as I've found writing this book (it was released on DVD in 2008).

It doesn't help either that some of the items in the Jean-Luc Godard filmography don't actually exist, or are apocryphal, and some have been withdrawn by the companies that commissioned them. [23]

A filmmaker such as Werner Herzog has made many of his films available, with some absolutely wonderful DVD audio commentaries by the director. It would be truly amazing to have Jean-Luc Godard release his films with commentaries – and to have additional commentaries by, say, Anna Karina or Raoul Coutard. (But there are many filmmakers who could have produced audio commentaries on their work but didn't or chose not to: Ingmar Bergman, Woody Allen, Walerian Borowczyk and Steven Spielberg).

As to books, there are many about Godard, but the two must-haves are: Colin MacCabe's 2003 biography, and Richard Brody's 2008 study.[24]

Websites about Jean-Luc Godard on the internet come and go, but some of the good ones include:

The Godard Experience: www.carlton.edu

The British Film Institute: www.bfi.org.uk

Senses of Cinema: www.sensesofcinema.com

Film-Philosophy: www.film-philosophy.com

www.geocities.com/Hollywood/Cinema/4355

23 You can see some of Godard's films and interviews on the excellent UbuWeb site (ubu.com), and also YouTube (youtube.com). Places such as the Centre Pompidou in Paris have excellent archives.

24 I would also recommend: R. Bellour & M. Bandy, eds., *Jean-Luc Godard*, W.W. Dixon, *The Films of Jean-Luc Godard*, B.F. Kawin, *Mindscreen: Bergman, Godard and First-Person Film*, P. Kolker, *The Altering Eye: Contemporary International Cinema*, R. Roud, *Jean-Luc Godard*, K. Silverman & H. Farocki, *Speaking About Godard*, and D. Sterritt, *The Films of Jean-Luc Godard*.

2

GODARD BIOGRAPHY

I once told Godard that he had something I wanted
– freedom. He said: 'You have something I want –
money.'

Don Siegel (1988)

Born in Paris on December 3, 1930 into a bourgeois family,
son of a Swiss physician, Jean-Luc Godard studied at the
Sorbonne between 1949 and 1951, obtaining a certificate in
ethnology.[1] Godard had two sisters (Véronique, b. 1937, and
Rachel, b. 1930), and a brother, Claude (b. 1933). His
childhood was dominated by Protestant religion (only later did
Godard become interested in Catholicism, especially in regard
to Catholicism's tradition of painting and image-making). The
two families of his father Paul Godard and his mother Odile
Monod were bourgeois, well-off, very large, and straddled the
Swiss-French border. It was normal for the Monods and
Godards to travel often between Geneva and Paris, for
instance. The two sides of Godard's beginnings, the French
and Swiss, need to be considered. Thus – he was born in
Paris, but Godard spent his childhood in Switzerland, in the
area bounded by Lausanne and Geneva, with Rolle and Nyon
between them. And that was where Godard returned to in the

---

1 I have drawn a good deal on Colin MacCabe's wonderful 2003
biography of Godard, and also Richard Brody's marvellous
2008 study of Godard.

later part of his life, living in the tiny town of Rolle[2] with Anne-Marie Miéville, between Lausanne and Geneva.[3] (Godard's film company, based in Rolle, was called Sonimage, then J.L.G. Films for a while,[4] but now it is Périphéria).[5]

Jean-Luc Godard described his family background as

> one of those huge Protestant families that behave like a tribe with their own ritual, their own ceremonies... you were protected. It was like a Greek legend, my grandfather and grandmother were gods, my parents were demi-gods and we children were humans. (Mac, 18)

Jean-Luc Godard's later attacks on the bourgeoisie, then, come from a specific place: his family was affluent, and his childhood was comfortable. Godard was as bourgeois as they come. As he put it in *Far From Vietnam*: 'I am cut off from the working class, but my struggle against Hollywood is related, yet workers don't come to see my films'. The rebellious, would-be revolutionary Marxist filmmaker was in fact the epitome of the bourgeoisie (he filmed bourgeois stories at first, he said, because 'I come from the bourgeoisie' [G, 226]). He called advertizing fascism, but of course he made commercials himself (into the Eighties. Well, you have to pay the bills). Godard admitted in *Variety*: 'I'm a capitalist. I'm a producer'.

Jean-Luc Godard produced ads for Darty (the chain-store), *Le Figaro*, France Télécom and Marithé & François

---

2 Some saw the move to Rolle as a flight from the big bad city – Paris... In this view, Godard was turning his back on the modernism and politics and neurosis of urban life, and embracing the natural world, conservatism, and great art of old times. But Godard also later complained about feeling isolated in Rolle: he didn't see much of his former colleagues, he said, and didn't feel connected to the film world (B, 556).
3 From Paris, Godard and Miéville first moved to Grenoble, before returning to Switzerland (Miéville was also Swiss).
4 It became Périphéria partly because Miéville was also making movies, rather than J.L.G. alone.
5 As Michel de Montaigne said in his *Essays* (1, 39): 'the greatest thing in the world is to know how to be self-sufficient.' Godard has exemplified that.

Girbaud (fashion designers) which were more like film essays (they ran up to 50 minutes). For F.J. Burrus, a tobacco manufacturer, Godard produced a commercial extolling Burrus' Parisienne cigars. Nike commissioned Godard to make 2 commercials for their shoes: inevitably, neither were shown. In one ad, the wolf catches Little Red Riding Hood because he's wearing Nike sneakers, and in the other ad, a bunch of youngsters out-run the Grim Reaper because they have Nikes.

Director Glauber Rocha said that his Cinema Novo pals didn't like the French New Wave films because they were too bourgeois: 'we like Godard now, but before we did not since we considered him very formalist, and very rational, very bourgeois' (in D. Georgakas, 22).

As a youth Jean-Luc Godard was into sports big time – skiing, tennis, swimming, and soccer, was a member of the Scouts, and played goalie for the junior football team in Nyon (elements of sport crop up many times in his films – basketball in *Hail Mary,* for instance, and tennis in *Weekend* and *Vladimir and Rosa*). Anna Karina said that Godard could swim like a fish, ski like a god and run like an athlete. Of *Pierrot le Fou*, Karina commented that 'everything that Jean-Paul would do in the film, Jean-Luc would do it ten times better'. Godard excelled at intellectual pursuits, including mathematics; there were always books in the family home (and books are everywhere in Godard's movies. No one in cinema has featured so many people reading books or reading aloud from books).

In his late teens, Jean-Luc Godard became something of a wayward personality, the black sheep among the Monods and the Godards, failing his baccalauréat in 1948 (in Lausanne), and turning to thieving. Some of the thefts were petty, others were fairly substantial. Godard spent three days in a jail in Zurich when he was caught, aged 22, stealing from the safe of a Swiss TV station (he seemed to get caught often). He stole from old women's handbags. He said he financed his fellow student Jacques Rivette's first film, *Le Quadrille*, from stealing. He stole a Pierre Renoir painting his grandfather owned and sold it. He had to leave Paris for Switzerland when he took petty cash from *Cahiers du Cinéma*.

Jean-Luc Godard would steal first editions of books in order to sell them at nearby *bouqinistes* at the Pont Neuf in Paris. One time Godard stole some first editions of Paul Valéry's poetry which belonged to his grandfather, Julien-Pierre Monod, and was found out when he sold them to a nearby bookseller. When Monod senior discovered the theft (he often visited the bookseller himself), Godard was cast out from the Monod family.

Following his spell in prison in Zurich, Jean-Luc Godard was taken to a mental institution by his father Paul Godard, who didn't know what to do with him (relations between Godard father and son appeared to be fraught). According to Godard, he was undergoing psychotherapy outside Lausanne for between two and three months, quite a long time for a young man (Mac, 40).[6]

But Godard didn't really know what he wanted, either. He was into painting in his late teens, and in 1949 his mother Odile Monod arranged an exhibition of his work in Mortriant (painting would remain one of Godard's obsessions. His late films delved into evoking the painterly aspects of video). He considered writing novels, but that seemed like too much work. He wanted to get into films, but no one in the Monod and Godard clans knew about that world. Godard said his father 'didn't understand what I wanted. With the other children it

---

6 Suspicious at first, only later was Godard more amenable to psychoanalysis, although his films clearly draw on Sigmund Freud, most of all (and some Carl Jung). Anne-Marie Miéville was possibly responsible for Godard's later interest in psycho-analysis (one of Godard's unmade projects was the Dora case history from Freud, with Paul Newman as Freud, in the early 1980s).

was clearer, but with me nobody knew and I didn't even know' (MC, 40).

Many commentators have noted J.-L.G.'s tendency to lie about his life — and lying so much he doesn't bother to hide the fact that he's lying (if you can't remember, make it up, Godard asserted in *I.T.* in '68). So some of Godard's accounts of his life have to be understood with that in mind. (Many filmmakers embellish the truth, or tell the same stories many different ways — Federico Fellini, Kenneth Anger, Michael Cimino, Werner Herzog, Orson Welles, etc).

❂

There were some famous people linked to the Monods and the Godards, including the poet Paul Valéry[7] and the writer André Gide. This is no ordinary heritage for Godard, then, not when you've got major artists like Valéry, Gide and Rainer Maria Rilke linked to the families.

Anne Wiazemsky said sometimes André Gide would come round to 78, rue d'Assas, Paris, where Jean-Luc Godard was staying with the writer Jean Schlumberger: 'the two of them would eat sandwiches in the kitchen' (Mac, 52).[8] Godard also stayed with Marc Allégret, a filmmaker (Allégret introduced Godard to his future producer, Georges de Beauregard). Godard's existence in Paris at this time — the 1950s — was fairly nomadic. He would disappear, Charles Bitsch recalled, but no one would know where he had gone.

To escape military service, Jean-Luc Godard used his Swiss nationality. Even so, Roland Tolmatchoff said that Godard ran into trouble with the authorities in Switzerland

---

7 Julien Monod, Godard's grandfather, was the literary executor of Paul Valéry after the poet's death in 1945, as well as his friend (B, 4). Godard said he was taught Latin by Valéry, and was also expected to recite Valéry's poem 'Le Cimetière marin' at his grandparents' wedding anniversary.
8 Godard fell in love with André Gide's wonderful book of travels in North Africa, homoeroticism and Rimbaudian intoxication with life, *Fruits of the Earth*. A spectacularly poetic book, *Les Nourritures terrestres* is one of the great pæans to youth and being alive.

more than once during the making of *Le Petit Soldat* (in Mac, 83).

Godard was determined to avoid the draft and undertaking military service in the Vietnam War. That was one of the reasons he travelled extensively as a youth in Chile, Argentina, Brazil, Bolivia and Peru (he started by joining his father in Jamaica). It was a reason why opted to film *The Little Soldier* in Switzerland rather than Paris.

❂

Paris in the 1950s was one of the best places in the world to see films (and it still is). Apart from Henri Langlois' Cinémathèque, one of the central cultural and social venues of the whole New Wave movement, there were many ciné-clubs and specialist cinemas. By the early 1960s, Godard was one of the leading lights of the film world in Paris, having been deeply involved in Parisian film culture since the early 1950s.

With his fellow cinéastes François Truffaut and Jacques Rivette, Jean-Luc Godard would regularly watch 3 or 4 movies a day. Godard and Rivette, for instance, saw Orson Welles' *Macbeth* repeatedly from 2 p.m. to 10 p.m. They haunted the famous Cinémathèque, as well as the C.C.Q.L.

Let's not forget that France has one of the strongest film cultures in the world: France produces more films than any country in Europe, and people go to the cinema more times a year in the French Republic than anywhere else in Europa. More European co-productions are made with French companies than any other country. In short, France is a very good place to make films.

❂

As well as sharing a cultural background in both France and Switzerland, Jean-Luc Godard was also exposed early on to different languages — French, German, English. He saw newsreels of WWII in Switzerland, for instance, in both German and English: 'the same fight but different victors'. A lesson in how voices can alter meanings.

Among the authors that J-.L.G.'s read in his youth were André Gide, Georges Bernanos, Jacques Chardonne, André Malraux, Julien Green, Edouard Peisson, Robert Musil, Hermann Broch, Thomas Mann, and adventure novels. Many of these writers would be quoted in his movies (Godard remained fond of adventure classics, as well as crime and pulp fiction).

Many commentators have noted that Jean-Luc Godard is small, secretive, quietly spoken, withdrawn, and something of a loner (and Godard's film sets tended to be quiet).[9] But he has a commanding presence.[10] He doesn't do small talk, and comes to the point straight away. If there's nothing to talk about, he doesn't chat for the sake of it (people say the same of Akira Kurosawa). Communicating with the crew could be problematic for Godard, despite being dedicated to collaboration, and a first-rate communicator. As Irving Teitelbaum, who worked with Godard in London on *British Sounds*, put it: 'it was all in his head but if you weren't in his head then that was your fault'.

In 1995, Jean-Luc Godard said: 'I am something of a loner... I've always considered myself marginal'. Gilles Deleuze remarked that although Godard was 'a man who works a lot, so he is, necessarily, completely alone', his solitude encompassed many people, with many collaborations.[11]

❂

Jean-Luc Godard's cinematic career has been well-covered by many writers: here's a brief summary: it started

---

9 Raoul Coutard and Charles Bitsch reckoned that they survived working with Godard so often because they didn't ask lots of questions, just got on with the job.
10 Colin MacCabe wrote in his biography of Godard: 'I was not surprised in the course of research for this book to discover that both Bernardo Bertolucci and Serge Daney had vomited on their first encounter with him' (Mac, 267).
11 In R. Bellour, 1992, 35.

with short films in the 1950s, coupled with, importantly, Godard's critical writing for journals (*Les Amis du cinéma, Arts, Gazette du cinéma*, which he founded and, most famously, *Cahiers du Cinéma*).

Jean-Luc Godard was a film critic before he made movies,[12] is the general view, emphasizing that Godard, like his fellow New Wave directors, was a film fan, a *cinéaste*, thoroughly immersed in cinema before he came to make films.[13] In the late 1940s Godard started attending the Paris Cinématheque Française, the Ciné-Club du Quartier Latin, and Left Bank film clubs. It was here he met André Bazin, mentor of the *Nouvelle Vague,* and some of the French New Wave directors (Truffaut, Rohmer, Chabrol and Rivette). Eric Rohmer said they would sometimes watch 4 films a day. (Paris remains one of the great cinema-loving cities of the world: in Paris, they are mad about film). Truffaut was the first of Godard's many collaborators: Karina in the 1960s, Gorin from the late 1960s to early 1970s, and finally Miéville from the early 1970s onwards.

As his critical writings show, by his late twenties Godard had a very wide and deep knowledge of cinema: he knew every classic from the U.S.A. and Western Europe; he interviewed many celebrated filmmakers (Renoir, Rossellini, Astruc); he happily referenced every great film director as if he knew them personally (Murnau, Griffith, Chaplin, Eisenstein, Fuller, Hitch, Vigo, Cocteau, Bresson, Ophüls, Visconti, Fellini, Ford, Walsh, Dreyer, Hawks, Preminger, Lubitsch, von Sternberg, Welles, Buñuel, Cukor, Bergman,

12 Godard would later remark that he and his New Wave cohorts knew nothing about real life, but only movies. He regretted his worship of cinema (and North American cinema), even though he couldn't help himself.

13 The *Cahiers* crowd were dubbed 'young turks' and the 'Schérer gang'. Godard once remarked that ironically by the time the New Wave filmmakers had the opportunity to make films, the kind of films that had made them want to make cinema no longer existed or were dying out (G, 192). And when *Cahiers du Cinéma* turned towards Marxist-Leninism and Bertholt Brecht, the founders were alienated – all except Godard.

Donen, Mizoguchi, Ray, Lang, Mann, Tashlin, etc – he did eventually meet many of them); many of these filmmakers were regarded with awe and devotion by Godard; he would talk about one film in terms of other films (i.e., one story in terms of other stories); he emphasized the viewer's experience of seeing a film; and recurring concerns included re-inventing cinema.

Jean-Luc Godard on film criticism, the impossibility of it:

> If you wake the woman you love in the night, you don't telephone your friends to tell them about it afterwards. Difficult, you see, to talk cinema, the art is easy but criticism impossible of this subject which is no subject, whose wrong side is the right, which draws close as it recedes, always physically let us not forget. (G, 215)

For Jean-Luc Godard, cinema is at the heart of life: Godard's passion for cinema and what it is capable of, its *potential*, is immense, and knows no bounds. From an early age, in his writings on cinema of the early 1950s, Godard formulated the notion of the inter-connectedness between the film, the filmmaker and the viewer, and how all three are inseparably linked to the real world. So when Godard says 'cinema is life' or 'everything is cinema', he really means it. Few filmmakers have had such a deep faith in cinema – and it's this faith and love which has sustained Godard's extraordinary career.

Godard dreams of cinema, but cinema also dreams (of) Godard.

Among Jean-Luc Godard's early jobs were construction work on a dam, in TV in Zurich, and an assistant in the PR department of 20th Century Fox's Paris offices (he took over Claude Chabrol's position). Godard worked for two years providing PR for Fox, which no doubt helped him to market his own films. Here he met producer Georges de Beauregard (1920-84), who financed his first feature film, *À Bout de*

Souffle (1960), made when Godard was 30.

THE FRENCH NEW WAVE.

The influences on the French New Wave are well-known: André Bazin, *Cahiers du cinéma*, Jean Renoir, Alfred Hitchcock, the Italian Neo-realists, American giants such as Orson Welles and William Wyler, and previously neglected Hollywood directors, such as Howard Hawks, Nicholas Ray, Douglas Sirk, John Ford, Vincente Minnelli, Sam Fuller and Frank Tashlin.

André Bazin's essay "The Ontology of the Photographic Image" is a key text for Jean-Luc Godard's cinema. Bazin's trio of key filmmakers were Jean Renoir, Orson Welles and Roberto Rossellini. And, had Bazin lived beyond 1958, no doubt Godard would have been added to that list.

What the French *Nouvelle Vague* brought to cinema, Jean-Luc Godard observed, was

> the love of the cinema itself. We loved cinema before loving women, before loving money, before loving war. It's the cinema that made me discover life and it took me 30 years, in fact, because I had to get through all those things which I myself projected on the screen. (1998, 132)

Jean-Luc Godard reckoned the cult of the director, which the French New Wave had helped to inaugurate, was overdone. Making the director God in auteurism had become too prevalent in film criticism and reception.[14] 'I don't believe in the solitude of an artist and the *auteur* with a capital 'A'', Godard commented (1998, 132).[15] In 2010, Godard insisted that he wasn't an *auteur* (political, yes, but *auteur*, no). Films had always been created by many people: behind the director

[14] The important word in the phrase 'la politique des auteurs' was 'politique', not 'auteur', Godard said.
[15] But he also insisted that the cinema 'is not a craft,' Godard asserted; 'It is an art. It does not mean teamwork' (G, 76).

'there are many other figures equally important in the making of the film' (ib., 133). Godard said (in 1980) that the New Wave filmmakers had emphasized the director partly because they themselves were not yet directors (1998, 103). 'It was in order to have our right to exist as directors, because we weren't authorized then'. Godard didn't differentiate significantly between the director and the writer, or the director and the artist. The roles were all part of the same thing, which was communication, using language, making a statement, having a point-of-view, or just *doing something*.

> People think of their bodies as territories [said Godard]. They think of their skin as the border, and that it's no longer them once it's outside the border. But a language is obviously made to cross borders. I'm someone whose real country is language, and whose territory is movies. (1998, 102)

And yet Godard enshrined certain film directors, and auteurism, throughout his career – up to and beyond *Histoire(s) du Cinéma*, Godard is always talking about Cocteau, Hawks, Hitchcock, Rossellini, Lang, whoever.

With *À Bout du Souffle*, Jean-Luc Godard produced one of the first, great, French New Wave movies, starring Jean-Paul Belmondo and Jean Seberg, and written by, among others, François Truffaut. *À Bout du Souffle*, with its cool, Parisian *milieu*, its filmic and *film noir* allusions, handheld camera, startling editing and stylized, self-conscious performances from Jean-Paul Belmondo and Jean Seberg, established Godard as one of the major voices of postwar cinema, a reputation which Godard built on in subsequent early feature-length films such as *Le Petit Soldat* (1960), *Une Femme Est Une Femme* (1961), *Vivre Sa Vie* (1962), *Le Mépris* (1963), *Les Carabiniers* (1963), *Bande à Part* (1964), and *Une Femme Mariée* (1964).

In these feature movies of the early to mid-1960s, Jean-

Luc Godard forged a radical, polemical series of films as film-essays[16] which confronted issues such as late consumer capitalism, prostitution, labour, youth identity, politics, ideology, gender, marriage, music, popular culture, modern French society, Hollywood and not forgetting cinema itself.

For Richard Brody, no other filmmaker has tackled more of the big political issues and philosophical debates in the modern era: Godard takes on WWII (and France's role in the war); the Shoah; philosophies such as Existentialism and Structuralism; Stalinism; the New Left; consumer capitalism; America; May, 1968;[17] Maoism; Marxism; French political life (such as the President Mitterand years); the permissive era of the 1960s; the global media; and of course cinema in all its forms and histories (B, xiv). When you stop to consider all of the subjects that Godard has tackled in his movies, it is simply mind-boggling.

In the mid-1960s, Jean-Luc Godard's films became increasingly politicized – the sci-fi film *Alphaville* (1965), the Existential road movie *Pierrot le Fou* (1965), the nihilistic *film noir Made in U.S.A.* (1966), the portrait of French youth *Masculine/ Féminin* (1966), a day in the life of a French housewife *2 ou 3 Choses Que Je Sais d'Elle* (1966) – until, by 1967-68, the Marxist and Maoist influences permeated Godard's films: the angry, roadkill movie *Weekend* (1967), the teens playing at being political radicals *La Chinoise* (1967), the early attempt at exploring ideology *La Gai Savoir* (1968), the guide to Marxist politics *Un Film Comme Les Autres* (1968) and the Rolling Stones in the recording studio in *One Plus One* (*Sympathy For the Devil*, 1968).

Jean-Luc Godard's concern was 'not to make political

16 His films were essays, Godard said, but he filmed them instead of writing them. 'If the cinema were to disappear, I'd go back to pencil and paper'. Expression is all one.
17 Godard was involved in the events of 1968 – he marched with workers on May 29, 1968, for example, and filmed the riots in Paris.

films, but to *make films politically* (my emphasis). Godard later told Andrew Sarris that he was never a Marxist, and had never read Karl Marx.[18] (Maybe, maybe not – surely Godard would have read page one and the last page of *Das Kapital*, at the very least, his usual preference). His use of Marx, he said, was 'only as a provocation, mixing Mao and Coca-Cola and so forth'. [19]

It doesn't matter if Godard is leftist, rightwing, or upside-downist, or pay-for-your-hotel-billist. He is *Godard*, that's all that matters. (Godard's great run of 1960s movies were produced during the right-wing de Gaulle administration, 1959-1969. That is what his films were reacting against).

In the U.S.A., J.-L.G. was not so well-known, until the late 1960s (the uneven releases of his movies in America didn't help). But by the time of *La Chinoise*, which was doing well,[20] for a lecture tour in the U.S.A. on the university circuit Godard was offered the very high fees of $1,000-1,500 per talk (B, 323).[21] Some of the lectures were sold out: 12 showings of *La Chinoise* were sold out in Berkeley. And the French director certainly knew how to play up to those radicalized student audiences.

Jean-Luc Godard shifted into what appeared to be wholly political, ideological filmmaking, forming the Dziga-Vertov Group with Jean-Henri Roger and Jean-Pierre Gorin (editor of *Cahiers Marxistes-Leninistes*), which made the following films between 1968 and 1972: *British Sounds* (*See You At Mao*, 1969), *Pravda* (1969), *Vent d'Est* (*Wind From the East*, 1970), *Luttes en Italie* (*Struggle In Italia*, 1971), *1 P.M.*

18 Some intellectual groups, such as the Situationists and Lettrists (in France), didn't like Godard at all; even the freedom he seemed to possess in his mode of filmmaking was stolen from elsewhere.
19 Quoted in A. Sarris, 1994, 898.
20 *La Chinoise* lays into the U.S.A. on numerous fronts, but was a hit in the New World.
21 At the time of the Museum of Modern Art retrospective in Gotham in 1968, J.L.G.'s fame in the U.S.A. was at its height.

(*One Parallel Movie,* 1971), *Vladimir et Rosa* (*Vladimir and Rosa,* 1971), *Letter To Jane* (1972), and *All's Well* (*Tout Va Bien,* 1972), with Jane Fonda and Yves Montand. (Not all of the films were made by the Dziga Vertov Group, but they have become known under that umbrella). Godard had met the young Maoist J.-P. Gorin during *La Chinoise*; with Gorin, Godard produced five pictures: *Vent d'Est, Lotte In Italia, Vladimir and Rosa, All's Well* and *Jusqu'à la Victoire* (unfinished).[22]

THE 1970s AND AFTER.

In the 1970s, Jean-Luc Godard moved into video and television territory, and worked with Anne-Marie Miéville on many projects: *Ici Et Ailleurs* (1974), *Numéro Deux* (1975), *Comment Ça Va* (1976), *Six Fois Deux/ Sur Et Sous La Communication* (1976), and *France/ Tour/ Détour/ Deux/ Enfants* (1977-78). With video, Godard said, he could preview his work, he could try out all sorts of things b4 deciding upon the final form.[23] He could shoot large portions of a movie too, edit it, and then move into 35mm celluloid. It changed the way he made films:

> Video lets me look first, and then I can begin to write from what I see. Before – just like most movie-makers and industry executives – I always wrote first, and then let the image come. (1993, 122)

It was effective in the TV films and video essays to have Jean-Luc Godard talking to camera with text superimposed over the images. And to have Godard talking over the images. In so many films, too, Godard, is playing on-screen with machines – tape machines, record players, film projectors,

22 The D.V.G. comprised mainly of Gorin and Godard. For Robert Kolker, the Dziga Vertov Group films 'were still the work of a middle-class intellectual trying to come to terms with his art, with his own means of production, with his own ideology, as well as with his own personality' (1985, 205).
23 Like Francis Coppola with his concept of 'electronic cinema'.

mixers, typewriters, cameras – a big part of Godard is the technofetishist.

In the late 1970s, Jean-Luc Godard made a 'return' to feature filmmaking, with the 'sublime trilogy', *Sauve Qui Peut* (a.k.a. *Every Man For Himself* and *Slow Motion*, 1979), *Passion* (1982), and *Prénom: Carmen* (a.k.a. *First Name: Carmen*, 1983). (Actually, it's *Passion, Prénom Carmen* and *Hail Mary* that seem more like a trilogy. Godard, though, regarded all four films as sharing similar themes).

This period of Jean-Luc Godard's career is always described as a 'return' or a 'comeback', as if Godard had been in the wilderness, or had retired from filmmaking. As the above list of projects shows, Godard has never retired.

It would be impossible for Godard to stop making films.[24]

Easily his most controversial film, *Je Vous Salue, Marie* (*Hail Mary*), appeared in 1985. Further films included: *Détective* (1985), made to help finance the completion of *Hail Mary, Grandeur et Décadence d'un Petit Commerce de Cinéma* (a.k.a. *Grandeur and Decadence*, 1986), *King Lear* (1987), which starred Peter Sellars, Burgess Meredith, Molly Ringwald, Norman Mailer and Woody Allen,[25] *Soigne Ta Droite* (a.k.a. *Keep Your Right Up*, 1987), *La Rapport Darty* (a.k.a. *The Darty Report*, 1989), *Nouvelle Vague* (a.k.a. *New Wave*, 1990), *Allemagne Année 90 Neuf Zéro* (a.k.a. *Germany Year 90 Nine Zero*, 1991), *Hélas Pour Moi* (a.k.a. *Woe Is Me*, 1993), *Les*

---

24 With some of his new films, Godard also produced video notes about the films, in which he discussed the projects. It's completely typical for a filmmaker such as Jean-Luc Godard to make a film about the film he's making, and one wishes that other filmmakers had done so. These films about films serve the same purpose as audio commentaries on DVD releases (which Godard doesn't do, unfortunately).

25 Jill Forbes suggested that, for Godard in the 1980s, in taking on famous works like the *Bible* in *Hail Mary* and Shakespeare in *King Lear* and great paintings in *Passion*, it was as if Godard were trying to 'reintegrate his films into the mainstream of western culture', and come in out of the cold of marginality (1992, 123). Maybe. But Godard has always been deeply engaged with the great works of Western history, from his early films onwards. *Breathless* is stuffed with high culture allusions.

Enfants Jouent à la Russie (1994), *2 x 50 Ans de Cinéma Français* (a.k.a. *2 x 50 Years of French Cinema,* 1995), *For Ever Mozart* (1997), *Éloge de L'Amour* (a.k.a. *In Praise of Love,* 2001), *Liberté et Patrie* (a.k.a. *Liberty and Homeland,* 2002), a best of *Histoire(s) du Cinéma* (*Chosen Moments of Histoire(s) of Cinema,* 2004), *Notre Musique* (a.k.a. *Our Music,* 2004), *Prières pour Refuzniks 1* and *2* (a.k.a. *Prayers For Refuseniks,* 2006), *Vrai Faux Passeport* (a.k.a. *The True False Passort,* 2006), *Une Catastrophe* (2008), *Film Socialisme* (a.k.a. *Socialism,* 2010), *Bridges of Sarajevo* (a.k.a. *Les Ponts de Sarajevo,* 2014),[26] *Goodbye To Language* (a.k.a. *Adieu au Langage,* 2014) and *The Image Book* (a.k.a. *Le Livre d'Image,* 2018).

❂

As well as the feature films and video projects noted above, Jean-Luc Godard has also produced many shorter pieces, many for television. There are good filmographies which list all of these productions.[27]

Jean-Luc Godard has also contributed segments to many anthology films, including *Sloth* (*La Paresse*) in *Les Sept Péchés Capitaux* (*The Seven Capital Sins,* 1961), with Sylvain Dhomme, Philippe de Broca, Jacques Demy, Edouard Molinaro, Roger Vadim and Claude Chabrol,[28] *The New World* (*La Nouveau Monde*) in *RoGoPaG* (1963), alongside Pier Paolo Pasolini, Roberto Rossellini and Ugo Gregoretti, *Le Grand Escroc* (*The Great Swindler*) in *Les Plus Belles Escroqueries Du Monde* (*The World's Most Beautiful Swindlers,* 1963), with Roman Polanski, Ugo Gregoretti, Claude Chabrol and Hiromichi Horakawa,[29] *Montparnasse-Levallois* in *Paris Vu*

---

26 *Bridges of Sarajevo* (2014) was an anthology film, released on 2014.5.22. Godard and 12 other directors contributed.
27 Such as in *Godard par Godard 2*, by Alain Bergala, or in C. MacCabe, 2003, or in R. Bellour, 1992.
28 Eddie Constantine featured in Godard's segment, *Sloth.*
29 Godard's episode, entitled *Le Grand Escroc,* starred Jean Seberg, Charles Denner and László Szabó. Seberg played the first of Godard's filmmaker characters.

Par... (*Six In Paris*, 1965), with Eric Rohmer, Claude Chabrol, Jean Rouch and Jean-Daniel Pollett, *Anticipation, ou l'Amour en l'an 2000* in *Les Plus Vieux Métier du Monde* (*The Oldest Profession, or Love Through the Ages*, 1967), with Michel Pfleghar, Claude Autant-Lara, Mauro Bologni, Philippe de Broca and Franco Indovina, *Caméra-Oeil* (*Camera Eye*) in *Loin du Viêtnam* (*Far From Vietnam*, 1967), with Alain Resnais, William Klein, Joris Ivens, Chris Marker, Agnès Varda and Claude Lelouch, *Amore e Rabbia/ Vangelo '70* (*Love and Anger*, 1969), with Bernardo Bertolucci, Pier Paolo Pasolini, Carlo Lizzani, Marco Bellocchio and Elda Tattoli, *Aria* (1987),[30] producer Don Boyd's opera anthology featuring Nic Roeg, Ken Russell, Charles Sturridge, Julien Temple, Bruce Beresford, Robert Altman, Frank Roddam, Bill Bryden and Derek Jarman, *L'Enfance de l'art* in *Comment Vont Les Enfants* (*How Are the Kids?*, 1990), and *Contre l'Oubli* (*Lest We Forget*, 1992), with Alain Resnais, Chantal Akerman, Costa-Gavras, and Anne-Marie Miéville among others.

Jean-Luc Godard has also collaborated with the National Film School of France (F.E.M.I.S.), between 1989 and 1991, and with camera companies such as Aaton (to develop a compact, 35mm film camera).

✪

The common view that Jean-Luc Godard moved into political cinema around 1968 then retired in the mid-1970s to the France/ Switzerland borderlands and relative obscurity is wrong, of course: he was still very active. The other common view, that Godard came out of the cultural netherworld to produce a couple of good feature films – *Slow Motion* and *First Name: Carmen* – before sinking back into obsolescence is also wrong. This is a filmmaker who simply could not stop making films, who has embraced each new technological develop-

---

30 Godard's segment in *Aria* is classic Godard, with body builders and nude women in a gym to the strains of *Armide* by Jean-Baptiste Lully.

ment and exploited it – principally, video production and digital video production (plus High Definition video and 3-D video).

In his later video and television pieces, Jean-Luc Godard has tackled a variety of themes and issues, including the new technology itself; the history of art (and painting in particular); the nature of images and image-making; ageing; memory; European history; literature and authorship; music (classical); autobiography; and, always, cinema itself (whatever else he is doing, Godard is always exploring cinema in every single thing he's ever done).

Is it even cinema at all? Some of Jean-Luc Godard's late work is like scraps of a documentary about a group of people discussing a movie they'd like to make, or grousing about some issue like WWII or the Americanization of all territories in the Western world (such issues remain vitally alive for Godard – he has never forgotten them).

At the end of *In Praise of Love*, the famous book by Robert Bresson, *Notes On Cinematography*, is quoted[31] (Bresson's stern, school teacherly mantras are favourites with wannabe intellectual filmmakers. Like: 'don't act'. Like: 'cultivate silence and stillness'. Like: 'make sure you get paid'). Well, one of Bresson's gripes is that 99% of cinema is really filmed theatre (i.e., talking heads), or even filmed radio (as Alfred Hitchcock asserted). Sadly, a good deal of Godard's late work is precisely that – people talking in chairs, or sitting at a table, smoking, staring out of the window...

By the time of his late works – say, the 1990s – Godard had accumulated a vast library of images and sounds, and numerous ways of making cinema and television. He had reached the stage where he could make a movie simply by raiding his library of previous works (in addition, working in the digital realm means that thousands of computer files can

31 I.e., read aloud.

be accessed quickly).

So if someone hired Godard to make a brand, new movie, he could do so without leaving his studio in Rolle simply by using footage and audio he's been creating and recording since the late 1950s. And in fact, this is what Godard actually did – not entire movies and TV pieces, admittedly, but many sections of his late works re-use material from earlier works (he was fond of quoting his own films, too).

As well as his feature films, Jean-Luc Godard has produced an amazing variety of shorter films and videos, some for TV, some as commissions – such as *Jean-Luc* (1976), *Lecons de Choses* (1976), *Lettre à Freddy Buache* (1981), *Oh s'est tous défilé* (1988) and *Contre l'oubli* (1991). And more recent shorts, such as *Reportage amateur Maquette expo* (2006), *Vrai faux passeport* (2006), *Ecce Homo* (2006), *Four Short Films* (2006), *Une catastrophe* (2008), *Journal des Réalisateurs de Jean-Luc Godard* (2008), *The Three Disasters* in *3 x 3D* (2010), *Tribute To Éric Rohmer* (2010), and *Khan Khanne* (2013). Some of these are dense, multi-layered film essays, where rapid images are vision-mixed on top of each other, as in *Histoire(s) du Cinéma*. In some, Godard is interviewing all sorts of people off-camera, as if he's searching for something.

Every single Godard movie is different, as Manny Farber pointed out: each has its own style and approach: 'the form and manner of execution changes totally with each film' (259). There is no other filmmaker in the history of cinema like this, exhibiting so many possibilities of making cinema – no one who has made a self-conscious musical (*A Woman Is a Woman*), gangster movies utterly uninterested in portraying 'action' or gangsterism (*Breathless, Band of Outsiders, Pierrot le Fou*), a Marxist-Maoist deconstruction of capitalism using a Hollywood icon (*Tout Va Bien*), a re-telling of the Christian myth and the Mother of God in modern-day Switzerland (*Hail*

Mary), a reworking of William Shakespeare without any Shakespeare in it (*King Lear*), and a densely-layered meditation on cinema itself (*Histoire(s) du Cinéma*).

In the early 1960s, Jean-Luc Godard said that movie musicals were dead as a genre, but he still wanted musicality in his films. His solution was to have characters half-singing, half-speaking. At times, one wishes that Godard had let rip, and really gone to town with a musical film. The segments of his cinema that are musical – the subway montage song and the Madison dance in *Bande à Part,* the songs in *A Woman Is a Woman*, Marianne singing to Ferdinand in *Pierrot le Fou* – are indications of just how unusual and lyrical a Godard musical might have been.

One genre or type of film that Jean-Luc Godard didn't produce, but which I think he would have been eminently suited to, was the artist's biopic. He could've delivered really intriguing accounts of the life of, say, Johann Sebastian Bach or Wolfgang Amadeus Mozart, or Pierre Renoir or Eugène Delacroix (some of his favourite artists). Godard did say in 1962: 'I would like to do essays, interviews or travel pro-grammes; talk about a painter or a writer I admire. Or simply do plays' (G, 191).

One of the barmiest of Uncle Godard's ventures was to travel to the cold, far North of Canada in 1968, at the invitation of Claude Nedjar: he and Anne Wiazemsky set up base in a local radio station, reading from the *Little Red Book* by Chairman Mao, and asking the locals if they wanted to get involved in revolutionary politics. Needless to say, nobody came to meet them at the radio station.[32] The North of Canada probably isn't the best place to stage a Maoist revolution.[33]

---

32 But there were 'violent protests' – against Godard and company, not protests in the streets about the Canadian government.
33 Godard's notion was to interview students and workers and develop a story out of the material, turning it into a 10-part series.

Another unusual venture, this time in 1978 with Anne-Marie Miéville, saw Jean-Luc Godard working with the Mozambique Ministry of Information to bring video technology to Africa. The goal was to train people to use video cameras and editing gear. (It's striking just how often Godard refers to Africa in his works – not only in terms of the French Republic's troubled political relations with Africa (such as Algeria in *Le Petit Soldat*), but Africa as an origin, a source).

SOME INFLUENCES ON GODARD

Among the influential people in Jean-Luc Godard's artistic life were André Bazin, Henri Langlois, Roberto Rossellini, Orson Welles, Alfred Hitchcock, François Truffaut,[34] Roger Vadim,[35] Jean Renoir, Anne-Marie Miéville, Robert Bresson, Jean-Pierre Gorin, and not forgetting actors like Karina, Wiazemsky, Belmondo, Brialy, Piccoli, Szabó, Léaud, Vlady, etc.[36] Godard knew quite a few of those people, and worked with them: Rossellini, Truffaut,[37] Renoir, Bresson, etc. Among musicians – Bach, Beethoven, Mozart, Schumann, Ravel, Fauré and Pärt. Among painters: Renoir, Delacroix, Monet, Picasso, Cocteau, and van Gogh.

Godard, François Truffaut remarked in a famous eulogy,

is not the only one who films as he breathes, but he is the one who breathes best. He is quick like Rossellini,

34 Over the course of his film career, Godard made enemies and there were fall-outs – with François Truffaut, for example, and Gérard Depardieu and Jean-Paul Belmondo.
35 Vadim was a model for Godard and Truffaut: his cinema offered a break with filmic tradition and the older generation of directors (W. Dixon, 14).
36 Jerry Lewis was one of Godard's favourites (Lewis is regarded as a titan for French *cinéastes*, as Woody Allen later was).
37 François Truffaut and Claude Chabrol were involved with *À Bout de Souffle*, of course, as writer and adviser.

wicked like Sacha Guitry, musical like Orson Welles, simple like Pagnol, hurt like Nicholas Ray, effective like Hitchcock, profound, profound, profound like Ingmar Bergman and insolent like nobody else.[38]

Some critics have pointed to Roberto Rossellini as the key cinematic influence on Jean-Luc Godard, above all of the other filmmakers enshrined by the 'Hitchcocko-Hawksiens' in 1950s Paris. Certainly Godard venerated Rossellini very highly. He never seems to have got over seeing *Voyage To Italy* (while I haven't got thru it even once). *Voyage To Italy* demonstrated to the young *Cahiers du Cinéma* crowd how one could make a movie big on themes and drama on a low budget: all you needed was two actors and a car. Godard stayed with Rossellini in Rome and was impressed with his lifestlye (including his affairs with women). But Godard disagreed with some of Rossellini's attitudes and ideas: Rossellini was not a total cinephile, like Godard, for instance. And Rossellini's emotional distance from his subjects Godard didn't care for.

Jean-Luc Godard, always the devotee of cinema, commented a number of times that certain films were so good it was not really possible to talk about them. One could only murmur, 'it is the most beautiful of films'. That was enough. *Voyage To Italy, Taboo* and *Le Carrosse d'or* were some of the films Godard was talking about not being able to talk about (that's certainly true of *Taboo*, an astonishing movie like no other, filmed by F.W. Murnau and a cast of unknowns in the South Seas with little to no crew and barely any money).

Jean-Luc Godard's work has always been piled high with literary, cinematic and cultural allusions and quotations. There are references in his early movie *Charlotte et Son Jules* to Goethe, Poe, Petrarch, Aragon, Chandler, Bataille, Baudelaire, Degas, Rasputin, Homer, Balzac, Éluard, Giraudoux, and

---

38 Truffaut, in J. Gerber, 113.

Queneau, among others. Early film criticism was filled with references to Manet, Ingres, Poussin, Botticelli, Titian, Diderot, Gide, Sartre, Stendhal, Dostoievsky, and Schumann. By the time of the 1980s, Godard had included more cultural references than any comparable film director in his works. And he continued into the 1990s, 2000s, 2010s, etc.

INGMAR BERGMAN.

Jean-Luc Godard was a huge fan of Ingmar Bergman's films. Godard called Bergman 'the most original filmmaker of the European cinema' (*Godard On Godard*, 76). Godard raved about the retrospective of Bergman's films that was showing at the Cinémathèque Française in Paris in 1958, and called *Summer With Monika* 'the most original film of the most original of directors', and likened it to *The Birth of a Nation*, no less, in terms of its significance for modern cinema, as D.W. Griffith's epic production was for classical cinema (G, 84). Godard had a go at doing his own version of *Summer With Monika* in *Pierrot le Fou* (and other movies). 'Because that which is precise, Bergman proves, will be new, and that which is profound will be precise' (G, 78).

However, the admiration didn't run the other way![39] Ingmar Bergman thought that Godard was 'a fucking bore'! Bergman griped:

I've never got anything out of his movies. They have felt constructed, faux intellectual, and completely dead. Cinematographically uninteresting and infinitely boring. Godard is a fucking bore. He's made his films for the critics. (Quoted in M. Kermode, 11)

Ingmar Bergman, J.-L. Godard reckoned, was

the filmmaker of the instant. His camera seeks only one

39 'It is easy to underestimate his passion for monotony, symmetry, and a one-and-one-equals-two simplicity' (Manny Farber, 263).

thing: to seize the present moment at its most fugitive, and to delve into it so as to give it the quality of eternity. (G, 85)

And the 'tricks' that Bergman employed – the unusual camera angles, the cuts to clouds or lakes, the mannered compositions – were not gratuitous, but integrated into the psychology of the characters.

For Jean-Luc Godard (writing in 1958), Ingmar Bergman was the last great Romantic, in the tradition of Beethoven or Balzac. This is from a *Cahiers du Cinéma* article by Godard:

The cinema is not a craft. It is an art. It does not mean teamwork. One is always alone; on the set as before the blank page. And for Bergman, to be alone means to ask questions. And to make films means to answer them. Nothing could be more classically romantic.

ROBERT BRESSON.

Jean-Luc Godard often referred to Robert Bresson, although they were very different filmmakers. There is of course no one quite like Bresson – he's a one-off, like Carl-Theodor Dreyer or Jean Cocteau. Unrepeatable – and impossible to emulate. For Godard, Bresson 'is the French cinema, as Dostoievsky is the Russian novel and Mozart is German music' (*Godard On Godard,* 47). In the early 1960s Godard was planning to make a movie of one of his favourite authors, Georges Bernanos: *La Nouvelle Histoire de Mouchette*, which Bresson later filmed (and Godard married Anne Wiazemsky, who appeared in Bresson's *Au Hasard, Balthazar*).

Robert Bresson's *Notes On Cinematography*, a wonderful book of ideas on how to make films – in which Bresson sets out his idiosyncratic ideas about actors as 'models', and his ascetic notions of sound, music and image – was influential on Godard, for example in his later films (a character reads aloud from it in *Elogie de l'Amour*). Here is a representative sprinkling of Bressonisms:

- It is not a matter of acting 'simple' or of acting 'inward' but of not acting at all.
- Build your film on white,[40] on silence and on stillness.
- Make visible what, without you, might perhaps never have been seen.
- No music as accompaniment, support or re-inforcement. *No music at all*.

In 1952 (age 22), Jean-Luc Godard wrote:

A beautiful face, as La Bruyère wrote, is the most beautiful of sights. There is a famous legend which has it that Griffith, moved by the beauty of his leading lady, invented the close-up in order to capture it in greater detail. Paradoxically, therefore, the simplest close-up is also the most moving. (G, 28)

Yes, and Jean-Luc Godard has provided many beautiful close-ups in his cinema, with those images of Myriem Roussel and Anna Karina among the most entrancing.

---

40 Godard followed that, but he built his later films on black (on black leader).

Roland Quilici©

3

THE *JOUISSANCE* OF CINEMA

> I need images in order to live and need to show them to others.

Jean-Luc Godard[1]

THE *JOUISSANCE* OF GODARD'S CINEMA

> One must film, talk about everything. Everything remains to be done.

Jean-Luc Godard

One shouldn't under-estimate the *joy* of making cinema that comes across in many of Jean-Luc Godard's films.[2] There are many other ways of making a living, and making movies is a stressful, difficult business. So Godard, like other filmmakers who are nuts about cinema, such as Werner Herzog, Steven Spielberg or Tsui Hark, must *really like* making films. He could probably have stopped a long time ago and been comfortably off, living in Switzerland, in retirement. He didn't need to keep making films and TV programmes for the money (and not in his seventies and eighties!). For Godard, speaking in the late

1 Godard in 1979, in *Travelling*, Documents Cinémathèque Suisse, 56-57, Spring, 1980.
2 Godard called *Une Femme Mariée* 'a film... where the cinema plays happily, delighted to be only what it is' (G, 208). The best of Godard's films have this quality of the sheer pleasure of making movies.

1970s, cinema was 'the paradise for the study of life while living it'.

Because the sheer volume, and diversity, of J.-L.G.'s output is staggering. This is a man utterly in love with making images and editing them together and adding sound effects and music and voiceover and directing actors and all the rest of it. And that *jouissance* does come across in his films. You can see it in *Contempt*, or *Weekend*, or *Éloge de L'Amour*. It's a seduction of the form, as well as the content, as well as the ability to make statements about the world. [3]

To make so many films, and so many *good* films, you've got to be very talented, obviously, and lucky, but you've also got to *love* doing it. And you've got to have immense stamina, and dedication, and numerous skills (most prominent being dealing with people. And patience).

The *quality* of Jean-Luc Godard's output is also astounding. I mean, there have been plenty of filmmakers who have churned out movies and TV shows but there have always been weaker entries and outright turkeys in their C.V.. Not for Godard. No. I don't think he's made a bad film or TV show or video. Ever. He's one of those film artists, like Woody Allen, or Carl-Theodor Dreyer, or Werner Herzog, who puts out an immensely high standard of work. (However, it's not a perfect filmography: there are one or two clunkers – *King Lear* and *Grandeur and Decadence,* for instance, and some that didn't really work – *Nouvelle Vague*. And Allen has laid some eggs, too – *To Rome With Love* and *Magic In the Moonlight*).

The *volume* of it, the *quality* of it, the *range* of it, the *intelligence* of it, and the variety of the *forms* of it make Jean-Luc's cinema among the most remarkable in the history of cinema. OK, we're dealing in superlatives on top of superlatives here, so we need to qualify what we're saying.

3 Godard's is a cinema of sounds and images: he said he preferred to speak of sounds and images instead of cinema or television.

There are filmmakers who are very talented, produce great bodies of work, but who, ultimately, are not what you would class as one of the 'great' filmmakers, who could rank alongside Chaplin or Griffith or Dreyer or Kurosawa. Godard is one of the very few film artists who can join that company.

Jean-Luc Godard is a 'filmmaker's filmmaker' at the level of production: even tho' he's been making movies for over fifty years, there is still a feeling of spontaneity and energy about his productions: few other directors of his stature and CV still transmit the youthful exuberance of simply going out with a camera with a few crew and a couple of actors and doing something, making something. Godard can come up with a film using a small van for the equipment and two cars for everyone else. By contrast, walk past a movie or TV production on the streets of New York or Los Angeles, and you'll see giant trucks, make-up trailers, honey wagons, and *lots* of cars – and all of that just for a simple dialogue scene featuring two actors!

WRITERS AND READING

> Poetry is what is truly and absolutely real, this is the kernel of my philosophy. The more poetic, the more true.
>
> Novalis[4]

Isn't it wonderful that Jean-Luc Godard can have characters quoting from Friedrich Hölderlin,[5] Arthur Rimbaud or Rainer Maria Rilke and not sounding like pretentious idiots? Isn't it great that Godard himself can quote from Rimbaud or

---

4 Novalis, *Works* (Minor), Schlegel, Paris, 1837, III, 11
5 It was Godard's father who introduced him to German Romanticism, Godard said in *Le Monde* (Sept 5, 1991), and references to Goethe, Novalis, Hölderlin and others can be found throughout Godard's cinema.

Hölderlin or Rilke and not sound like an arrogant snob?[6] That's another difference between British and French filmmakers. British artists can just about get away with citing William Shakespeare, but not much else, while North American filmmakers might stretch to evoking Ernest Hemingway or William Faulkner.

It's not only Hölderlin, Rimbaud and Rilke, though: Jean-Luc Godard's *œuvre* is amongst the most well-read and well-informed and literary cinema in the history of the medium.[7] This is a filmmaker *utterly in love* with books and writers. There are numerous images of people picking up books, or reading aloud from them, or using the covers to communicate with each other, and numerous close-ups of book covers (no other director has included so many book covers in their films. Maybe Godard received funding from Gallimard or Editions de Minuit?). And the books are always those French softbacks with the uncut pages. Wonderful.

Favourite writers for Jean-Luc Godard included Honoré de Balzac, Arthur Rimbaud, Ferdinand Céline, Rainer Maria Rilke, Raymond Chandler, William Faulkner, Fyodor Dostoievsky, Dylan Thomas, André Bazin, Michel de Montaigne, Bertholt Brecht, Lewis Carroll, Elie Fauré, James Joyce, Thomas Hardy, Jean Giraudoux, Marguerite Duras, David Goodis, Louis Aragon, Paul Éluard, Paul Valéry and Jean-Paul Sartre. (The influence of Sartre and Existentialism is easy to spot in Godard's cinema and thought: Godard hung out in St-Germain-des-Prés in the 1950s, soaking up the philosophical culture: 'I wanted to read everything. I wanted to know everything. Existentialism was at its peak at that time. Through Sartre I discovered literature, and he led me to

6 Pauline Kael remarked that sometimes 'there is a disarming, an almost ecstatic innocence about the way he uses quotes as if he had just heard of these beautiful ideas and wanted to share his enthusiasm with the world' (1969, 21).
7 Godard pointed out that people don't say they read an 'old Stendhal book', but they do say they saw an 'old Griffith' or an 'old Chaplin' film (G, 219).

everything else,' Godard later recalled in 1964. Sartre had showed him how to unify his work and life, Godard said).

Michel de Montaigne was another influence – Godard thought of himself as a film essayist.[8] Among philosophers: Friedrich Nietzsche, G.W.F. Hegel, Karl Marx, Vladimir Lenin, Sigmund Freud, Simone Weil and Mao Zedong. Jean-Jacques Rousseau's *Émile* was the basis of *Le Gai Savoir*, a commission from the French TV channel ORTF.

And don't forget Lewis Carroll (1832-98) – Jean-Luc Godard loves word games and puzzles. There are numerous references in Godard's cinema to *Alice's Adventures In Wonderland* (1865). Sometimes his actors meet characters from Lewis Carroll (as in *Weekend*). Godard once described *Breathless* as more like *Alice In Wonderland* than *Scarface* (he was aiming for *Scarface*, but it came out like *Alice*). Easy to see how the illogical logic, or the logical illogic, of Carroll's fiction, the emphasis on speaking, on words, and philosophizing, would appeal to Godard (as well as the undercurrent of violence, and the healthy doses of surreality).

Thomas Hardy was another writer Jean-Luc Godard admired (another Brit, by the way), referring to him a number of times in his work. Godard made many films from novels, but how wonderful would it have been to see Godard tackling *The Woodlanders* or *Jude the Obscure*? The most obviously Godardian novel, though, is of course *Tess of the d'Urbervilles;* in fact, Godard hoped to make a version of *Tess* around 1962 with, of course, Anna Karina to star. The virulent anger and social rebellion that suffuses Hardy's two late novels – *Tess* and *Jude the Obscure* – is something I'd love to see Godard exploring. (But we know that a Hardy adaptation *à la* Godard would be as far away from twee heritage cinema and quaint TV dramas as possible!).

---

8 Godard said he regarded his films as 'essays': 'I am an essayist with a camera'. An essayist 'producing essays in novel form, or novels in essay form: only instead of writing, I film them'.

Jean-Luc Godard's sister Véronique remembered Godard telling her often that you only needed to read the first and last page of a book. He was famous for it (Francois Truffaut said he would read the first and last pages of every book on people's bookshelves). As Sam Goldwyn put it, 'I read part of the book right the way through'. It's clear from films such as *King Lear* (1987) that Godard only dipped into William Shakespeare's play, and it's quite likely that he didn't actually sit down and read the whole thing through. It's just as possible that Godard took up a students' study guide to the Bard, like *Brodie's Notes* or *York Notes*.

One of Jean-Luc Godard's favourite phrases by Rainer Maria Rilke – for me the greatest poet of the twentieth century – was: 'beauty is the beginning of the terror that we are able to bear'. There's another Rilke connection with Godard: *Lou n'as pas dit non* (1994) was Anne-Marie Miéville's film based on the letters of Rilke and Lou Andreas-Salomé, one of the most fascinating of creative relationships in recent history. Andreas-Salomé (1861-1937) is a truly intriguing woman: not only was she associated with Rilke, she was apparently the only woman that Friedrich Nietzsche ever loved, and she later worked with Sigmund Freud.

A favourite device of Godard's in his 1960s films was to introduce a real philosopher to mull over some of the themes and issues raised by the stories. The philosophers typically pop up in the final act, usually chatting with the main character: Brice Parain (one of Godard's former tutors) turns up in a café to talk with Anna Karina in *Vivre Sa Vie*; Roger Leenhardt is introduced in *A Married Woman*; Francis Jeanson appears on a train to assess the political committment of Anne Wiazemsky in *La Chinoise*; and Jean-Pierre Melville plays a similar role in the airport scene in *Breathless*.

But these are not conversations between the actors and the philosophers, but between Godard and the philosophers:

either the questions are scripted by Godard, or Godard feeds the questions to the actors through an ear-piece. The Chat With a Philosopher scenes lift us out of the fiction of the films, and into the realm of ideas, of debates in universities and coffee houses.

GODARD COLLABORATORS

Jean-Luc Godard said he was only 'half' a person unless he was collaborating with someone:

> I think I'm the only person, apart from perhaps Mao or other people that I haven't heard about, who thinks of himself as half, as not complete. Movies and communic-ation help me to think that way and working together with someone else. (M, 103)

Consequently, Jean-Luc Godard has had some signific-ant collaborations in his film career: with filmmakers such as Anne-Marie Miéville, Jean-Pierre Gorin, Jean-Henri Roger and D.A. Pennebaker. (He could do everything in film himself, though. Godard has been described as an artist, theoretician, boss, artisan, actor, businessman, producer, prophet, historian and critic.)

Jean-Luc Godard's career has included many important collaborations: with Raoul Coutard, his cinematographer of the 1960s films (he was re-united with Coutard for 1982's *Passion*); actors such as Anna Karina (Godard's first wife), Jean-Paul Belmondo, Jean-Pierre Léaud, Anne Wiazemsky (his second wife),9 László Szabó, Jane Fonda (as well as appearing in *Tout Va Bien*, Fonda was also the subject of

9 In 2001, Godard remarked of the women and actresses he'd loved: 'When I hear about them, I think about it, but it seems like another life to me. I think they were more disappointed than I was'.

Godard's 1972 *Letter to Jane*); assistant directors Charles Bitsch[10] and Romain Goupil; make-up artist Jackie Reynal;[11] the composers Michel Legrand and Georges Delerue; the editors Agnès Guillemot and Lila Lakshman; sound in many earlier films was by René Levert and Antoine Bonfanti, and in later films by François Mussy;[12] production manager (and later producer) Ruth Waldburger;[13] and filmmakers such as Jean-Henri Roger and Jean-Pierre Gorin, of the Dziga-Vertov Group. Producers should be noted, too: Carlo Ponti and Georges de Beauregard in the earlier films, Philippe Dussart and Anatole Dauman in the mid-1960s, and Alain Sarde from the late 1970s onwards (producers Sarde and Ruth Waldburger were important supporters and enablers of Godard's later films).

The Polish Anatole Dauman (1925-98) was one of the key film producers of the 1950s-1990s period. Dauman had credits that included art house classics such as *Hiroshima Mon Amour, Masculin/ Féminin* and *Mouchette*. Dauman founded Argos Films in 1951, with Philippe Lifchitz.

One of Anatole Dauman's specialities was the combination of softcore porn and art cinema (or arty films with plenty of erotic components, taking advantage of the relaxation of what was deemed acceptable in the film market in the late 1960s and early 1970s): Dauman produced *Immoral Tales* and *The Beast* (dir. by Walerian Borowczyk); *In the Realm of the Senses* (Nagisa Oshima), *Fruits of Passion,* and *The Tin Drum.* Dauman's *resumé* on the art cinema circuit (via his company Argos Films) is impeccable: Alain

---

10 Bitsch was one of the old *Cahiers du Cinéma* crowd, having met Rohmer and Truffaut back in 1949.
11 Jackie Reynal did all of Anna Karina's make-up, beginning with *A Woman Is a Woman.* So Reynal is another vital collaborator, helping to give the Karina-Godard films their astonishing beauty.
12 François Mussy was an important adviser on the technical aspects of Godard's later cinema, too, when Godard set himself up in Rolle and Grenoble with his own filmmaking facilities.
13 Art directors or set designers are not often noted credited on Godard films, although there are set builders.

Resnais (*Hiroshima Mon Amour, Night and Fog, Last Year At Marienbad, Muriel*), Robert Bresson (*Au Hasard Balthazar, Mouchette*), Jean Rouch (*Chronicle of a Summer*), Alexander Astruc (*Crimson Curtain*), Nagisa Oshima (*Empire of Passion*), Andrei Tarkovsky (*The Sacrifice*), Volker Schlöndorff (*Circle of Deceit*), Wim Wenders (*Paris, Texas, Wings of Desire*), Chris Marker (*Sunless, Sunday In Peking*), and Jean-Luc Godard's *Masculin-Féminin* and *Two or Three Things I Know About Her*. (At least 8 of those films are regarded as masterpieces).

Many of Godard's movies were financed with deals with distributors and exhibitors: Godard took a dim view of them, likening them to civil servants, people who had no idea about cinema. Producers, on the other hand, were colleagues, showmen:

> Crazy, stubborn, half-witted, innocent or stupid, they are kindred spirits. They chance their money on things with no idea how they will turn out, often just because they want to. (G, 184)

Anne-Marie Miéville, his private and professional partner, collaborated with Jean-Luc Godard from the 1970s to the 21st century. Miéville (b. November 11, 1945, Lausanne, Switzerland) was politically active in Switzerland and France[14] (and like Godard, she moved between the two countries regularly).

Anne-Marie Miéville is *hugely significant* in Godard's cinema, and must always be taken into account – and not only as co-author and editor and co-director, but as a major influence on Godard's art.[15] (Solely as the editor of many of Godard's later movies would make Miéville a major collaborator, but she has been much more than that). Miéville co-directed *France/ tour/ détour/ deux/ enfants,* co-directed

14 For instance, the bookstore Miéville worked in was pro-Palestine (B, 359).
15 Their marriage broke down around 1976, but they continued to live together, or in adjacent apartments.

Six fois deux, co-wrote *Comment ça va?,* wrote *Prénom Carmen,* co-wrote *Détective,* co-directed *Soft and Hard,* co-directed *Le Rapport Darty,* and art directed *Nouvelle Vague.* (However, Godard's cinema made with Miéville is patchier than his 1960s work, with more failures. Also, one can't help noticing that the staging and blocking (of actors) in Godard's later work is much more static, much more about people sitting down, at tables, making phone calls, drinking, smoking, talking, and being, well, very middle-aged (and bourgeois). And one wonders if this dissatisfying dramatic development is also a result of Miéville's influence).

Let's emphasize one vital point here: Jean-Luc Godard *did not* write the scripts for all of his films. Most of them, yes, but not all of them. *Slow Motion,* for instance, was written by Anne-Marie Miéville and Jean-Claude Carrière. *Detective* was written by Miéville, Alain Sarde and Philippe Setbon. *Tout Va Bien* was co-written by Jean-Pierre Gorin (who also co-directed), as was *Letter To Jane. Vent d-Est* was co-written with Gorin and Daniel Cohn-Bendit. *British Sounds* was co-written with Jean-Henri Roger. *Les Carabiniers* was co-written with Jean Gruault and Roberto Rossellini. And some of Godard's later TV and video pieces were co-directed and co-written by Miéville.

If you read lots of Jean-Luc Godard criticism, you'll find the same Godard collaborators cited again and again – the actors, the cameramen, the writers sometimes, the producers sometimes, sometimes a designer, very occasionally an editor or assistant director, but no one else. Film criticism routinely ignores make-up, hair, costume designers, prop men, 2nd units, sound people, and a host of other crew. What? Did the actors walk on set in their street clothes and go straight into shooting without hair or make-up? Did those props appear out of nowhere? (Someone had to source all those guns and cars, for instance).

In the 1980s, Jean-Luc Godard again attempted to surround himself with a group of collaborators who would work with him not on one production, but as regular employees. They included DPs Caroline Champetier, Jean-Pierre Menoud and Julien Hirsch, sound man François Mussy and assistant Hervé Duhamel. The bid for independence included buying an Arriflex camera and some super-speed lenses.16 (Note that Godard has worked with female DPs, such as Sophie Maintigneux and Caroline Champetier).

And there's one person who's absolutely vital but who is *never* cited in film criticism, and that's the casting director. This all-important function on a Jean-Luc Godard production seems to have been over-seen often by Godard himself, and as the casting director doesn't appear on many Godard filmographies, one guesses that casting was undertaken by the producers, as usual on a movie.

THE POETRY OF IDEAS

> All experiences are moral experiences, even in the realm of sense perception.

> Friedrich Nietzsche, *The Gay Science*

I haven't seen every scrap of film or video that Jean-Luc Godard has produced (who has? Very few people on the planet), but as far as I can tell he hasn't delivered a single conventional film or TV programme. Maybe his TV commercials are traditional, but I bet they aren't.

Jean-Luc Godard's not a cinema of absolutes but processes, not endpoints but departures and journeys, not static but eternally restless, not closed but open, not modern

---

16 Godard liked to shoot in very low level conditions, so fast lenses were essential.

but postmodern. Godard emphasizes *process*, a cinema in the process of being constructed,[17] a cinema of ideas which give birth to further ideas, a cinema of developments and suggestions (J. Rosenbaum, 1995). Though Godard can seem to be getting up on his soapbox and ranting about a myriad of targets (as yet another Left Bank philosopher and Parisian intellectual), his cinema is rather one of questions, ideas for debates, not fixed in some dogmatic worldview. His films are not 'traditional' nor 'classical' narratives or forms; they are film-essays, a series of disquisitions, theses, suggestions, questions, which freely mix a variety of cinematic forms, from documentary and *cinéma verité* to Hollywood melodrama and extreme stylization. They are not fixed, definite, finished, but in flux: works in progress. Some of the early films have a conventional narrative form, but the later ones, such as *Socialism* or *Nouvelle Vague*, do not.

Godard simply leaves out scenes which other films and screenwriters would automatically put in – the exposition scenes, the explaining scenes, the watering-hole scenes, the transition scenes. As Pauline Kael put it, Godard had a nonchalant, irreverent tendency towards narrative: 'it's the casual way he omits mechanical scenes that don't interest him so that the movie is all high points and marvelous "little things"' (1969, 140). As if Godard has the film in his head, and has already thought up the exposition, made the connections, and done the transition scenes, so he doesn't put them in the film – and the audience is expected to keep up, to make the dramatic links, and to invent their own exposition.

Although they are usually categorized as European art movies, in the same cultural arena as the films of Truffaut, Fellini, Bergman, Wajda and Buñuel, they are quite different from the usual kind of European art film. 'I am half a novelist

17 A Godard film 'gives the impression not of the complete but of the ongoing,' said Gilberto Perez, 'a world in process of taking place' (*The Material Ghost*, Johns Hopkins University Press, 1998, 337).

and half an essayist', Godard said,[18] identifying the twin strands of his artistic make-up, the poet and the philosopher, the writer and the critic.[19] Part of Godard's cinema recreates fictions, adventures, fantasies, characters, situations (more often in the early films); at the same time, Godard's cinema is also taking apart those fictions and conventions, and continually asking questions. There has rarely been such a *curious* cinema, such a cinema so interested in the world and how it works. ('I am constantly asking questions. I watch myself filming, and you hear me thinking aloud' [G, 239]).

No filmmaker has asked more questions on screen to his actors, stopping the action in the middle of a fiction film.

No filmmaker has included so much voiceover, nor delivered so much voiceover themselves (and in a whisper, too!).

Peter Wollen drew up a table of the characteristics of the art film or 'counter cinema', in a piece on Jean-Luc Godard and *Wind From the East*; Colin MacCabe suggested three types of film (classic realist, progressive realist and *avant garde*); Paul Willemen offered four types of film, depending on whether a film prevents, allows, encourages or requires an 'active reading'; Noël Burch and Jorge Dana suggested three types: classical films, films which depart on stylistic grounds, and films which question dominant codes. Clearly, Godard's films have been part of each of these definitions, and there's always a strong element of questioning cinema in every Jean-Luc Godard film.

Godard's is a cinema about cinema, a cinema that never tires of deconstructing cinema. It is a cinema in which the filmmaker is taking apart and revealing the grammar, the

18 In D. Sterritt, 1999, 35.
19 As a youth, Godard had ambitions to be a novelist, and sometimes bragged (to Suzanne Schiffman) that he wrote 30 pages each morning. Cinema in the end saved Godard from having to write those promised Great Novels, and match himself up to the Great Writers. Instead, he became a Great Filmmaker.

conventions, the traditions, the genres, the star system, the expectations, the perceptions and the ideologies of cinema. Godard's project has, in part, been a radical exploration of what cinema is, and what it can do. Godard's cinema refuses to accept cinematic conventions without questioning them; Godard's cinema refutes the notion that films 'capture' reality, that they transcribe the real world unadulterated, and that cinema can somehow render psychological and social aspects directly.[20]

If Godard has renounced mainstream cinema, as he insisted, it becomes more difficult to assess his work. That is, you can't apply the usual criteria of assessment to his cinema, because he has stated he is trying for something different.

Jean-Luc Godard's cinema can seem disruptive, like a filmmaker playing at acting the intellectual rebel, revelling in overturning traditions, genres, conventions, fictions.[21] It's not like that at all, though: rather, Godard's project is to interrogate the very mechanisms and forms that filmmakers as well as audiences take for granted.[22] Godard's arguments – social, political, æsthetic, ideological – are not set in stone, but are continually being revised with each film, and within each film. Godard does not lay out a carefully-structured argument in each film, that proceeds from point to point, with scenes illustrating his themes. Rather, Godard suggests possibilities for discussion, proposing ideas that can be considered. One of the ways Godard does this is by foregrounding the apparatus

20 For Godard, the real and the unreal fuse with one another, there is a continuity between the imaginary and the real (R. Roud, 54).
21 Godard said he always worked from the margin, from the margin looking in, and the margin was the 'real position of the public', 'a necessary position', because '[t]hat which is seen cannot be seen without those who see it' (1998, 135).
22 For Gerald Mast and Bruce Kawin, 'Godard unsentimentally depicts both irrational moments of fleeting sensation and long-winded speeches of abstract rational argument, both moments of violent action and hours of inactive discussion, outrageous intrusions and the director's favorite film sequences and book titles and long unedited scenes in which the director attempts to efface himself completely' (359).

of cinema, in the manner of Bertholt Brecht, exposing the usually hidden mechanisms of film, the way it produces seemingly seamless fictions. Godard wants to investigate what lies *behind* cinema's fictions, what is 'invisible' in cinema, what creeps into the audience's subconscious without them realizing it. Godard does not simply want to reproduce reality, or fictions, he wants to take apart how they are constructed. Assumptions are smashed, as are expectations (though not pleasures – Godard's is an extremely pleasurable cinema).

Thompson and Bordwell explained in *Film History* how Brecht aimed to create the alienation effect:

> Brecht proposed several techniques that might accomplish this: breaking the play into episodes, interspering titles, separating text from music or performance, and letting performers speak the lines as if quoting them. (521)

For Manny Farber, the Godard-character is eternally rebellious, always opposed to whatever the established social order is (rebellion for rebellion's sake, a mere stance), and self-consciously primitive: for the Farbster, the Godard-character is

> the feeling of a little boy drifter, a very poetic and talented self-indulgent Tom Sawyer, who can be a brainy snot throwing doctrinaire slogans or coyly handling books so that the hip spectator can just barely make out the title. (264)

Jean-Luc Godard is one of the most 'poetic' of filmmakers, in a number of ways. He alludes to many poets, such as Lorca, Rimbaud, Valéry, Goethe and Hölderlin, among others (in voiceovers, in written texts on screen, in his montages). His cinematic style is intensely poetic, with its hypnotic combinations of sounds, images, words, and voiceover. One can imagine that Arthur Rimbaud, if he could see Godard's films, would really enjoy them – for their anarchic approach, their (apparently) improvized performances, their radical politics, their simultaneous attacks on and eulogies of popular culture. (That is, Rimbaud before he went to Africa and became utterly disenchanted with life).

Allusions to Arthur Rimbaud occur in *Vivre Sa Vie*, *Made in U.S.A.* and *Pierrot le Fou*. In some ways, Jean-Luc Godard is the most Rimbaudian of directors, developing Rimbaud's sense of radical Romanticism, his extremism, his anarchic politics, his artistic rigour, his philosophical purity, his overarching curiosity, his love of travel and movement (Godard's 'between'), his love of the city, and his total dissatisfaction with French society and politics.

Spontaneity is another key weapon in the cinematic arsenal of Jean-Luc Godard's project: he encourages spontaneity in actors, and crew, in an approach to cinema. If the phone rings during a take in a real café, he will use it (as in *Masculin Féminin*). Some aspects of his cinema are obviously well-rehearsed (the lengthy tracking shot in *Weekend*, for example), because they have to be. One can't set-up a scene like that without rehearsing nearly all of it. There is, though, a greater degree of spontaneity in Godard's cinema than in most. Or there *appears* to be: because if you see Godard at work, and hear from his actors, you'll realize that pretty much everything is worked out in detail.[23]

Another way of defining what *seems* like improvization (to onlookers) in the cinema of Godard is that sometimes he decides what do at the last minute, rather than planning it all months before. If you decide what to do just before shooting, that's not improvization, Godard asserted, it's just making a last minute decision. (Anna Karina recalled that sometimes

<hr>

23 True: Pauline Kael commented that Godard's 'technical control is superb, so complete that one cannot tell improvisation from planning' (1969, 21).

the Maestro would tell them what to do half-an-hour before they were shooting, so they were working on nerves, and there was no time to plan).

EMOTIONS

> Things are entirely what they appear to be, and *behind them*... there is nothing.

> Jean-Paul Sartre, *Nausea*

Some critics have called Jean-Luc Godard's films emotionally cold and distant. The same criticisms have been levelled at Stanley Kubrick, Andrei Tarkovsky, Ridley Scott and Peter Greenaway. It's true that Godard's films are clever, witty, ironic, stylized, radical, bombastic, but rarely emotionally engaging, in the sense of sentiment. His films are enjoyed on other levels; at least, I can't think of being moved by Godard's films in that respect, except by *Hail Mary, Pierrot le Fou* and *Vivre Sa Vie* (and the opening ten minutes of *Our Music*, which is overwhelming). Godard doesn't produce films of uplifting waves of emotion, like *Mr Smith Goes To Washington* or *The Wizard of Oz*. No romantic weepies, no stories of one man fighting against the social system and winning, no stories of aliens befriending boys and flying away. (Filmmakers who *can* generate big emotions are cherished by viewers).

And it's true that the dramas of Jean-Luc Godard's most famous films, of the Sixties (usually involving a bunch of young people and assorted lovers),[24] are not particularly emotionally gripping. His characters seduce each other, flirt, argue, fall apart, and betray each other, but I don't think viewers are (meant to be) emotionally involved with these

---

24 'Had he done nothing else, Godard should be remembered for having invented an army of graceful, clumsy, feeble oddballs' (Manny Farber, 265).

people.[25] You watch them for the wit of their rejoinders, or the speed of their gestures, their frowns and stares, their rebellious attitudes. It's a dance, a polemic in the style of a screwball comedy, but it doesn't compel the feelings.

Does Godard 'believe in' the stories he tells in the movies he directs? Presumably, yes – partly because he often he says he *didn't* shoot, or *didn't* take up a subject or book or whatever, because he wasn't inspired, didn't feel connected to it, or didn't know what to film. 'The important thing, as Douglas Sirk demonstrates, is to believe in what one is doing in order to make it believable', Godard wrote in 1959 (G, 138).

Jean-Luc Godard's films are moving in other ways: the sense of elegy, of melancholia, of isolation – of the sadness of contemplating history – are part of the later films. It's impossible not be moved by the orchestration of imagery from recent times that the *maître* includes in films like *Éloge de L'Amour, Notre Musique* and *JLG/ JLG.* I mean the images of wars, of the concentration camps, of suffering in so many parts of the globe. (Godard included his own explorations of the Holocaust in *Histoire(s) du Cinéma* and *Éloge de L'Amour:* he had famously put *A Place In the Sun* and Elizabeth Taylor next to footage of death camps.)

And yet, altho' Godard has explored the issue of the Shoah, drawing attention to it many times, he has been accused of anti-semitism. Well, it's true that Godard does sometimes make controversial statements (knowing full well that they'll wind people up), but few other major filmmakers address so many vital issues, including one of the most important events in human history.

25 For Manny Farber, Godard's characters were always incomplete: they required the director himself to complete them (264).

CAMEOS

Another aspect of Jean-Luc Godard's cinema that shouldn't be ignored is his vanity and love of performance himself. Godard often appears in his films – like Rainer Fassbinder or Pier Paolo Pasolini or Werner Herzog (and, like them, he isn't a great actor). His image is easy to spot: a middle-aged guy with short, dark hair in a long coat or raincoat, always with tinted glasses,[26] behind which beady eyes gleam, always with a cigarette (later it was cigars), and a hoarse, croaky, low voice (which comedians in France send up – everyone can do their 'Godard voice' and recite pretentious Godardisms). Godard was a regular feature on French television, on intellectual shows or in the news. Godard has, in short, a celebrity status that very few filmmakers ever achieve. He was the Orson Welles, the Sergei Eisenstein of French culture. (Godard has also appeared in other films as an actor – starting in 1950, and including movies like *Paris Belongs To Us, Cléo From 5 to 7, Shéhérazade, The Defector, Ciné-girl* and *We're Still Here*).

No one would take Jean-Luc Godard for a great actor appearing in his own films like, say, Orson Welles or Charlie Chaplin. But, like Alfred Hitchcock, Godard can't resist cameos, often playful ones. Sometimes, and more particularly in his later work, Godard takes on larger roles, with lines and cues and everything. You can see the other actors around him in scenes are a little wary and in awe too – after all, this guy is one of the most noteworthy European filmmakers.

In the later films, Jean-Luc Godard's cameos are like those of a kindly but stern, cool but implacable university professor, given to pithy one-liners and caustic observations.

26 At one point in *Alphaville,* Caution dons tinted shades *à la* Godard. David Thomson noted that Godard tried to appear impassive, cold, yet also emotional: 'European yet besotted with Americana, emotional but cold, an avant-gardist but eager for movie hits to surpass the rest of the gang' (2012, 331).

And, quite often, fond of lecturing (nay-sayers can point to Godard's tendency to lecture his audience. It's true: sometimes his films do come across like the work of a man with a thousand chips on his shoulder and a thousand 'issues' to address). In *Notre Musique* the Maestro plays himself as an affable guy who even smiles!

Had Godard been a fine actor and had he taken some lead roles, he might've been a titanic on-screen presence, equivalent to Orson Welles or Charlie Chaplin, a director-writer-producer-actor combo that could've been almost too powerful, too much. Instead of scenes where he asks questions thru his actors, we would've had Godard there, on screen. And instead of the actors, Godard himself would've performed the life-and-death scenarios. A scary thought! (Even so, Godard's presence is still powerfully felt in the interview scenes where he questions the actors thru another actor).

Godard references his fellow French (New Wave) directors many times in his movies (with posters, or in dialogue, or giving them cameos): Demy, Resnais, Miéville, Rouch, Rivette, Truffaut, Varda, Duras, Chabrol, etc.

One of J.-L.G.'s most endearing – and important – qualities is his honesty. The man is out-spoken and *doesn't give a hoot about what people think*. *Very* few artists in the global media arena are *truly* out-spoken and honest, even the ones who boast about speaking the 'truth'. Godard is. For many he probably goes too far. And the press – particularly in the French Republic – are fascinated by him (B, xv).

> For a long time, I tried to make a film in the United States
> but never succeeded. I'd meet people, and they'd say,
> "Very honored," and shake my hand; that's all. So I'd
> say, "If that's true, at least give me $10." The only one
> who did was Mel Brooks. "Oh, yes," he said, and gave
> me $10."

Jean-Luc Godard[27]

Jean-Luc Godard's cinema has always been a low budget
cinema. He's never had thousands of extras to command, or
vast sets built on backlots, or complex visual effects[28] costing
$80m (and produced by thousands of geeks at computers), or
enormous action set-pieces. He could have – no doubt
Godard, like many other successful filmmakers, will have had
studios and producers coming to him with big budget
projects. But Godard has always declined them. Godard could
easily have moved from his base in Paris or Rolle working on
low budget, personal films to be a director for hire from time
to time. Many European filmmakers of Godard's generation
did just that – sometimes to direct big European co-
productions, and sometimes to go to 'Ollywooood.

So the fact that Godard has based most of his films in
the contemporary era is partly a budgetary consideration. It's
simply cheaper (and more efficient) to set a film in
contemporary Paris than in Ancient Rome.[29] When Godard
directed a futuristic science fiction film in 1965 (*Alphaville*) of
course he staged it in Paris, as usual (but that's actually a
standard practice in futuristic sci-fi movies – *THX-1138, A
Clockwork Orange, Total Recall, Gattaca*, etc. You just chose

27 Quoted in A. Riding, 1992.
28 'Godard probably spent more on lunch than on special
effects', quipped John Scalzi (60).
29 *Breathless* was typical among New Wave films in being
filmed quickly, on a low budget, with amateur actors among the
secondary characters, a small crew, using lightweight 35mm
equipment, and available light. The conditions of creating New
Wave cinema inevitably led to contemporary-set stories.

the bits of architecture that look kind of futuristic).

I reckon that Jean-Luc Godard could have been one of the most fascinating of directors of big, historical films, had he chosen to do so. One wonders what Godard would have done with the gigantic budgets and resources of the large-scale historical films of the 1960s, for instance. If Godard instead of Sergei Bondarchuk had made *Waterloo* (1970), about Napoleon. Or if Godard had helmed *The Fall of the Roman Empire* (1964) instead of Anthony Mann (Mann was another of Godard's favourites among U.S. directors). But *Weekend* (1967) must have had a sizeable budget: there are scenes with extras, scenes with camera cranes and tracks, it's all location shooting, plenty of cars, and a big special effects crew for all of those fires, smoke and car wrecks. Yet in 2010 Godard estimated the budget of *Weekend* as 180,000 Euros! (= US $210,000. But $210,000 is equivalent to $1.95 million in 2025).

Jean-Luc Godard didn't make the historical and costume dramas that have been staples of French as well as European and North American cinema since the 1910s. Godard's reason for avoiding such genres was typical of the director: he couldn't make the costumes or designs real or authentic. He wasn't a costume designer, he hadn't lived in those times, so the film couldn't be 'realistic'. In the 1960s, Godard said if he made a film set in Ancient Rome (a very popular genre in the early 1960s), he'd have the actors speak in Latin, and so wouldn't be able to do it. (There have been some filmmakers who've attempted films set in the ancient world with characters speaking authentic languages – Derek Jarman and Paul Humphress made the lamentable *Sebastian* (1976), and, more recently and famously, the controversial and relentlessly violent *The Passion of the Christ* (2004), which grossed over $600 million worldwide, used ancient languages, and proved, for the zillionth time, that 'no one knows anything' in the movie business).

Nearly all of Jean-Luc Godard's films are set in the present day. That's a very significant element in his cinema. Very rarely has Godard gone back into the past to recreate it. Many of Godard's heroes in cinema of course did historical films (Ophüls, Renoir, Murnau, Welles, etc). Even a filmmaker like Alfred Hitchcock, whose films seem fixed in the contemporary era, in the 1950s and 1960s, produced historical films (*Rebecca, Under Capricorn, Jamaica Inn,* etc).

Jean-Luc Godard, though, is deeply immersed in the past, and history impinges on all of Godard's films – but he's really interested in the relationship between the past and the present, how the present arises out of the past, and how history is interweaved in the contemporary world. If Godard includes a historical figure, it'll be someone dressed in a costume who appears without explanation, like Jean-Pierre Léaud in *Weekend*. So his historical recreations are short skits. (Also, I reckon that Godard simply couldn't be bothered with all of the effort and complexity that a historical movie demands. He'd much rather turn up at a real airport, a real hotel, a real café, and film whatever's there, without wasting time in dressing sets or getting costumes just right. Historical movies are a lot more work. If Godard wants to evoke history, what does he do? He simply grabs a clip from another movie! Why bother recreating the past if another movie has already done it?).

Also, structurally, Jean-Luc Godard's movies start and run on until they finish, all in the contemporary era. Godard isn't interested in chopping up his narratives into segments of time: you don't find captions such as 'six months later'.[30] There are no flashbacks. No exposition. No origins. No childhood sequences, which're central to the cinema of, say, Federico Fellini, Hayao Miyazaki or Ingmar Bergman. No

---

30 Even tho' Godard employs captions more than anyone else.

JEAN-LUC GODARD ❂ 82

scenes explaining motives, experiences in childhood, or the family, or past lives. No parallel scenes (instead scenes occur one after another). No set-up scenes., No transition scenes. *La Chinoise* is unusual in including a sequence where, during the interview with the member of the Maoist cell who leaves (Henri), there are flashbacks.

One of the curious aspects of Jean-Luc Godard is that he doesn't discuss his early works much at all, and at times they seem to have been erased from his memory. That's not unusual among artists, who are chiefly concerned with the work in progress, and with future projects (to keep being pulled back to your early works is not healthy, like going over past relationships). But Godard also doesn't define himself or his current works in terms of his old works. He just doesn't go back there at all.[31]

Jean-Luc Godard isn't interested in discussing the New Wave era much. 'It's a past life,' he says. He doesn't keep in touch with his collaborators from that period either. 'It's like with any family. You see your relatives and then you don't. All of a sudden, they disappear and you don't know what has become of them.'

Godard has concentrated on filming in France and Switzerland, with the odd jaunt into Eastern Europe (Czechoslovakia – *Pravda*) and Italy (*Contempt*), twice to Britain, once to Morocco, once to Jordan, abandoned projects in the U.S.A., and once to Sweden (for budgetary reasons – *Masculine Feminine*). We might have expected him to visit Russia and China as a location at some point, particularly during the politicized years. Germany is also curiously left aside, as is Spain.

Jean-Luc Godard's production company, Sonimage, was based in Paris from the early Sixties (partly financed through Gaumont); it moved to Grenoble in the early Seventies, and to

31 Except in his *Histoire(s) du Cinéma* project, which quotes from his earlier films.

a suburb of Paris (Neuilly); in 1982 Godard changed the name to J.-L.G.; Godard had lived in Rolle on Lake Geneva since the early 1970s. (Krzysztof Kieslowski said that Geneva was one of the most unphotogenic cities in the world: after you'd filmed the fountain, there was virtually nothing else inspiring).[32] Jean-Luc Godard has refuted that numerous times: you could put Godard in the dullest, scuzziest place on Earth, and he would still be able to create magical cinema.

In 1981 Jean-Luc Godard described his production company set-up with Anne-Marie Miéville (at Sonimage) as basically two small apartments and two cars, with the company running on a small amount of money each month (1998, 123). 'We tried to live together and we failed, so we now have two separate apartments', Godard explained.[33] There was also a print room, a library, an editing room, and a record library nearby.

Most of Jean-Luc Godard's later films were made not far from Rolle, his base in Switzerland, and on schedules that Godard prepared himself, rather than being imposed by a studio. He is his own producer, then (but more successful than, say, Orson Welles was in his later career). However, Godard does work with producers, too – Alain Sarde and Ruth Waldburger, for instance, from the 1980s onwards.

In the 1980s, Hervé Duhamel, one of Godard's assistants, remembered seeing the Master write out an entire budget by hand once, including the entries for tax. But that's not so amazing, really, for a filmmaker who by then had made over 25 feature films, and who has been intimately involved in every aspect of filmmaking – including, and above all in some respects, the money.

It is not true that only if you have a great deal of money

32 That is kind of true, as *The Little Soldier*, the Algerian War thriller made there, showed.
33 Quoted in P. Kael, "The Economics of Film Criticism", in M. Temple, 2004, 417.

can you make a film [commented Godard]. If you have a lot of money it is just a different kind of film that you will make. If you have no money, you can still make a film. (1998, 135)

Although Jean-Luc Godard's films had low budgets (typically $70,000, $90,000, $120,000 and $180,000 for the films thru the 1960s – Godard said (in 2010) that they cost about 45,000 Euros, which equals 1.1 million Euros), Godard said he liked to have the crew and cast around all the time during shooting, even if they had to wait all day before he was able to decide what to do. In the early films, Godard remarked that the crew worked with him, but in later films like *Passion* and *Slow Motion*, there were more battles with the crew (they seem to have found it trickier to understand what the Maestro was after).

As Jean-Luc Godard was fond of repeating, the art of making films is the art of raising money. 'The mark of your standing as a filmmaker, he claims, is defined by the percentage of the budget you can spend on yourself and your friends'.[34] Godard told Hal Hartley that he built his living expenses into the budget of his films: that was what he lived off.

Money was one of Jean-Luc Godard's chief concerns when it came to filmmaking. It was all about time for him, having money meant being able to turn it into time for filming. Controlling the money was thus vital for Godard, and his deals became famous for the way that Godard would try to control the money ('for Godard to be happy, there must be something crooked in the deal', remarked Claude Chabrol [Mac, 329]). If a film budget was quoted, for instance, Godard would know there was a way to make it for less. He took his second film, *Le Petit Soldat,* to Switzerland because he knew it could be produced there cheaper than in Paris. Controlling the money

34 In J. Boorman, *Money Into Light: The Emerald Forest: A Diary*, Faber, London, 1985, 17.

meant being your own producer, too. And keeping the budgets down, because when budgets went up film producers had more say.

Some have accused Jean-Luc Godard of quoting a figure for a budget then pocketing some of it after he's found a cheaper way of delivering the product. Well, good for him, if that's what it takes to get the film made (some of the money was/ is used to buy new equipment, or for new films). Others have accused him of being stingy.[35] Some have reckoned that Godard didn't steal as a youth as a cry for attention, but because he wanted to be able to have money, to spend money.

What's certain is that Jean-Luc Godard has never liked to work for film producers who won't allow him to operate the way he likes, especially in the area of spending money. But Godard is no different from most filmmakers in requiring a film producer who's just going to sign the cheques and let him get on with it. Unfortunately, even at the low budget level of film production, those sorts of decent film producers are rare.

Godard will spend his own money to re-shoot something if he isn't happy about it. He re-shot his contribution to the opera compilation film *Aria* because it wasn't what he wanted. *Aria*'s producer Don Boyd visited Rolle and watched in amazement as Godard and an assistant edited the film right in front of him, in one day.

'Uncompromising' is a term often used about Jean-Luc Godard. With many a filmmaker, that's not really true, but Godard does seem to compromise far less than many other film directors – in his choice of material, his approach to filmmaking, the way he makes and distributes his films, and over his career as a film artist.

35 Godard also ran into trouble with his taxes in the 1960s. At the time, he claimed he didn't know how to fill in a tax return, which's rubbish, of course (Mac, 395).

Of course, Godard has touched on the subject of the lure of Hollywood and big money many times in his films. There's the Hollywood movie producer in *Contempt*, for example, who's making an ancient world epic. And, over the years, Godard has poured thousands of tons of scorn over much of 'Ollywooood's output – he derides Steven Spielberg, *Avatar*, *Titanic*, etc (if you look at Godard's film criticism, he tends to prefer smaller films from Tinseltown, rather than the *Ben-Hurs* or the *Cleopatras*).

Jean-Luc Godard simply isn't interested in pursuing many kinds of genres and types of film, however. He is interested mainly in the contemporary world (although he is always referring to history). The typical Godard film is a drama with comedic and romantic elements, often moving into film essay territory then back into fiction. Godard has played around with genres like the gangster film and *film noir* (many Godard films are based on or use thriller/ gangster forms/ novels, from his first feature film onwards – partly because they're cheap to make, and they're in contemporary dress), as well as the quasi-musicals, *A Woman Is a Woman* and *One Plus One* (imagine Godard doing a full-blown, \$120 million musical!). But most of the standard genres of Hollywood and films in the West have been ignored: horror, action, Western, animation, etc.[36]

Wait – that's not wholly true. In fact, Godard has directed genre movies such as marriage-in-crisis movies (*Contempt, A Married Woman, A Woman Is a Woman*), science fiction (*Alphaville*), modern religion (*Hail Mary, Woe Is Me*), a sort of opera (*First Name: Carmen*), a kind of Shakespeare play (*King Lear*), thieves on the run movies (*Pierrot le Fou*), political thrillers (*The Little Soldier*), and movies-about-movies (*Passion, Contempt* again). And, yes, he has made a sort of

36 Robin Wood complained that Godard's films shifted from scenes of textual complexity to scenes 'whose significance and interest strike one as thin in the extreme' (R. Wood, in I. Cameron, 62).

cowboy film (*Wind From the East*).

❂

Obtaining accurate information on the box office takings and rentals of Jean-Luc Godard's films is difficult. In his biography of Godard, Colin MacCabe offers a picture of many of Godard's movies not doing very well at all. *Contempt* sold 220,000 cinema tickets when it opened in Paris, but that wasn't good for a Brigitte Bardot movie. *Les Carabiniers* (also 1963) bombed in Paris – less than 3,000 seats sold in two weeks of its Paris run – 2,000 in the whole run according to other reports[37] (but it's a far, far lesser picture than *Contempt*).[38]

It's a pity, but understandable. A pity, because Jean-Luc Godard's films are so enjoyable, and so expressive of their time – *Bande à Part* or *Pierrot le Fou* or *Weekend* are as important (and enjoyable) as famous movies of the Sixties like *Blow Up* or *Bonnie & Clyde* or *Help!* But the films of J.-L.G. have often had to fight to reach an audience, or at least to get beyond the audience that regularly sees his films. Godard has never had a really big film, financially. (Godard and Miéville have spoken of their audience in terms of 100,000 friends around the world.)

Jean-Luc Godard commented in 2001:

> In France there are perhaps 100,000 or 200,000 people more or less like me, who might go and see my films. They're fewer than they used to be, because it's too difficult, because the world has changed. They go to the

37 In Richard Brody, 153.
38 Certainly, *Les Carabiniers* is tough going. Pauline Kael called *Les Carabiniers* 'hell to watch for the first hour', but then it comes alive in the postcard sequence, which 'is so incredible and so brilliantly prolonged. The picture has been crawling and stumbling along and then it climbs a high wire and walks it and keeps walking it until we're almost dizzy from admiration. The tightrope is rarely stretched so high in movies' (1971, 130).
    It didn't help that the actors in *Les Carabiniers* were virtual unknowns without much experience (and were badly dubbed). However, the crew were really enthusiastic about the movie, according to Charles Bitsch.

cinema a lot less, and so do I. But if they do go, they'll give 80% of themselves to the film. If you go and see *Titanic*, you only give the film 10% of your personality. Good films get smaller audiences, but more of the viewer.

RIGHTS.

Jean-Luc Godard famously plays fast and loose with copyrights and rights to clips — i.e., he ignores them. Which means that broadcasting Godard's *meisterwerks* such as *Histoire(s) du Cinéma* and *Notre Musique* is problematic, because Godard packs those films with clips from movies and television. Which's a shame, because works such as *Histoire(s) de Cinéma* are central to Godard's cinema. But Godard is not copying or re-presenting the TV and film clips as his own work, or exploiting them in the usual manner of commercial movie-making, he is using them as a poet collages words, or a painter collages bits of newspaper or posters or postcards.[39] Or it was science and research: it wasn't art or the media, but scholarship, Godard asserted. Godard sees the clips as material he can use, like words, or light, or sounds. But Canal Plus's René Bonnell knew that nobody would try to legally oppose Godard's quotations. [40]

In *2 x 50 Years of French Cinema* (which includes many film clips), this caption comes up repeatedly:

NO
COPY
RIGHT

Jean-Luc Godard has also made films from books for which the rights weren't cleared, it seems, so that showing

39 Filmmakers like Godard used 'collage structures, disjunctive editing, stylized framing and acting, and interspersed titles to achieve "anti-illusionist" works that would provoke reflection' (K. Thompson, 1994, 521).
40 And Gaumont had apparently given the rights to their film library free to Godard. However, writer Viviane Forrester sued Godard and Bodega Films over quotations from her essay about Cordelia in *King Lear*, and won damages of 10,000 Euros.

these films in some territories can be tricky. In that respect, Godard is again ahead of his time, as new technologies, such as digital recording, streaming and the internet, offer further threats to copyright.

No artist gets paid, however, if they've been dead long enough: thus, Ludwig van Beethoven, Johann Bach, Wolfgang Mozart and Joseph Haydn don't receive a cent when their music is included in Jean-Luc Godard's movies (or anyone's movies). If they did, Wolfgang Mozart and William Shakespeare, among many other artists, would be billionaires (Shakespeare, a keen and careful businessman, would be utterly stunned by how much money his texts have generated. And he'd definitely want his share!).

WIDESCREEN.

One doesn't think of Jean-Luc Godard as a widescreen filmmaker, but he was on a few projects (I mean proper widescreen – not the 1: 1.66 or 1: 1.85 or 1: 1.85 masked that manufacturers of TVs and broadcasters and film distributors call widescreen these days. True widescreen is at least 1: 2.2 or 1: 2.35).

Contempt, Made In U.S.A., Two or Three Things I Know About Her and *Pierrot le Fou* were filmed in widescreen (and colour). In fact, Godard has directed in widescreen more often than many filmmakers.[41] In those films, Godard and his team of filmmakers proved they could compose in the wide aspect ratio, and move the camera in it too.

Jean-Luc Godard was of course a passionate devotee of North American cinema, and much of his film criticism and movie-buff-watching occurred in the 1950s, the Era of Widescreen. In a piece about Douglas Sirk, for instance, Godard talks about the 'astonishingly beautiful' camera

---

41 The films were made in the Techniscope process, an anamorphic film process in which two images are photographed on each frame of 35mm film. So twice as much footage could be shot.

movements that Sirk and the great Russell Metty deployed in Universal's *A Time to Love and a Time To Die* (1958). The movements were so rapid and so fluid they looked as if they were done 'by hand instead of with a crane, rather as if the mercurial brushwork of a Fragonard were the work of a complex machine' (G, 139). So when Godard was able to shoot widescreen himself, he tried out some of those moves and compositions and transitions that he'd admired in the films of the Fifties.

CREDITS.

The credits on a Jean-Luc Cinéma Godard film are inevitably not your usual credits. Sometimes there isn't a title card at all (*Comment Ça Va*), or no credits at all: *Two or Three Things I Know About Her*, *Breathless* and *La Chinoise*. For *Pierrot le Fou* the title card comes up with different coloured letters, piece by piece. Very often the crew isn't cited at all (which legalized, unionized films wouldn't allow). Or just the DP and crew and the sound crew. Often Godard plays word games in the credits ('un film entre l'actif et le passif' is the caption opening *Comment Ça Va*). And *Weekend* is 'a film found on a scrapheap'.

CENSORSHIP.

Inevitably, Jean-Luc Godard had his run-ins with the censors and authorities over his films, as every good European *auteur* has to do (a tussle with the censors adds the mandatory layer of cool). *Le Petit Soldat* was suppressed for three years (and was released with omissions);[42] the newsreel of Eisenhower and de Gaulle was ✄ from *Breathless;* and some of the Dziga Vertov Group documentaries were withheld.

---

42 *Le Petit Soldat* was suppressed by the authorities, due its subject matter of the Algerian War. It wasn't shown until 1963. In *Le Petit Soldat*, Bruno works for an anti-F.L.N. group, which aligns him with the French government. That didn't stop *Le Petit Soldat* being banned until January, 1963.

The title of *Une Femme Mariée* was altered; the censoring of *A Married Woman* by de Sogogne and the censorship board (20 cuts, and changing the title), led to Prime Minister Georges Pompidou getting involved.

And when Jean-Luc Godard's films entered the international market, there were different kinds of censorship to contend with: when Godard's films were subtitled, lines were changed or elided. Anna Karina's 'baise-moi' in *Pierrot le Fou* became 'be quiet' instead of 'fuck me'. In numerous other ways the sense of Godard's films has been altered by subtitling. You only have to see his films with an audience that understands the original language (i.e., usually French) to realize that subtitling doesn't carry everything (Godard prefers dubbing– it's more honest, he says). [43]

43 There are other ways in which Godard's films are altered: broadcasters regularly show films with bits cut out, sometimes whole scenes. Or they're sped up, or shown in the wrong aspect ratio.

Some of Godard's films (this page and over).

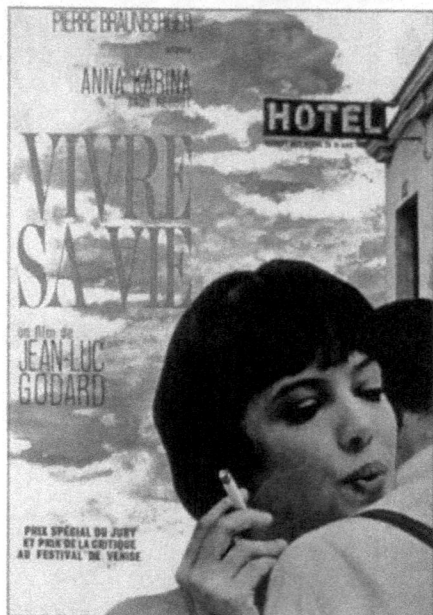

PIERRE BRAUNBERGER

ANNA KARINA

HOTEL

VIVRE
SA VIE

un film de
JEAN-LUC
GODARD

PRIX SPÉCIAL DU JURY
ET PRIX DE LA CRITIQUE
AU FESTIVAL DE VENISE

COCINOR présente

BRIGITTE
BARDOT

dans un film de
JEAN-LUC
GODARD

LE MÉPRIS

d'après le roman d'ALBERTO MORAVIA

TECHNICOLOR   JACK PALANCE   FRANSCOPE

MICHEL PICCOLI · GEORGIA MOLL et FRITZ LANG

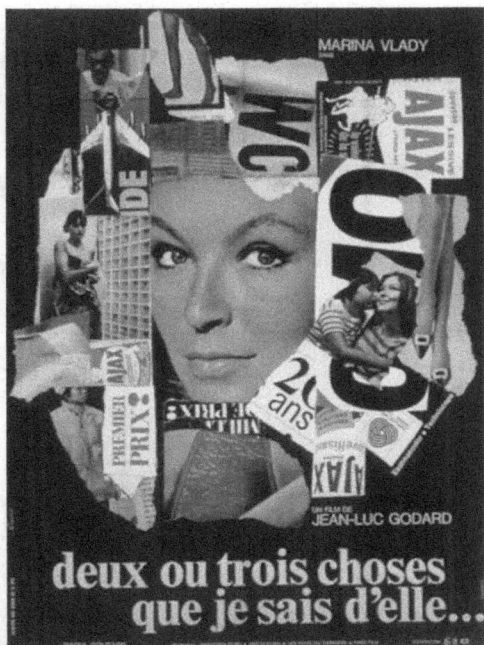

MARINA VLADY

UN FILM DE
JEAN-LUC GODARD

deux ou trois choses
que je sais d'elle...

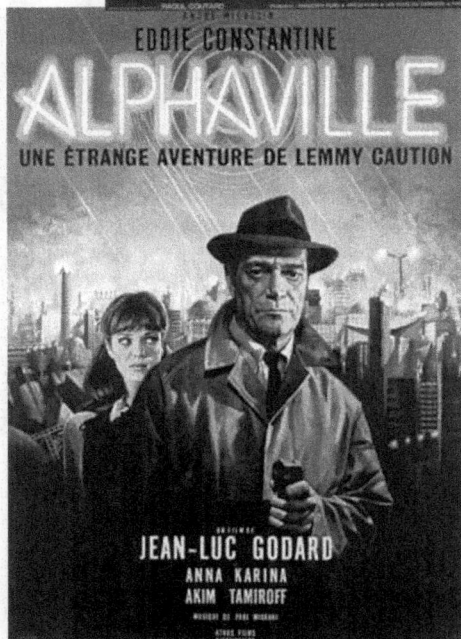

EDDIE CONSTANTINE

ALPHAVILLE

UNE ÉTRANGE AVENTURE DE LEMMY CAUTION

UN FILM DE
JEAN-LUC GODARD

ANNA KARINA
AKIM TAMIROFF

MUSIQUE DE PAUL MISRAKI

ATHOS FILMS
DISTRIBUTION

JEAN-PAUL
BELMONDO

ANNA
KARINA

JEAN-LUC
GODARD'S
PIERROT
LE
FOU

"ONE OF THE MOST IMPORTANT FILMS GODARD HAS EVER MADE."
-THE NEW YORK TIMES

WEEKEND
A FILM BY JEAN-LUC GODARD

ISABELLE HUPPERT
JACQUES DUTRONC
NATHALIE BAYE

un film composé par
JEAN-LUC GODARD

SAUVE
QUI PEUT
(LA VIE)

scénario
JEAN-CLAUDE CARRIÈRE
ANNE-MARIE MIÉVILLE
musique
GABRIEL YARED
produit par
ALAIN SARDE
réalisé par JEAN-LUC GODARD
avec la collaboration de
MARIN KARMITZ

YVES MONTAND
JANE FONDA
VITTORIO CAPRIOLI

TOUT
VA
BIEN

un film de
JEAN-LUC GODARD
et
JEAN-PIERRE GORIN

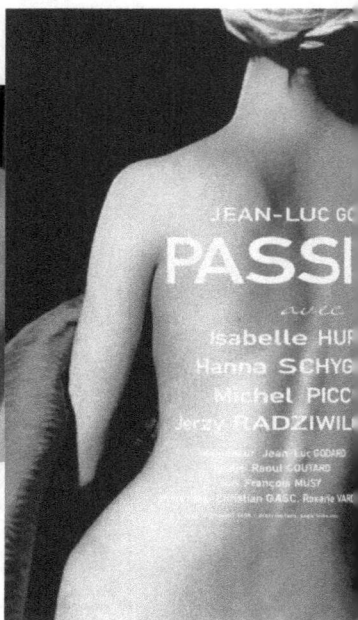

JEAN-LUC GO

PASSI

avec

Isabelle HUF
Hanna SCHYG
Michel PICC
Jerzy RADZIWIL

Jean-Luc GODARD
Raoul COUTARD
François MUSY
Christian GASC, Rosarie VARE

SELECTION OFFICIELLE
CANNES 2001
ÉLOGE
DE
L'AMOUR
DE JEAN-LUC GODARD

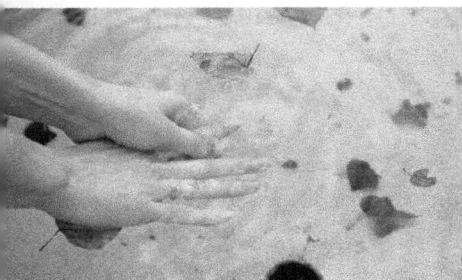
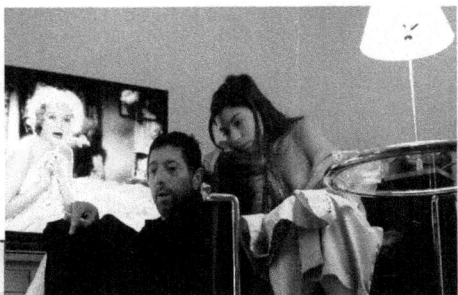

GODARD AND LOVE AND BEAUTY

> The only film I really want to make I will never make,
> because it is impossible. It is a film on love, or about
> love, or with love. To speak in the mouth, to touch the
> breast, for women, to imagine and see the man's body,
> his sex, to caress a shoulder, things as difficult to show
> and hear as horror, and war, and illness. I don't
> understand why, and it makes me suffer.

Jean-Luc Godard[1]

Jean-Luc Godard was no different from many a film director
in having relationships with his actresses: Anna Karina, Anne
Wiazemsky, Marina Vlady, and apparently with Myriem
Roussel. Godard was famously married to his leading actress,
Karina, between 1961 and 1966.[2] Godard and Karina were one
of European films' star couples (others of the time included
Ingmar Bergman and Liv Ullmann, Michelangelo Antonioni
and Monica Vitti, Dino de Laurentiis and Silvana Mangano,
Carlo Ponti and Sophia Loren, and Roberto Rossellini and
Ingrid Bergman).

Jean-Luc Godard married the actress, Anne Wiazemsky,
in 1967 (they later divorced). Wiazemsky (b. May 14, 1947),
was the grand-daughter of the novelist François Mauriac (and
Polish aristocracy on her father's side).[3] Wiazemsky had
appeared in the Robert Bresson-directed *Au Hasard, Balthazar*
(1966), and Godard had met her on set. It's worth noting that
Godard had first seen both Karina and Wiazemsky on screen
before meeting them. Wiazemsky had written a fan letter to
Godard after seeing *Masculin Féminin* and *Pierrot le Fou*
(*Pierrot le Fou* 'struck me like an artistic thunderbolt',

1 Quoted in *Godard par Godard*, 294f.
2 They were married on March 3, 1961, in Béquins, Switzerland.
3 Anne Wiazemsky's background was privileged, Richard Brody
pointed out, like Godard's: 'she was, in effect, a bourgeois
bohemian of a similar stripe, less of an omnivorous intellectual,
perhaps, but emotionally more spontaneous and less guarded'
(310).

Wiazemsky said in 2003 [B, 271]). It was really a love letter – 'one of the craziest things that I've ever done', admitted Wiazemsky, who up until then had been 'very prudent and shy'.

Godard was 36, Wiazemsky was 20; like Eddie Murphy, Woody Allen and Mick Jagger, Godard has a penchant for young women. During their courtship in the Fall of 1966, they would go and see a film at 6 o'clock, have some food at 8 o'clock, and see another movie at 10 o'clock (it's the perfect Godard courtship).[4] Wiazemsky and Godard split up because of Godard's intense jealousy, she says; there was also the age difference, and the influence of Jean-Pierre Gorin.[5]

There's quite a *lot* of anger in Jean-Luc Godard's films[6] – relationships are often fraught and sometimes come to blows (including the romantic pairings). The silly tapping and slapping that Godard has his actors perform maybe masks deeper rages. Commentators, including Godard's wife Anne Wiazemsky, have noted the deep feelings of fury and hatred expressed by Godard in the late 1960s.[7] Sometimes that hate would manifest itself in some nasty comments. When Sharon Tate and others were killed by the Manson family, Godard quipped, good, because Roman Polanski had beaten him over a deal to buy the film *Une Animal Doué de Raison* (Mac, 212).

In a Godard movie, you hear these phrases repeated:

tu m'emmerde
tu me dégoûtes
sans blague

In a Godard movie, everybody emmerdes or dégoûtes

---

4 Henry Miller spoke about his ideal day involving a good meal, a good talk and a good fuck. Godard's would be the same, but a good film would replace a good talk.
5 Godard hadn't wanted Wiazemsky to take up acting.
6 Rainer Fassbinder used to say about the people he deliberately irritated at film festivals: 'I wanted to make them angry. As angry as I was'.
7 Godard told André Malraux in 1966 that he was 'submerged in hate'.

each other, all the time. Name-calling is a recurring motif – Belmondo repeatedly derides Seberg in *Breathless* (the word *dégueulasse* is a refrain in *Breathless*).

Over his career, Jean-Luc Godard has worked with some very beautiful women, putting them in the lead roles in his films: Brigitte Bardot, Anna Karina, Myriem Roussel, Juliet Berto and Juliette Binoche (there are many others).

That brings us to one of the most unusual aspects of Jean-Luc Godard's cinema. It's so obvious one might miss it: many of his films have female characters in the lead role. Oh sure, there are other male filmmakers who've done that: Ingmar Bergman, famously, or Pedro Almodóvar, or Walerian Borowczyk. But it's actually very rare. If one goes back over Godard's career, the number of films with female leads is very striking: *Une Femme Est Une Femme, Vivre Sa Vie, Une Femme Mariée, La Chinoise, Hail Mary, Deux ou Trois Choses Que Je Sais d'Elle, Sauve Qui Peut, Éloge de L'Amour, Slow Motion, Prénom Carmen, Struggle In Italy,* and *Notre Musique.* And the films which contain couples are pretty clear that the woman is the stronger character: *Pierrot Le Fou, Masculin Féminin, Bande à Part, Passion, Made In U.S.A., First Name: Carmen,* etc.

A recurring motif in Godard's movies depicting men and women in romantic relationships is how hungrily/ yearningly/ bemusedly the men look at the women: there are numerous scenes where women are moving about a room, doing their hair, pouring coffee, whatever, while the men can't keep their eyes off them.

Jean-Luc Godard, though, isn't known for being one of the great 'women's directors', or directors of 'women's films'. But he is – way more, really, than many of the film directors usually noted for it. And he's also dealing with all those things that film critics love to talk about, like the representation of women, like the history of women in art (in painting and cinema especially), like the role of women at work and play in contemporary society, like the exploitation of women, and so on.

And Jean-Luc Godard has had many creative collaborations with women in his films: Miéville for his career since the early 1970s, and Karina and Wiazemsky before that. There are many women in key positions in Godard's film crews – and not just in the usual ones of wardrobe, hair and make-up, or editing. (He has worked with female DPs, production managers, and producers).

TRAVEL

> For my part, I travel not to go anywhere, but to go. I travel for travel's sake. The great affair is to move.

> Robert Louis Stevenson, *Travels With a Donkey*

Jean-Luc Godard spoke about the value of travelling, the journey, being 'between places'. He didn't like to rush from one place to another, because that wasn't moving:

> I think and I work better when I'm travelling – when you're supposed to be doing nothing. Sometimes I need two hours to get to the station. To go five minutes before kills me. That's not moving... you're in one place then you rush to another one and between them doesn't exist. For me it's the between that exists and the places are more immaterial. (M, 77)

For Jean-Luc Godard, the journey was precisely the point. The in-between time was the really interesting area of existence.

> A lot of tourists, when they go from New York to Honolulu, don't think that between New York and Honolulu they still exist, even if it's a 10-hour flight. To

me, what exists is *mainly* between. And I try to put this between in my films. (1998, 104)

Most of Jean-Luc Godard's films have been filmed in France and Switzerland, but, for all his anti-Americanism, Godard has also made films in America (*One A.M.*), been linked with American producers (Joe Levine on *Contempt*, Francis Coppola and Zoetrope, D.A. Pennebaker and Richard Leacock), and visited the United States many times, including for lecture tours, and to promote his movies.[8] (Godard also travelled in North and South America in his youth – the South American jaunt was extensive: Godard visited Peru, Chile, Argentina, Bolivia and Brazil. In the 1960s films, when Godard's young characters dream of escaping Somewhere Exotic, it's Mexico or Brazil).

Jean-Luc Godard has also shot films in Italy (*Contempt*), Czechoslovakia (*Pravda*), Morocco (*Le Grand estroc*),[9] Jordan (*Jusqu'à la victoire*), Sweden (*Masculin Féminin*), and Britain (*British Sounds* and *One Plus One*).

ANNA KARINA AND JEAN-PIERRE LÉAUD

While for some the image of the Beatles or the Rolling Stones may embody the Sixties, for me the young Jean-Pierre Léaud encapsulates much of that era. The Léaud of the films of Jean-Luc Godard and François Truffaut, dressed in a jacket and sweater (or sometimes a tie), constantly flicking cigarettes into his mouth, slouching against walls, riding the Metro, sitting around in cafés, spraying anti-Vietnam slogans on walls, looking longingly at girls, earnestly discussing

8 When Godard showed *La Chinoise* in L.A., for instance, Fritz Lang, King Vidor and Jean Renoir were in the audience.
9 *Le Grand Estroc*, part of *Les plus belles escroqueries du monde* (1963), featured Jean Seberg as a journalist (a clip was used in *Pierrot le Fou*).

Existential philosophy, and spouting polemical views. Léaud, the alter ego of Truffaut and Godard, in many films, embodies a certain aspect of the Sixties: youth, intensity, high-blown idealism, lust, political activism, Existential angst, melancholy and lassitude. As well as a certain Gallic cool.

If ever there was an actor born to play the anti-heroes of the Existential novels of André Gide, Albert Camus, J.-K. Huysmans and Jean-Paul Sartre, it was Jean-Pierre Léaud. The 'faces' of the Sixties in cinema are usually thought to be, in Anglo-American terms, Julie Christie, Jane Fonda, Terence Stamp, Dirk Bogarde, David Hemmings, Warren Beatty, Alan Bates, *et al*, but one should not forget European stars, such as those of the French cinema: Léaud, Jean-Paul Belmondo, Jeanne Moreau and Alain Delon, and Italian stars such as Marcello Mastroianni, Monica Vitti, Silvana Mangnano and Sophia Loren.

Best known for playing Antoine Doinel in Francois Truffaut's movies, beginning with *The 400 Blows,* Jean-Pierre Léaud also worked for both Truffaut and Godard (the two fathers of the French New Wave) as an assistant, when acting jobs were not forthcoming (particularly in the first half of the 1960s). Godard employed Léaud as an assistant on *A Married Woman, Alphaville, Pierrot le Fou* and *Weekend.*

✿

Among French actors, as well as Jean-Pierre Léaud, one should mention Anna Karina, star of many of Jean-Luc Godard's early movies. If Léaud embodies the masculine aspect of the French New Wave (along with Jean-Claude Brialy, Delon and Belmondo), Karina is the feminine aspect. Godard was clearly in love with her face, her eyes, her voice, her body, her motion, her whole presence on screen (she was also his wife at the time, between 1961 and 1966; and she played lead roles).

Anna Karina is not just one of the faces of the Sixties, but one of the great faces of film. She is one of the Goddesses of Cinema, as luminous as any of the deities routinely trotted out by film buffs: Lillian Gish, Gloria Swanson, Marilyn Monroe, Judy Garland, Greta Garbo, etc (and Karina can act most of the Goddesses of Cinema off the screen). In some films, Godard allows the camera to linger on Karina much longer than might be thought necessary. In lesser directors or producers, this adoration can be embarrassing and awkward, but Godard manages to integrate it into his films.

And Anna Karina was only 20 when she starred in her first Jean-Luc Godard film (*Le Petit Soldat*), and she was incredible from the beginning – very witty, a very appealing personality on screen, and very sexy. And Karina could act, *and* sing, *and* dance. Although there seems to be many performers who can do all three, they are actually very few (and from the beginning Godard was indulging his wife with scenes where she would sing and dance as well as act. However, these are not professionally choreographed scenes. What? Godard is going to hire a choreographer and set aside two days of rehearsal solely for a dance number? Not on a Godard movie!).

The camera absolutely adored her, and she was never less than brilliant. Remarkable. So remarkable is Anna Karina, I reckon, that Jean-Luc Godard's early films took an enormous boost from her involvement. They are not, then, just 'Jean-Luc Godard films', they are also very much 'Anna Karina films'. No *auteur* does *everything* on their films – and Godard's collaborators should always be noted: Raoul Coutard, Anne-Marie Miéville, Agnès Guillemot, François Mussy, Charles Bitsch, etc. And Anna Karina is up there with the foremost Godard collaborators. Critics often note Coutard's cinematography, and quite rightly, but without Karina to look at, Jean-Luc Godard's early films would be so much *less*. (One can see that the replacement for Karina in *Masculin Féminin*,

Chantal Goya, was adequate, but not a patch on Karina).

And Anna Karina wasn't French, either. She seems to be the epitome of the smart, cool French star – funny, talkative, independent. No: born on September 22, 1940 in Copenhagen, she lived in Denmark until she moved to Paris when she was 17. So that disarming French accent of hers was only worked up in three or so years.

In Denmark, Anna Karina had appeared as an extra in films, and also a short film called *The Girl With Shoes*, in which she was the lead. Karina had also appeared in a British comedy, *She'll Have To Go* (1961).[10] Karina has spoken of her unhappy home life, not getting on with her mother (her father had left when she was one), or her mother's second husband.[11]

Karina was born Hanne Karin Bayer; it was Coco Chanel who helped her to find a better name when Karina modelled for *Jours de France*. It seems that Karina was discovered as a model by being spotted on the street in Paris: after the *Jours de France* job, Karina was modelling for *Elle*.

After her movies for Godard, Anna Karina appeared in *Lo Straniero* (Luchino Visconti, 1967), *Before Winter Comes* (J. Lee Thompson, 1968), *The Magus* (Guy Green, 1968), *Michael Kohlhaas* (Volker Schlöndorff, 1969), *Laughter In the Dark* (Tony Richardson, 1969), *Rendezvous à Bray* (André Delvaux, 1971), *Chinese Roulette* (Rainer Werner Fassbinder, 1976), *L'Ile au Trésor* (Raul Ruiz, 1985) and *L'Oeuvre au Noir* (André Delvaux, 1988). She also directed *Vivre Ensemble* (1974).

Jean-Luc Godard became aware of Anna Karina when she appeared in some commercials (for Palmolive and Monsavon). He offered her a small part in *Breathless*. Their

---

10 I haven't seen this film, but Leonard Maltin describes it thus: 'broad farce about two brothers who compete to win the family inheritance left to attractive Corsican cousin (Karina)'. It starred Bob Monkhouse, Alfred Marks and Hattie Jacques.
11 A footnote: Karina's mother did the wardrobe for *Gertrud*, Carl-Theodor Dreyer's last film.

first meeting didn't go well, according to Karina: Godard said she would have to go nude, and Karina stormed out (and Karina kept that promise of no nudity – at least in Godard's movies).[12]

Jean-Luc Godard tried again in Summer, 1959, when he was preparing *Le Petit Soldat*, this time offering her a lead role. Karina first made sure she wouldn't be disrobing, and then accepted. The courtship of Karina and Godard (she was going out with someone at the time) took place during the shooting of *Le Petit Soldat* in Geneva.[13] Godard said his romance with Karina was his first proper relationship: 'I started very late with girls'.

Their relationship was one of extremes, ups and downs – 'on the moon or in hell', as Anna Karina put it.[14] 'It was mad love. Love, jealousy, revenge,' Karina explained in 2001. 'We adored each other. We were rather passionate'. Jean-Luc Godard was apparently intensely jealous of Karina (forgetting that he wooed (or stole) her from someone else),[15] and Karina often felt abandoned by Godard when he went away to work for long periods.[16] Sometimes he was violent, and hit her.[17] (Godard's explosions of anger were well-known – some said

12 Godard later insisted that he was offering Karina the photographer's model role, at the end of *Breathless*, not the former girlfriend role at the beginning. But either role might have required disrobing – in fact, Godard decided not to have Virginie Uhlman go topless, after having gone to some trouble finding an actress who would (Mac, 393). The part was played by Truffaut's mistress, Liliane David.
13 Karina married Daniel-Georges Duval, a French director, in 1978. Later in life Karina took up singing, and giving concerts.
14 Quoted in M, 135.
15 He apparently slapped her in front of everybody at a nightclub in Rome when she danced with someone else (B, 165). And Karina being Karina, she took it as further proof that he loved her.
16 Colin MacCabe characterized their relationship thus: 'for Godard, the story is of crippling jealousy; for Karina, of desperate solitude' (Mac, 131). Later came the suicide attempts by Karina, and 'a constant strain of horrific sorrow' (142).
17 When Karina told Godard she was leaving him, in November, 1961, he wrecked everything in their apartment, including clothes, furniture, teddy bears, etc. He left, and Karina took an overdose of barbiturates (B, 126).

they were the rages of a frustrated child, angry most of all at himself; and some said that side of his character has been overdone. Observers have noted how Godard would sometimes yell at an actor. But some of Godard's outbursts seem really directed at himself, at being unable to express himself, or to communicate what he was after. I would think too that Godard is one of those filmmakers that you don't dare say 'no' to in the middle of shooting).

Anna Karina later said: 'he was and will remain the greatest love of my life' (Mac, 178). But there's a tragic undercurrent to the golden couple of the 1960s: during *A Woman Is a Woman* Karina became pregnant, but had a miscarriage[18] which deeply affected her emotionally (and she was also infertile afterwards). Karina tried to kill herself at least three times – on the third attempt, she survived only because the painter who was working on the Godards' Paris house in rue Toullier had come back to get his keys (Godard said there had been two previous suicide attempts, which he had been able to prevent) [19]

GODARD AND TRUFFAUT

The friendship between Jean-Luc Godard and François Truffaut was one of the most well-known in European cinema, and their falling-out was also much publicized. They had met in 1949 (when Truffaut was 17 and Godard was 19). Both were film critics completely devoted to cinema, so in love with cinema that they were enslaved by it. Truffaut and Godard are probably the most famous examples of film critics who went

18 And when Karina was in hospital, she said that Godard was very rarely there. He would disappear for weeks (B, 116).
19 Suicide also loomed at this time in the private lives of, among others, Brigitte Bardot, Sami Frey (her one-time boyfriend, and star of *Bande à Part*), and Godard himself.

on to become major film directors. (Godard includes several references to Truffaut in his TV/ cinema work; they shared collaborators, too – Raoul Coutard and Georges Delerue worked on *Jules and Jim*, for instance).

Their friendship had been already deteriorating for some years b4 their final disagreement in 1973 (which lasted up to François Truffaut's death in 1984): Truffaut wanted to pursue a classical form of cinema, and Jean-Luc Godard, by the late 1960s, had become wildly politicized. Truffaut simply didn't want to go there, to explore those radical, ideological areas. Godard had famously stormed out of a screening of *Day For Night* (compare *La Nuit Américaine* with *Tout Va Bien* to see how far apart the cinemas of Truffaut and Godard had become around this time, 1972-73). For Godard, Truffaut had descended into a comfortable, self-righteous form of bourgeois cinema which betrayed their idealistic origins as *cinéastes* (even tho' plenty of the film directors they both revere are comfortable, bourgeois directors: Hitchcock, Mann, Ophüls, Hawks, Renoir, and most of the American cinema that the *Cahiers du Cinéma* crowd exalted propounded right-wing, conservative values). For Truffaut, Godard had become full of shit, as he put it in his 20-page reply to Godard's letter to him. From Truffaut's perspective, Godard had become dangerously blinkered in his pursuit of radical politics.

Godard was disappointed by Truffaut partly because his younger brother in cinema had been so critical of the 'cinema of quality', the old school of French film, throughout the 1950s. As Dudley Andrew put it, Truffaut embarked on 'an incessant, nearly indiscriminate strafing of the established film industry' (1987, 4). But then he reversed his position, and started to make those bourgeois films in the Seventies.

JEAN-LUC GODARD AT WORK

JEAN	LUC
JOHN	LUKE
HANS	LUCAS

What is Jean-Luc Godard like as a director on set? There's not much decent footage of the director at work. There seems to be few of those 'making' of documentaries that one finds on DVDs and home entertainment products. (Apart from those 'making of' documentaries, which only show certain aspects of the production, and they're usually PR/ marketing devices, so any conflicts, any big bust-ups on set, any troublesome areas of production, won't make it into the show.)

Judging by the accounts from crew members, the director's comments, and the footage of the director himself, I would guess that Jean-Luc Godard was a challenging and sometimes difficult director, and probably drove people nuts quite often, but he certainly pulled incredible performances out of his cast and crew. He could get actors to do extraordinary things, like drive cars into the sea, or leap off buildings. Any director who survives that long, and makes that much work, is clearly a strong leader, organizer, and inspirer. And Godard has his regular bunch of collaborators, who come back for more. (He even persuaded his crew to work on Christmas Day for *A Woman Is a Woman* – try getting a unionized film crew to do that!).

On set, I would guess that Jean-Luc Godard works very fast, and gets pretty much what he wants from one or two takes, as with Werner Herzog or Woody Allen. I wouldn't imagine him demanding take after take, like Jackie Chan or Michael Cimino. Going to 50 or 60 takes would be against so much of Godard's mode of operation. Hell, you could make three or four movies with the film stock if you regularly went to 50 or 60 takes! (Talking about working fast – Raoul Coutard said that *Une Femme Mariée* was conceived, written, planned, filmed, edited and dubbed in one month [Mac, 164]).[20]

Jean-Luc Godard is clearly a filmmaker who gets right in there during filming, and never sits down. He's on his feet all the time.[21] There are directors who sit by the video monitors and yell instructions, of course, or those that pass on a few comments then retire to their trailer. Godard loves to be in the thick of things. Footage of Godard at work shows him revelling in directing – the bigger and more chaotic the set-up is, the better. In the documentary for *One Plus One*, Godard can be seen skittering around the final scene at Camber Sands in England like a kid: he's directing the camera, the actors, the crew, the extras. You can see Godard pouring fake blood on his cast, or lining up shots, or showing a performer what he wants them to do by doing it himself, or pushing the camera (some film directors would *never* push a camera dolly).

I would guess that if he can Jean-Luc Godard doesn't give much direction, but relies on the actors to just do it. On the other hand, if actors are finding it difficult, I imagine he would go through it all slowly until they got it. Filmmakers can be very patient in getting what they want. Indeed, they'll do anything to get what they're after, even if it means leading an actor through a scene beat by beat.

Godard wouldn't explain things at length, Raoul Coutard recalled, and wasn't talkative on set; sometimes they would film a scene several times because Godard saw mistakes that weren't clear to everyone else.

I bet there aren't halts in production on a Jean-Luc Godard movie while the director sits down with an actor to go

---

20 Truffaut once remarked that Godard was mercurial and changeable and lost interest in projects rapidly. He is 'very fast-moving by nature. He quickly exhausts what amuses him', Truffaut said.
21 Stephen Sommers noted that someone in the production of *The Mummy* brought a chair to the set for him to sit on every day, until they realized that he never sat down.

through motivation and character points for an hour. No Method acting deconstructions, preparations, explanations. Giorgia Moll, who played the translator in *Contempt,* recalled that Godard would tell her to do simple things like 'you come down the stairs and you cry' and Moll would ask, 'why do I cry?', and the *Maître* would reply, 'I don't know' (Mac, 161). Godard's is a cinema of effects, not motivations, results not reasons. It's the visual, the mood, the sound, not the meaning, the interpretation, the analysis.

Being a filmmaker for J.-L. Godard was a 24-hour-a-day activity: 'I make my films not only when I'm shooting, but as I dream, eat, read, talk to you'. 'Filming is a way of life', Godard stated.

Jean-Luc Godard wanted input from his actors and crew in his later works. He wanted them to get over feeling intimidated by him and his reputation. During *Forever Mozart*, he suggested that his actors (Bérangère Allaux and Frédéric Pierrot) should give him some feedback on the script. If they wouldn't, he told them he should have asked them to pay for the text, so they would've felt they had the right to tell him it didn't work (paying for a script! only Godard would suggest something insane like that! And this is a guy who's made at least ten all-out masterpieces of world cinema!).

Colin MacCabe reported that Godard was demanding too much of his crew during the making of *Slow Motion*. They were loyal and idolized him, but 'there can be no doubt that the terms Godard set for collective work were entirely personal' (Mac, 269-270). Godard appears at times to be one of those filmmakers or artists who expect other people to do as much as he does, to put as much of themselves into the project as he has.

Anna Karina said that Jean-Luc Godard was 'one of the directors who has done the most variation' in terms of films, 'and done the possibilities for the actors to give all kinds of sentiment'.

Anna Karina said the atmosphere on set was like a family.

> It was a family thing, like in a family. Even though you don't really know what you have to do next, you know anyway. It's kind of a love story; you knew without knowing. How can I explain it? It's very difficult to explain.

Jean-Luc Godard had different techniques for dealing with actors. Jean Seberg had lines yelled at her during takes (and Godard did that on other films). During *La Chinoise* Anne Wiazemsky had her dialogue coming from Godard via an ear-piece. For the long monologues, done in a single take, a Godard actor clearly has to have a good memory, or to cheat with idiot boards, ear-pieces, or the director giving them the lines some other way. Handily, Godard's actors are often reading aloud from a book, so no problems there (they've still got to be able to read aloud well – not everyone can do that). Sometimes actors would be required to tell a story to camera with an actor next to them doing the same (as in *Made In U.S.A.*).

I can't be sure, but from the directing I've done myself, I bet that when actors like Anna Karina were on set they probably absorbed much of the director's time (and Karina was Jean-Luc Godard's wife, too), so that the other actors (the guys, for instance), would be left to their own devices. I don't mean that Karina or Bardot or Wiazemsky or Roussel were demanding divas, I mean they would kind of automatically attract all of the attention to themselves.

There probably wouldn't be much rehearsal time for the actors, though the many sequence shots in Jean-Luc Godard's cinema demand long periods of concentration and stamina from cast and crew, and some of the long takes clearly took hours and maybe days to set up. And you've got to have fantastic actors to get through such long scenes, with so many marks to hit and bits of business and dialogue. You can see Godard rehearsing his actors and camera crew again and again in the junkyard scenes in the *One Plus One* documentary, until everyone delivers what he's after.

There is an aspect of the bully, the self-righteous dictator in Jean-Luc Godard's cinema: it comes out when his characters are interviewing people, as in *Masculine/ Feminine* or *Two or Three Things I Know About Her,* that barrage of questions about revolution, or politics, or popular culture. It's as if Godard in his filmmaker guise assumes that everyone should want to be a radical or revolutionary, and that not to know about Mao Zedong or Karl Marx is pitiful ignorance. (Critics have drawn attention to the bullying way that the woman, Elsa Leroy, in *Masculin Féminin,* is questioned by Paul, off-screen. But Catherine in the same film gives back as good as she gets – and in her long interview scene with Robert, she bests him, refusing to answer his intimate questions). And with lines fed to the actors thru an ear-piece, Godard is embodying the characters at a real, physical level. (Some film directors have been worse than Godard in their treatment of personnel – James Cameron, David Russell, Michael Bay, etc).

Jean-Luc Godard didn't get his own way all the time – even the greatest or most dictatorial film directors don't,[22] but it's likely that he prevailed many times when problems arose. As Anna Karina put it:

> I did as I was told. I had my character; we'd discuss it – what she'd wear, what she'd think... C'mon, this was Jean-Luc! You didn't interrogate him. People would

---

22 As a controlling presence, Godard can be sensed throughout his films. The director's management of the material is felt from the beginning of *Bande à Part,* for instance: he is credited as 'Jean-Luc Cinéma Godard'; his commentary recaps the plot a few minutes into the film, for the benefit of latecomers to the cinema.

always accuse us of improvising, but it's absolutely not true. Jean-Luc's scripts were always carefully revised, red pages, blue pages, yellow pages. Sure, often he'd make up dialogue on the spot, but everything was rehearsed, particularly the dance sequence in *Bande à Part*. When I hear about actors trying to control their movies – tsk, tsk. When I work with a director, he's the director; what he wants me to do, I do. Especially with Jean-Luc: he's such a genius; you must trust him completely. And I did.

Of course the films weren't 'improvized' – how could they be? This is *Jean-Luc Godard* we're talking about! – a director who's intensely obsessive about language, words, and communication, a man who fetishizes the act of writing, of keeping a journal, of putting words on screen, of captions and quotations, more than anyone in the history of cinema! *Pace Breathless*, Godard commented: 'Belmondo never invented his own dialogue. It was written' (G, 173).

Or put it this way: you *don't* walk onto the set of a Godard movie, hand a script over and say, 'I've written my own dialogue. This is what we're shooting today, Jean-Luc'. You don't do that with Ingmar Bergman, or Akira Kurosawa – or, in fact, with *any* director or producer.

Film critics often talk about the famous sequence shots in the cinema of, say, Orson Welles or Andrei Tarkovsky, but Godard actually uses more than almost any other contemporary filmmaker, and their complexity is on a par with anyone else's (Theo Angelopoulos springs to mind – his films are entirely constructed from incredibly long sequence shots, commonly five or six or eight or nine minutes long).

'We didn't have a script, we didn't have the dialogue until the very last moment, but we still had time to rehearse, to talk about it, and time to get into the characters,' Karina recalled. And the lengthy, complicated shots that Jean-Luc Godard and his team put together would take ages to rehearse and set up, so there was plenty of time for the actors to 'get into the characters', as Karina noted.

Withholding the script until the day of shooting, which Godard often did (writing the lines is an exercise book the night before), is a classic way for directors to exert their control over a production. (Some actors hate it – they like to prepare, they like to know what they're going to be doing).

Vivre Sa Vie took four weeks to shoot, but nothing was filmed during the 2nd week. Jean-Luc Godard said he usually asked for five weeks from his producers. Shooting would normally take two weeks (that's what I meant when I said Godard worked fast).

So that's 5 x 6 days a week = 30 days (or 3 x 6 days a week for *Vivre Sa Vie* = 18 days). By contrast, the average shooting schedule for a drama film in the Hollywood industry (between 2006 and 2016) was 90 days.

Some filmmakers, Jean-Luc Godard said, had everything planned out in advance, and the shooting meant following as closely as possible the imagined vision: Hitchcock, Resnais, Eisenstein, Demy. The other sort of filmmakers tended to search as they made the film. 'Shooting is going out to meet something,' remarked Robert Bresson (94).

Pace Pierrot le Fou, Jean-Luc Godard mused that 'the only great problem with cinema seems to me more and more with each film when and why to start a shot and when and why to end it' (G, 214).

In 1965, Jean-Luc Godard said that he staged scenes not knowing how long they would be or how long the overall film would be (G, 222). 'I never have any time scheme. I shoot what I need, stopping when I think I have it all, continuing when I think there is more'. Well, sure, a lot of filmmakers would go along with that. The overall length of the film can be decided later. At the same time, Godard is working within the professional, European filmmaking industry, and knows full well how long films are expected to run commercially, and it is stated clearly in the contract. (Actually, one of the great things about Godard is that most of his feature films are *not* too long, but come in at one hour twenty, one hour thirty minutes, and *don't* run to over two hours, or 2h 20m, like so many North American movies).

However, Godard admitted that he finds it difficult sometimes to make the running time of 90 minutes (G, 182): his scenarios are two-page outlines, with the script being written the night before. Hence his films do feature padding (tho' sometimes the padding is outrageously obvious – like playing the same shot twice, repeating captions – and, in the later films, adding black leader).

You will notice that many of Godard's movies contain padding, as the filmmakers struggle to reach the 80-90 minutes of a regular feature film (even so, some Godard movies fall short of even 80 minutes). Godard has acknowledged this. Often, the padding occurs *before* the final scenes. The final scenes might be worked out, or at least contain some incidents that seem to round off the movie (tho' not always). But before them, there's padding (inserting the padding *before* the finale is so you won't notice it).

The padding might be a scene that shamelessly repeats material (like the interview between Robert and Catherine in *Masculin Féminin*); or it might be a scene extended far beyond its time (like the two-hander between Belmondo and Karina towards the end of *A Woman Is a Woman* or the central hotel scene in *Breathless*); or it might be a montage of material we've already seen (*Contempt*); or the second half might shamelessly repeat the first half (*Goodbye To Language, Struggle In Italy*).

Partly it's because Godard's natural running time as a film director is 60-70 minutes, like a film essay or documentary, and many of his movies would be improved by deleting the padding and repetitions before the finale.

Actually, this also occurs in Hollywood/ Western cinema, which typically runs to 1h 50m or more (over four, not three, acts). The danger time is around 1h 10m or 1h 20m. It's striking just how many Western/ Hollywood movies flounder at this point. They've said everything they want to say, they've delivered all of the action they intended to deliver, then they lose their way, before rallying for the final act.

❂

Jean-Luc Godard tended not to use much in the way of lighting. He liked available light, or to light a scene with a minimum of lights.[23] (Maybe Godard should take off his dark glasses from time to time!). Godard said he disliked the tendency in television to light everyone and everything the same, 'all the people with the same fill, no shade, nothing' (1998, 193). He also liked to mix daylight with artificial light. Not all cinematographers like to work that way, but Raoul Coutard was happy to. (Godard said he only discussed lighting with Coutard, but never anything technical). Sometimes actors became anxious about Godard's penchant for under-lighting. Godard related that Isabelle Adjani was due to make a film with him (*First Name: Carmen*), and she was scared that she wasn't pretty enough to look good under those sorts of lighting conditions. In the end, her part was taken by another actress (Marushka Detmers) because she and Godard couldn't agree on the way to light the film (1998, 137).

Films have to be either one or the other, Jean-Luc Godard asserted, in 1959:

> there are no half-measures. Either it is reality or it is fiction. Either one stages something or one does reportage. Either one opts completely for art or for chance. For construction or for actuality. Why is this so? Because in choosing one, you automatically come round to the other... All great fiction films tend towards

---

23 If the light was sufficient to shoot already in a setting, Coutard said that Godard would go ahead and shoot, without asking for more lighting.

documentary, just as all great documentaries tend towards fiction. (G, 132)

Jean-Luc Godard of course didn't apply those rules to his own output, and happily mixed fiction and reportage all the time. His fictions are often deliberately fake, yet also look like documentaries. And in the midst of fictions, Godard would add mini-documentaries about workers or landscapes, or a collage of street signs and posters, or a whole extract read aloud from a book.

Alain Robbe-Grillet's comments (made at the time of 1962's *Last Year At Marienbad*) summarize the position of this sort of film neatly:

> I don't think either the cinema or the novel is for explain-
> ing the world. Some people believe there's a certain
> definite reality and all that a work of art has to do is
> pursue it and try to describe it… I don't think believe a
> work of art has reference to anything outside itself. In a
> film there's no reality except that of the film, no time
> except that of the film… The only reality is the film's,
> and as for the criterion of that reality, for the author it's
> his vision, what he feels. For the spectator, the only test
> is whether he accepts.[24]

GODARD AND PERFORMANCE ART

While we're discussing some of the crazy stunts that Jean-Luc Godard has his actors perform from time to time, it's worth recalling that the 1960s films were made in the great era of performance art, in which similar events took place around the globe. Performance art is a vast area, taking in live art, happenings and action art. There are artists who talk to dead hares in their arms (Joseph Beuys), sculptors who stood and sang in suits (Gilbert & George), artists who carry out

24 A. Robbe-Grillet, *The Observer*, Nov 18, 1962.

weird, post-Catholic rituals or cut up sheep carcasses (Hermann Nitsch), artists who perform nude with film, video and installations (Carolee Schneemann), artists who sat in rooms and menstruated (Catherine Elwes), artists who had themselves bound and gagged in a gallery, holding a pig's heart (Tania Bruguera) – very Godard – artists who replayed the physical martyrdom of Catholic saints (Ron Athey), artists who re-enacted car crashes at a happening (Jim Dine and Judy Tersch), artists who doused themselves in water (Nam June Paik), artists who drew on their bodies (while naked, of course), artists who set themselves on fire (Tomas Ruller), or ignited gunpowder charges (Roman Signer), groups who threw paint and food over each other while singing vaudeville songs (the Kipper Kids), artists who painted gallery floors with their long hair (Janine Antoni), artists who masturbated with cuddly toys, while naked, of course (Mike Kelly), artists who meditate, chant, sing and play music (Caryle Reedy), groups who burn U.S. flags and protest against war (while naked, of course) on Brooklyn Bridge (Yayoi Kusama), artists who hid under wooden ramps in galleries and masturbated while speaking to visitors (Vito Acconci), artists who hung between bridges (Dennis Oppenheim), artists who shot guns at paint-filled balloons (Niki de Sant Phalle), artists who burnt books (John Latham), groups who staged a protest 'blood bath' in a New York street (Guerrilla Art Action Group), artists who sat on horses in galleries (Jannis Kounellis), performers who locked themselves in rooms for six days while covered in paint (Stuart Brisley), artists who hung themselves upside-down in galleries (Jill Orr), creative couples who walked and bumped into each other for an hour (while naked, of course), artists who scrubbed cow bones (Marina Abramovic), groups who sat naked in healing baths (Cai Guo Qiang), performers who had their clothes cut off by the audience (Yoko Ono), artists who signed semi-nude women as 'living sculptures' (Piero

Manzoni), and artists who crucified themselves on the roof of a Volkeswagen (Chris Burden).

From that brief list (I could go on), it's easy to see that the things that occur in a Jean-Luc Godard film aren't that out>rage>ous after all. An actor walking around with a book and declaiming from it (a common Godardian performance) is, well, very boring in the Wacky World of Performance Art. The scene in *Weekend* where Roland sets Emily Brontë on fire, while brutal, seemed to be a fairly average kind of happening in the art world of the time (but the *rage* in the act and running throughout *Weekend* is very alarming). Glauber Rocha, one of the directors of Brazil's New Cinema, remarked: 'I think a truly revolutionary film is Godard's *Weekend* because it is a film that provokes the public' (in D. Georgakas, 14).

SOUND AND MUSIC AND LIGHT

> Godard claimed to have a 'dialectical' notion of film-making: adapt the scenario against its source, shoot against the scenario, edit against the footage, and mix sound against the images.
>
> David Bordwell, *The Classical Hollywood Cinema* (383)

SOUND.
Jean-Luc Godard's use of sound is extraordinary, one of the most distinctive features of his cinema. Like editing, sound and music are part of the 'invisible' devices in cinema which viewers and critics often don't notice. But with sound effects and voiceover Godard added many further layers to his films, while his use of music is among the most appealing aspects of his cinema. 'People never attach any importance to sound,

but that's what interests me most', Godard remarked. [25]

Typical Godardian strategies include: direct or sync sound, which captures all the other sounds in the area (i.e., not close-miked); often the direct sound[26] is miked from one position, so the actors' voices are drowned by traffic noise or the clanking of a pinball machine; the direct sound can be harsh, grating, or too trebly, making dialogue indistinct. (And the sound isn't cleaned up – there are techniques for tidying up production sound, but they're not used in a Godard film).

Jean-Luc Godard often dispenses with fades and smooth links between sounds and images, so sounds will be suddenly cut off, or will abruptly burst onto the soundtrack after a moment of silence; sounds will be stopped halfway through a scene or a shot; sometimes the title cards are silent, but the sound will enter a scene after the image.

Jean-Luc Godard said many times in interviews that he worked very carefully on the sound in his films. His usual practice was to 'put only that which is the most important sound of the moment', and to leave all the other sounds out (1998, 134). For composer Jean Schwarz, Godard's way of working with music in his later movies was like sculpture. 'For him, everything was music – voices, sounds. He had a way of making it come alive like a symphony' (B, 529).

When he was mixing the sound for his films, Jean-Luc Godard said he liked to have the sounds split up into two channels on a mixer: dialogue on one, sound effects or music on another. He would then mix between the two live, in relation to the picture. It's typical of Godard to use only two tracks for the sound in his movies. With these sounds, rather than the many more of the typical Hollywood flick, Godard would 'sculpt with sound', as he called it.

Jean-Luc Godard's sound technique is diametrically

25 Quoted in A. Martin, 268.
26 As Coutard put it, Godard used 'direct sound under any and all conditions'.

opposed to Hollywood's, which carefully mutes background sounds, often to silence, with the actors miked-up; meanwhile, background sounds, such as traffic, horns, birds, are placed in the pauses in dialogue in post-production. Hollywood prefers sound to swing by unnoticed, to recreate a 'naturalistic' setting, replicating 'real life', which Godard's cinema continually rejects. While the typical Hollywood movie has edits and changes in volume occurring continuously over a film, Godard's cinema highlights the 'transparency' or 'inaudibility' of Hollywood sound practice. Godard's preference for recording all of the sound for a scene directly, as the scene is filmed (and onto a single track) – taking in the dialogue, jukebox, café noises, traffic, and so on – is the opposite of classical Hollywood, which prefers to separate each sound and layer them later.

The use of direct sound favours diegetic sound, but Jean-Luc Godard often favours non-diegetic sounds, sometimes poetic (the sea, birds, wind, rain), sometimes didactic (voiceovers, television news, gunfire, etc); Godard built up sounds for their concrete qualities, their abstract qualities, their connotations; typical sounds in a Godard movie include: gunshots, traffic noise, car horns, construction site sounds, pinball machines, the clink of cups and cutlery, birdsong, and ocean waves.

In a typical Jean-Luc Godard scene (the Parisian café), the actors are competing with the clank of a pinball machine[27] or a jukebox playing French pop music, plus the clink of cups and the cars outside, not to mention the chatter of other people in the café. (Some of the sounds do get tiresome in their constant repetition – I'm thinking of that bloody crow sound that crops up in *JLG/ JLG, King Lear, Hail Mary* and other films. Maybe the crow's croak symbolizes the Decline of

27 No filmmaker has ever included more pinball machines in their films than Jean-Luc Godard, have they? Forget the Who and 'Pinball Wizard' and *Tommy*, Godard is *the* pinball wizard.

Global Capitalism Seen From the Viewpoint of a European Filmmaker Living In Switzerland or something, but it's also irritating).

Few directors have so many voices reading aloud in their films: it is one of the hallmarks of Jean-Luc Godard's cinema (doesn't Godard say somewhere that reading aloud is going out of style?). Characters pick up books and read passages from them; sometimes characters walk around, declaiming; sometimes reading aloud will be on the soundtrack, in voiceover; sometimes it will be Godard himself reading aloud from a text.

It's endearing. Surely, in the past, when the number of people who could read was far smaller, reading aloud would have been more common. These days reading aloud is associated with certain contexts – parents reading to children, teachers and pupils at school, courts, police stations. The broadcasting media, of course, is entirely founded on people reading aloud. (The global media's a world of images, certainly, but words and voices still dominate – especially in regard to meaning and value. People with their cel phones are *reading words* – they aren't looking only at images (and they're typing messages and reading them); people watching TV (2-4 hours per day on average in the West), are *listening* to it).

Jean-Luc Godard's films feature reading aloud from pulp novels, from poetry, from pornography, from newspapers, from political treatises, and from advertizing. Godard also favours radio announcements, quotations from TV adverts, and interviews.

Jean-Luc Godard's cinema abounds in voiceover, from characters, from an omniscient narrator, from Godard himself. In this single respect, Godard's cinema is one of the most dazzling in the history of the medium. Even on a sub-standard outing like 1987's *King Lear,* Godard's control of voiceover is extraordinary. Godard is a genius at separating voices from shots and laying them over other shots.

Orson Welles is probably the king of employing voiceover in cinema for dramatic effect, but Jean-Luc Godard is Welles's equal in the manipulation of images and sounds, and his use of voices off is even more sophisticated than that of Awesome Welles. And Godard's control of the voices is 'invisible', so you can miss the skill and subtlety of the manipulations he's delivering. And often Godard combines two levels of voiceover: one is someone reading aloud from a book, and on top of that is narration. Or two characters are speaking to each other and Godard lays another voice over the top. In films like *JLG/ JLG*, Godard combines the voice track from a movie with his own voiceover. (More recently, Godard's films have placed different voices on the right and the left in the stereo spectrum; and 5.1 sound mixes are perfect for the way Godard works, putting sound all around the room).

Critics have remarked on the outstanding voiceovers in films like *Apocalypse Now* or Martin Scorsese's films *The Age of Innocence* and *Casino*. Yes, all very fine, but Jean-Luc Godard is adding multiple narration to his films (particularly the later pieces), *and* layering them on top of dialogue, and diegetic sounds like TVs playing films.

For Jean-Luc Godard's films new terminology needs to be invented: film criticism talks about *off*-screen sounds, but not so much about *on*-screen sounds, remarked Roland-François Lack; similarly, there are voices *off* but not voices *on*; and the image is never *off* screen. [28]

Visitors to Jean-Luc Godard's film facilities in Rolle have been struck at the sophistication of the equipment, particularly the sound technology.[29] An obsession with sound wouldn't describe it — sound in many Godard films takes

28 R. Lack, in M. Temple, 2004, 312.
29 Bob Last said that 'sound seemed a dominant theme in all my dealings with him' (Mac, 303).

precedence over the image, despite how vital the image is to Godard's cinema. One of the chief reasons that films such as *Hail Mary, JLG/ JLG* and *Éloge de L'Amour* are masterpieces is the soundtrack.

Film critics have written of the sound designers of U.S. cinema, particularly the Bay Area filmmakers, such as Ben Burtt, Walter Murch, Richard Beggs, and Gary Rydstrom (including those associated with George Lucas's Skywalker Sound and Francis Coppola's Zoetrope Studios). Jean-Luc Godard is in that same class – but many would place him also far above.

MUSIC.

Jean-Luc Godard's use of music is eclectic, idio-syncratic: classical music is a favourite (Bach, Debussy, Mozart, Stockhausen, Schumann, Ravel, Dvořák, Fauré, Chopin, Strauss, Franck, Bartok, Schubert, Liszt, Beethoven), with Beethoven, Bach and Mozart being recurring choices, as is popular music (Françoise Hardy, Chantal Goya, the Rolling Stones, Tom Waits, John Coltrane, Ornette Coleman, Bob Dylan, Janis Joplin, and Joni Mitchell, often coming from a jukebox within a scene).

Jean-Luc Godard mixes 'high' and 'low' music, the élite and the popular. Godard's cinema is full of musical quotations, from radios or jukeboxes, or characters singing (and dancing). Godard employed film composers (such as Michel Legrand, Philippe Arthuys, Maurice Leroux, Paul Mizraki, Antoine Duhamel, and Georges Delerue), but also preferred to create his own soundtrack from existing pop and classical sources. (Legrand scored many Godard movies, including *Une Femme Est Une Femme, La Chinoise, Vivre Sa Vie* and *Band of Outsiders*, while Delerue added the unforgettable, sweeping, romantic strings in *Contempt*. Some of the composers hired for Godard's films were highly regarded, and scored many well-known movies, including: *Julia*, *Day of the Dolphin*, *Silkwood*, *Platoon*, *Twins*, *Women In Love*, *Agnes of God*, *A Man For All Seasons* – Delerue, and *Yentl*, *The Thomas Crown Affair*, *The Three Musketeers*, *Atlantic City*, *Summner of 42*, *F For Fake*, *The Go-Between*, *Never Say Never Again* – Legrand).

As Jean-Luc Godard himself acknowledges, he is not a musician, but that hasn't prevented him from being one of the most subtle and penetrating users of music in films in the history of cinema.

In 1965, Jean-Luc Godard admitted that he always asked for the same sort of music from his composers – it was 'film music', music that would be 'worthless' outside of the film (G, 233). This is kind of true of some of the film scores for Godard's films. Compare the music for *Contempt* with *Pierrot le Fou*: the string music swells to a highpoint then dies. Godard, though, is highly unusual in simply cutting off music without fading it. [30]

Jean-Luc Godard was involved with rock music, particularly in the late 1960s, when he made *One Plus One* with the Rolling Stones, one of the biggest bands in the world, and filmed Jefferson Airplane for the abandoned *One A.M.* There was also talk of John Lennon starring in a film about Leon Trotsky, which Godard offered to Lennon. [31] (The Beatles met with the French genius at the Apple offices, but nothing came of it. Paul McCartney was more amenable, and met with Godard and Anne Wiazemsky a number of times. Apparently Lennon wasn't sure at all about Godard, and didn't want Godard filming the Beatles in the studio. If Lennon had seen how Godard filmed the Rolling Stones in *One Plus One*, it's

---

30 Godard also once said that he would prefer to use bad Stravinsky than good Stravinsky, if he asked Stravinsky to score one of his films, 'because if what I use is good, everything I have shot becomes worthless' (G, 234).

31 To be written by Robert Benton and David Newman, the team behind *Bonnie & Clyde*.

understandable why he wouldn't want the same treatment for the Beatles).

But you wouldn't think of Jean-Luc Godard as one of the great rock 'n' roll filmmakers, although there's plenty of pop music in Godard's films (the problem being that much of that music is really dreadful, and has dated badly. Is that because French pop music is usually regarded as fairly paltry? But it *is*! It's certainly true that the in-your-face freshness of Godard's films is let down when the jukeboxes in the cafés play something your fuddy-duddy, tweedy aunts and uncles think is really 'with it'. Now if the films has selected Eddie Cochran or Little Richard or Duane Eddy or Otis Redding or the Beach Boys or Jimi Hendrix, it might be another story).

More recently, Jean-Luc Godard has produced films which are founded on music (such as *Notre Musique*),[32] in collaboration with Manfred Eicher (b. 1943) and the wonderful Edition of Contemporary Music record label (founded in 1969).

But although Jean-Luc Godard is forever foregrounding music – and some sequences in his films are constructed in order to let the audience listen to music for a while (as in the middle of *Weekend* with the piano sequence) – he is not afraid to manipulate music any which way he likes. I'm sure some of the composers who've had their music cut to pieces – stopped and started, or reduced to a reverby din by Godard in his films – have hated it. Godard is not afraid of simply stopping a piece of Bach or Dvorák mid-stream, simply nixing it in the middle of its flow. No gentle fade, just an abrupt cut. (Musos and classical music devotees also hate it).

You can imagine some film composers delivering a score they've laboured over for weeks to J.-L.G. in Switzerland only to have the director use a tiny bit of it, and the same bit,

---

32 Many of Godard's features from *Nouvelle Vague* onwards have incorporated music from the E.C.M. record label. 'I had the feeling, the way he was producing sound, that we were more or less in the same country, he with sounds, me with images,' Godard remarked of Eicher in 1996 (B, 528).

over and over again, and every time he uses it, he cuts it off abruptly, so it sounds like nothing. Of course, every film composer knows that filmmakers will cut their work to shreds – use 15 seconds here, to follow Penny kissing her lover goodbye at the door of her Santa Monica apartment, and a 4-second sting there, when the Green Goblin comes face to face with Spider-man in a rain-spattered, Gotham alley. But a Jean-Luc Godard composer is going to be treated much more severely.[33]

LIGHT.

Jean-Luc Godard talks about light as matter, a real thing, and he has to shoot looking towards the light. 'So when I go in front of the light – go towards it – it is because it brings me energy.' Or, in ancient terms, it's sun-worship.

> I've decided that what interests me most is that you can only capture the light at a certain time [Godard said in 1994]. But after that, five minutes after that, then it's a different thing. So if you don't have the right aperture, you've missed it.

As with direct sound, Jean-Luc Godard liked to shoot without additional lighting. His watchword was to keep it 'real'. For *Alphaville*, for example, source lighting was used, resulting in thousands of feet of film having to be scrapped. Godard didn't reshoot everything: he put some of the very dark shots in anyway (R. Roud, 71).

Later films, such as *JLG/ JLG, King Lear* and *Éloge de L'Amour,* are especially dark. Maybe it's the gloomy Swiss Winters and Autumns, when Jean-Luc Godard seems to make so many of his later films (like Woody Allen, Godard seems to

---

33 Godard, though, probably didn't ask for a 4.5-second sting here or a 25-second cue ending on a note of wistful melancholy from his composers. He probably asked for some general purpose, atmospheric pieces which he could then cut up as he liked.

wait until Fall/ Winter to shoot, when everybody else opts for Summer). No – it's that Godard prefers to use source lighting often, and to leave the brutes, the 2Ks, the dinos, the arcs and the space lights outside in the camera truck. 'Under-lit' would be an under-statement for some of Godard's later films (some scenes are lit by nothing but a candle or a cigarette lighter, or the glow of a TV screen. The later films play with darkness to the point where light flickers then dies, revealing then hiding paintings or faces). It's the opposite of conventional cinemato-graphy, especially in the era of Classical Hollywood, when sets tended to be lit into the corners (or modern TV lighting, which blasts everywhere with light, making every-thing look blank and bland). Maybe Godard simply doesn't like bright light – he always wears dark glasses, for instance.

It doesn't mean, though, that Jean-Luc Godard's films aren't often visually breathtaking, and lush, and sensual. *Contempt* and *Pierrot le Fou*, for example, are fabulous cameraman's movies, lit by the hot, blue light of the Mediterranean, and filled with saturated colour. And films like *Weekend, Une Femme Est Une Femme, Vivre Sa Vie* and *Bande à Part* are very much films that delight in the movement of cameras, their ability to frame and focus and all the rest of it.

Jean-Luc Godard is acutely conscious that a film or video production has to be squeezed through a camera or optical/ electronic device at some point – it's got to be caught on 35mm or 16mm film, or digital video, or high definition, or pixels and bytes.

The notion of 'projection' is one Jean-Luc Godard has explored a number of times (there are so many scenes of movies being screened in Godard's cinema). Because movies are *projected*, Godard claimed they had a bigger history than books, which were 'reduced' ('let us not forget that a film is nothing if it is not seen, in other words if it is never projected'

Jean-Luc Godard has said he is always aware of the technicality and craftsmanship of making films, and it always comes across in his cinema. A devotee of the image *par excellence,* Godard is a filmmaker who clearly loves cameras (and all the associated technology – lenses, televisions, projectors, tape recorders, but not so much computers). You can get into the issues of surveillance, and voyeurism, and postmodernity, and specularity, and projection, and communication, and all those issues beloved of cultural critics, but it's also very much about the fundamental pleasures of making images and using technology.

It's also worth noting that Jean-Luc Godard is very much the all-round filmmaker, having editing and camera credits for many of his films (especially the video and TV productions). The short video pieces are often produced with the director himself working the camera, and doing the editing. And Godard is sometimes depicted in his films operating tape recorders, or editing machines, or cameras. (In some interviews, for instance, he has discoursed at length on the technical merits of particular movie cameras like Mitchells and Camaflexes and Debries, or aspect ratios, or film stocks.[34] Godard isn't usually thought of as a techno-nut, but he is).

---

34 For instance, in *Godard On Godard*, 183f, 187f.

> Film people are pointless if they aren't American. What does it mean if a Frenchman says 'I'm a scriptwriter' – no such creature exists. Whereas it doesn't matter with an American if it doesn't exist: things American have a mythical element which creates their own existence.

Jean-Luc Godard (G, 183)

Jean-Luc Godard said he didn't write scripts, but wrote out the 7 or 8 moments or points he wanted. He also said that he didn't really like telling a story, but that he used stories to put across what he wanted to say. 'A conventional one serves as well, perhaps even best', Godard remarked (R. Roud, 49).

About Jean-Luc Godard's method of directing, Anna Karina said that 'he doesn't really direct anybody, you know… he never tells anybody anything. We never had a script.' No script – except for pages which would be handed out to the actors not long before shooting. 'We never knew before what we were going to do,' Karina explained, 'so we were so involved with learning the text that we're not even asking what's going on'.

Where was the script? It was inside Uncle Godard's head. 'He would write it every day. He had that kind of structure in his head, and a kind of story, and probably the dialogue too'. The script for *Masculin Féminin*, for example, was only a few pages long – and wasn't a conventional script, but more like a short treatment.

For Jean-Luc Godard, all of the work in making a film had already been done before the cameras started rolling. The real work of making the film was the scriptwriting and the preparation. 'Most people think they work only when the camera is rolling, but that's not it. When the camera rolls, everything is done already' (1998, 174). Hence Godard stating that writing and directing were part of the same thing, and not that different. For an observer, seeing a film crew on the street or a film set or a location is the only time when they see a film being made, and that's the moment when it all seems to be happening. What they don't see is the enormous amount of preparation and organization that had to happen before that moment could be attained. But the real work, for Godard, was achieved even before pre-production or casting or location scouting, and that was conceiving and writing the film.

Jean-Luc Godard liked the idea of cinema being used for research, for science, for documenting the world, for showing people a different way of looking at life. In that sense, Godard regarded himself as 'half a novelist and half an essayist' (1998, 176). Godard said he liked both the documentary and the fiction aspects of films, the spectacle (Méliès) and the research (Lumière). 'I have always wanted, basically, to do research in the form of spectacle' (G, 181).

Having a good script and a good subject were not the same thing for Jean-Luc Godard. Having a *subject*, 'a meaning, a belief in something', was more important than having a good script or story. 'A pretty woman is not a subject', Godard asserted (1998, 177).[35] North American cinema tended to have 'no subject, only a story'. For Godard, it's a 'good script when you know the subject and try to [explore] it' (ibid.).

A beginning, middle and an end, as Jean-Luc Godard famously observed once (in Cannes in 1965), 'but not necessarily in that order'. (But that is precisely what frustrates some critics about Godard: a recurring criticism is that his films present fascinating subjects/ themes, but refuse to create the stories and the storytelling to explore them).

---

35 American pictures usually have no subject, only a story. A pretty woman is not a subject. Julia Roberts doing this and that is not a subject. Yet Godard's view here could be contradicted by one of his own movies: *A Woman Is a Woman* seems to be a movie with a pretty woman as the story (who just happened to be the director's new wife, Anna Karina).

Writing was 'already a way of making films,' Jean-Luc Godard said in 1962 of his time as a movie critic, 'for the difference between writing and directing is quantative not qualitative' (G, 171). Godard often said he wouldn't stop creating if cinema died: he would move into TV, and if that disappeared, he would move into writing again (ibid.).

The general view of Jean-Luc Godard is someone committed to the image, to sound and images, but literature suffuses his work. Few filmmakers make more literary allusions in their art than Godard.[36] Everybody bases films on books or plays, of course, but Godard's dialogue with literature goes way beyond that. In Godard's cinema, characters discuss writers, read aloud from books, quote authors, and some characters are even trying to be writers (like Patricia in *Breathless* or they are writers, like Paul in *Contempt*). It's quite ordinary in a Jean-Luc Godard film for characters to refer to Faulkner, Rilke, Rimbaud or Montaigne. And it's equally normal for the film to put up captions with quotes from books (that is a common practice in cinema, though, but usually only for a single quote, as an epigraph; Godard, however, does it very often). And then of course there's Godard's love of the written word – words that are literally written down, in front of the viewer. And Godard's use of captions is a whole other level to his cinema. Godard 'uses words in more ways than any other filmmaker,' Pauline Kael observed (1971, 94).

What all this boils down to is that although Jean-Luc Godard's art is a modernist/ postmodernist collage of sounds and images and music, it is also very much about literature and literary references and written words and captions. The joy of texts. And alongside the countless references to literary figures from Homer to William Shakespeare to Goethe to Rimbaud to Duras, there are also plentiful allusions to painters

36 As Godard quips in one of his films, *pace* reading aloud, 'the classics always work'.

and paintings, and composers and music.

Once again, this is most unusual. While directors such as Cecil B. DeMille or D.W. Griffith used paintings as an inspiration for lighting (DeMille's 'Rembrandt lighting') or set designs or costumes, Godard's films discuss painters in the foreground of the text. (Part of this is again pedagogical: Godard's films constitute a history lesson in painting, literature and music. Except of course there's nothing like a standard lecture in Jean-Luc Godard's cinema. Like his conversation, it's a loose, scattershot approach, assuming the viewer/ listener already knows everything about the topic anyway. Godard would make the most fascinating but also the most frustrating of university lecturers. Unless you had the time to take the course first in the regular manner, then again with Godard teaching it. For myself, I'd rather attend a Godard lecture than the countless dull ones I've sat through).

Typewritten texts are a favourite, but so are handwritten ones – as captions and intertitles, and notes on paper. There are postcards, and letters, and films-as-letters, numerous book covers, newspapers, magazines, graffiti on walls, street signs, neon signs, credit sequences, subtitles, and super-impositions of writing over the screen. No major filmmaker has used writing on screen as much as Jean-Luc Godard – and especially their own handwriting.[37] (How many important film directors can you name who include their own handwriting in their films? That was partly about the budget – if you can't afford proper film captions, just write them yourself and film them on a wall or a table).

As well as enshrining writing, Godard has also attacked it, saying that seeing should be privileged over writing, that writing denotes the Law, and death, while the image means desire, and life.[38]

37 Godard introduced his own handwriting in *Le Nouveau Monde*, his segment in *RoGoPaG*. Actually, it also appears in *Breathless*.
38 See P. Dubois, in M. Temple, 2004, 232.

*

A genius, certainly, a one-off the like of which cinema has never seen before or since, absolutely, but is Jean-Luc Godard an *auteur* to the extent that he creates *everything* from scratch? No. For instance, a large proportion of Godard's films as director are based on existing works – most of which (as with many movies) are books (and usually novels, but also plays, operas and even movies).

Thus, even if Jean-Luc Godard alters/ restructures the story, changes the emphasis, edits it drastically, and 'makes it his own', he is still drawing on the original material, which provides (1) characters, (2) their relation to each other, (3) the set-up or hook, (4) scenarios, (5) settings, (6) themes, etc. So even tho' the novels, plays and short stories are Godardized, the starting-points are still novels, plays and stories, containing characters, situations, relationships, themes, etc.

Among the writers that Jean-Luc Godard has adapted for his movies are: James Hadley Chase, Judge Marcel Sacotte, James M. Cain, Edgar Allan Poe, Fyodor Dostoievsky, Alberto Moravia, Jacques Audiberti, Beniamino Joppolo, David Goodis, Lionel White, Guy de Maupassant, Richard Stark (Donald Westlake), Catherine Vimment, Jean Giraudoux, Geneviève Cluny, Jean-Jacques Rousseau, Julio Cortázar, Dolores and Bert Hitchens, William Shakespeare, and the *Bible.*

TARGETS AND THEMES AND GODARDISMS

What's bad is that students think that because they've got a little camera [one of the new digital cameras], they can film something. The manufacturers, even the critics, say: 'It's great! Everyone can make cinema!' No, not everyone can make cinema. Everyone can think they're making cinema, or say, 'I make cinema.' But if you give someone a pencil it doesn't mean they're going to draw like Raphael or Rembrandt.

Jean-Luc Godard

Capitalism, consumerism, labour and the 'free market economy' were some of Jean-Luc Godard's perennial targets. He was simultaneously critical of capitalism, and seduced by it (especially in its manifestation in Hollywood cinema and popular culture, or technology, or even cars). Godard sent up commodity capitalism even as he exalted it.[1] (It was the same with the French *Nouvelle Vague*'s critique of Hollywood cinema, which they loved as well as loathed). North America was often the focal point for Godard's attacks on capitalism, but the Western form of capitalism has of course overrun not only Europe but the Far East and many other territories.

(When the Soviet Union broke up in the early 1990s, Hollywood movies were one of the products of Western capitalism that Russians clamoured to see – to the point where it destabilized the home-grown film industry. I, like many others, and like Jean-Luc Godard, loathe many aspects of popular Americana and Western pop culture and the Western lifestyle, but it's what many people seem to want).

Glauber Rocha reckoned that American distribution had destroyed the Italian Neo-realist cinema and the French New Wave cinema, except for Godard and a few others (in D. Georgakas, 17).

[1] 'Cinema is capitalism in its purest form... There is only one solution, and that is to turn one's back on the American cinema', Godard affirmed in the mid-Sixties. But *he* didn't.

Elio Petri takes the same view of the imperial colonization of Europe's culture by the U.S.A. and Hollywood cinema: America was 'already occupying Italy and Europe' by the 1930s, Petri reckoned, with its invasion of an army of movies (in D. Georgakas, 54).

Despite his later anti-Americanism, expressed in numerous incredibly derogatory and even racist statements, Godard was wholly under the spell of Americana in the post-WWII years. Look at his film criticism of the 1950s-1960s: he is utterly overwhelmed by North American cinema, to the point where he comes out with idiotic assertions like: film people are laughable unless they're American, or a French screenwriter is pitiful beside an American writer.

Uncle Godard raved about *Man of the West* (Anthony Mann, 1958), a film which, he claimed, was re-inventing cinema, was both course and discourse, where each shot was 'both analysis and synthesis', 'an admirable lesson in cinema':

> *He* [Mann] *does reinvent.* I repeat, reinvent; in other words, he both shows and demonstrates, innovates and copies, criticizes and creates. (G, 117)

One notes something of Godard's own ambitions in producing a cinema which both creates and criticizes, copies yet innovates. (*Man of the West*, one of Gary Cooper's last films, was not a hit with film critics at the same time, but it has since gained a cult following).

Prostitution was used by Jean-Luc Godard as a vivid manifestation of late capitalism (prostitution could stand in for any kind of exploitation, including that of the filmmaker in the movie industry).[2] And European intellectuals have a long history of exploring prostitution as a theme – not least, it

2 'The truth of our world is prostitution. Advertising? Prostitution! Writing? Prostitution! Even making films! Capitalism is that', Godard asserted in 1967.

allows filmmakers like Godard to put women on the screen in states of undress. And for Godard, prostitution was viewed from the Marxist-Leninist perspective of capitalist exploitation.

Jean-Luc Godard also explored the economics of filmmaking, labour in factories, and cultural imperialism. 'During the projection of an imperialist film the screen sells the voice of the boss to the people', a voiceover asserted in *British Sounds*, while 'during the screening of a militant film the screen is no more than a blackboard offering a concrete analysis of a concrete situation'. Maybe Godard's politics at this point, the late 1960s, were too simplistic, or a little too polarized: 'us and them', left and right, Europe and North America, Communism and capitalism.[3]

A leftist movie doesn't have to show people at work, Godard maintained. For Godard, a movie such as *Saturday Night and Sunday Morning* was not left-wing, but right-wing. 'Reactionary, paternalistic, in the sense that it imposes on the spectator an idea that the spectator enjoys', Godard said in 1961. I totally agree with him.

Jean-Luc Godard loved (and has always loved) to provoke (that side of his personality and art has never disappeared). For example, in *British Sounds,* the narration states: 'if a million prints are made of a Marxist-Leninist film it becomes *Gone With the Wind*' (except that it's unlikely that a million prints are going to be made of a Marxist-Leninist film[4] – not the kind of Marxist-Leninist film Godard envisaged at the time). In *Made In U.S.A.,* the voiceover remarks that 'we were certainly in a film about politics: Walt Disney plus blood'.

Jean-Luc Godard's is a cinema of dialectics, oppositions, pairings, montages – this *and* that, him *and* her, these *and*

3 'All my films are reports on the state of the nation', Godard said, stating the obvious (G, 239).
4 Except maybe in Communist China, the only nation which might consider a million prints of a film (and have the resources to accomplish it).

those. As soon as you mention that, Godard automatically knee-jerks with, what about this?

A list of oppositions and dualities and montaged pairings in Godard's cinema would include:

men	women
right-wing	left-wing
America	Europe
America	China
America	France
West	East
fascism	democracy
capitalism	Communism
city	country
bourgeoisie	working class
bosses	workers
light	dark
past	present

At its simplest the dualisms and oppositions of Godard's cinema are evoked with numerous duologues, non-stop conversations of thesis and anti-thesis (often with two actors facing each other, with a lamp or a train window between them).

Jean-Luc Godard is fascinated by divisions and borders and dualities – this AND that: either/ or: he AND she: documentary AND fiction. Godard asserted:

> I have always tried to make what is called documentary and what is called fiction two aspects of a single movement, it is the relation between the two which produces the true movement.

The late 1960s political films revolve around ridiculously over-simplified oppositions. While the filmmaking is very sophisticated, the political/ ideological arguments are often childishly reductive: left-wing vs. right-wing, Marxism vs. capitalism, proletariat vs. bourgeoisie, activism vs. consumption, political militancy vs. capitalist consumerism, Russia vs. America, China vs. America, Europe vs. the West, France vs. America, etc.

One of Jean-Luc Godard's provisos was not to be fixed to particular meanings or readings: 'not to be definite; don't pretend to mean this or that. American people like to say, "What do you mean exactly?" I would answer: "I mean, but not exactly."' (1998, 186)

Jean-Luc Godard is not interested in notions of 'good' and 'evil', or what constitutes a 'good life', or the 'right' way to live, or morality in the conventional manner (his films don't have conventional villains, usually, they have targets that're issues or social systems). Ethics and morality are never that simple for him, and, although he is very interested in education and informing audiences, he isn't a philosopher or teacher in the traditional mold. And he doesn't have a 'system', or a structured worldview which could be classed as a 'philosophy'. There is no Godard 'religion', no Godard 'philosophy', no standard, Godardian way of doing or being.

Some Godardisms:

• One of my favourite Godard quips comes from Barbet Schroeder, who recalled that once when Godard was accused of plagiarism, he retorted, 'of course. When one of my character says 'I love you', the 'I' is taken from one context, the 'love' from another and the 'you' from a third' (Mac, 397). That's classic bonkers Godardian thinking.

• Another favourite Godardism: when someone says 'I saw a bad film', Godard's retort is to say, 'it's your own fault. What did you do to improve the dialogue?' Only Godard could tell someone it was their own fault if they saw a bad film! And then go on to suggest that they improve the dialogue. *Godard classique, n'est-ce pas*?

• 'To show and to show myself showing' is one of Godard's mantras. One of Godard's maxims of the 1970s was: 'instead of making films, we'll make cinema'.

• 'I have no ideas' is another oft-used phrase. That's part of an artist's humility (but not really frustration). Humility because if any one in the history of cinema has never lacked for an idea, it's Jean-Luc Godard. The Maître sometimes calls himself someone who 'transfers' ideas, but can't originate them. Maybe. Certainly Godard seems to need an initial impetus or inspiration to make a film often – a book usually, or an event (or a title). He needs that book to get him going, but once he's started, the book is cast aside and the film catches fire.

• 'There is nothing invented in the cinema. All one can do in the cinema is observe and put in order that which one has seen *if* one has been able to see well', remarked Godard (1998, 135). Yes, but at the same time Godard quotes Paul Klee, who said that art doesn't reproduce the visible world, but reveals what isn't there.

• 'Cinema is life', Jean-Luc Godard said often, and in *Histoire(s) du Cinéma* it's all happening at the same time, the images overlapping and falling upon each other. A continuous cinematic present.

• In *Wind From the East*, a pregnant woman carrying a film camera asks the Brazilian filmmaker Glauber Rocha, 'I beg your pardon for disturbing you in your class struggle. I know it is very important. But which is the way to the political film?' An *Alice's Adventures In Wonderland* scene.

• It's necessary to struggle on two fronts at the same time is another Godardism. In *La Chinoise,* that means 'music and words', as Véronique puts it.

• One of Jean-Luc Godard's chief concerns, particularly

in his later work, is montage. For Godard, montage isn't simply editing in cinema, but could apply to many areas of existence. Montage was what made cinema different from painting or literature, Godard remarked, and many have said the same thing.

• One of Jean-Luc Godard's skills, as he knew, was being able to combine things, to create montages from disparate elements. He could put 'Raymond Chandler in contact with Fyodor Dostoevsky in a restaurant on a particular day with well- and lesser-known actors'.[5]

GODARD AND AMERICA

Jean-Luc Godard and his films are absolutely steeped in North American cinema. Godard's films are always about cinema itself, as well as everything else, and that very often means North American movies.[6] Dip into Godard's critical writing on cinema anywhere (not only in his 1950s critical work), and he's always discussing U.S. films and filmmakers. And that becomes ambivalently fused with the love-hate relationship Godard has with N. Amerika, N. Amerikan culture — and N. Amerikans.[7] 'I have always detested America and adored the American cinema', Godard admitted in 1988 (B, 530).[8]

Despite his well-known loathing of North America, Godard is happy to use many North American writers for the basis of his movies: Edgar Allan Poe, James M. Cain, David

5 In *Godard par Godard 2*, 201.
6 Godard revered North American movie folk, in spite of his virulent anti-Americanism. He would praise Ben Hecht to the skies. He would come out with rubbish like, 'Film people are pointless if they aren't American' (G, 183).
7 It's significant that the love affair in Godard's first feature (*Breathless*) is between a French and an American character. And it's the guy who's French.
8 'Godard himself has made a habit of badmouthing everyone who isn't Godard, particularly if they are American, and especially if they've had hits,' as Mark Kermode put it (12).

Goodis, Lionel White, Richard Stark, Bert & Dolores Hitchens, etc.

It's a classic Godardism that America has no name: it is the 'United States', but of what? of where?: in *Elogie de l'Amour*, a character (Berthe) complains about the definition of the 'United States', maintaining that Brazil also comprises united states, and so does Mexico – and Canada. So when you say the 'United States', do you mean Mexico? Brazil? Canada?

> So what is the name of what you call your United States? You see, you have no name. This agreement has been signed with the representative of a country the inhabitants of which have no name. It's no surprise that they need other people's stories, other people's legends.

Godard, incredibly intelligent as he is, has forgotten that all stories are shared, that stories are being continually changed, re-told and re-made, that no story is 'original' or permanently 'belongs' to a particular place or time, that stories're travelling around the globe all the time... He also forgets that France has taken up stories from everywhere else, just like any other nation or national culture, and for a lot longer that the U.S.A. (to cite one example: the French fairy tale writers of the 17th century (the *salonnières* or *conteuses*) drew upon Greek and Roman mythology, ancient fables, Italian mediæval tales (Giovan Francesco Straparola and Giovanni Boccaccio), Apuleius' *Golden Ass,* and numerous other sources and influences.)

GODARD AND BRITISH CINEMA

What a bastard Jean-Luc Godard was about British cinema at times! In a review of *Woman In a Dressing-gown* (J. Lee Thompson, 1957), Godard complains:

> Like football, the British cinema today is an enigma as much as legend. How have the descendants of Daniel Defoe, Thomas Hardy and George Meredith reached such a degree of incompetence in matters of art? ...No, it really is enough to make one despair. Except that to despair of the British cinema would be to admit that it exists. (G, 86)

And in *Histoire(s) du Cinéma*, Uncle Godard sneers that the British did what they always did (in cinema during WWII): nothing. To rise to the defence of British cinema of that time for a moment: how about *A Matter of Life and Death, The Red Shoes, A Canterbury Tale, Gone To Earth, Black Narcissus, The Life and Death of Colonel Blimp, Great Expectations, Oliver Twist, The Third Man, The Lady-killers, Kind Hearts and Coronets* and *Brighton Rock*? Yes, Jean-Luc, much of British cinema sucked in the 1940s-1950s, but you can't really be serious by saying that the best films of Michael Powell, Alex Mackendrick, David Lean, Carol Reed, the Boulting brothers and Alfred Hitchcock (a guru for Godard) were not the equal of Hollywood cinema or French cinema, or European cinema, or Japanese cinema?![9] (Godard also adapted British authors, such as Chase and Shakespeare).

That's the bitter irony – that North America – the land of rampant capitalism and everything Marxists, Maoists, militants and liberal intellectuals despise – is also the place where they make the best films. Or the films that dominate world cinema. Or the films that have impressed filmmakers like Jean-Luc Godard more than many others. (In relation to

9 Godard made some films Britain, two of which were *One Plus One* and *British Sounds*, in his politico-anarcho-comico period.

this French-American ambiguity and anxiety, one of Godard's favourite filmmakers, Alfred Hitchcock, was very, very *British*, but Godard seemed to prefer to think of Hitch as American, or maybe an honorary American (he also called him 'profoundly Germanic'). Hitchcock, though, only went to North America to make movies when he was 40. Godard's relationship to British cinema is ambivalent at best. 'One really has to rack one's brains to find anything to say about a British film', Godard complained in 1958 [G, 85]). But Godard revered Hitchcock as he exalted few other filmmakers. 'Throughout his entire career, Hitchcock has never used an unnecessary shot', Godard said in 1957 [G, 48]. And Godard wrote at length about Hitchcock's movies in his film criticism, raving about pictures like *The Wrong Man* and *Strangers On a Train*). For Godard, Hitchcock's genius was in creating images that you couldn't forget, rather than being the 'master of suspense'.)

CARS ('GET IN YOUR ALFA, ROMEO!')

Cars! Was there ever a director so in love with cars, or who used cars so often in their films? Cars are like cowboy flicks with their horses for Jean-Luc Godard, a constant presence: in every Godard film, people are getting into and out of cars; there are numerous scenes inside cars; cars over-take other cars; sometimes they jump in or out of them while they're moving; sometimes they drive next to another car so they can kiss the other driver; sometimes cars are piled high as wrecks, or they're on fire. Only the Yanks go as far in their enshrinement of the motor car.

The more you look at Jean-Luc Godard's films the more you realize that this guy fetishizes cars as much as anyone in the history of cinema. Big American cars, like Ford Galaxies and Cadillacs, classic, French cars like old Peugeots, Renaults and Simcas,[10] the occasional luxury car like a Rolls Royce or a limo, and of course the dream cars – the opentop sports cars, and not forgetting the brand that's always trundled out as the car of choice for the young, hip Godard character: the Alfa Romeo: 'Get in your Alfa, Romeo!' (no surprise that it's a classic, Italian automobile).[11]

Cars are part of Jean-Luc Godard's technofetishism. Godard admitted he was a bit of a technofetishist, and had 'always been instinctively interested in technical things' (1998, 160). He made a whole movie about cars – *Weekend*. However the car stunts in Godard's movies are scrappy – *Weekend*, *Pierrot le Fou*, *The Little Soldier*. Road accidents, for instance, are staged *after* they've occurred, with the smashed vehicles already in place in their final positions (as in *Contempt*). Had a professional stunt co-ordinator been hired, the results might be incredible (especially in an apocalyptical car movie like *Weekend*).

In the 1960s, classic car moments that ciné-fans rave about include the Dodge Charger and Mustang GT that Steve McQueen and co. drive in *Bullitt*, or the Minis in *The Italian Job*, or the DB5 that James Bond drives, or David Hemmings' Rolls Royce in *Blow-Up*. But Godard's films, though not as nearly well-known, rival the *James Bond* films for the sheer number of cars on show. (And Godard's films do many of the same things as *James Bond* movies: cars and women, cars and sex, sports cars, car chases, and car crashes.)

Jean-Luc Godard turns Paris into Los Angeles, the City of the Car, and the flat landscapes around Paris into the North American desert, with vehicles hurtling along the autoroutes. (And from *Breathless* onwards, scenes in cars are everywhere). And cars are employed in a large number of the

---

10 But not the 2 C.V. (which has a weedy engine).
11 Godard created a name for his character if he had appeared in *Germany Year 90*: 'Gulf Oscar Delta Alfa Romeo Delta'.

endings of Godard's movies (characters die next to cars, in cars, or they manage to flee in cars).

Gas stations: no one in the history of cinema has ever used gas stations and garages like Jean-Luc Godard. He is without question the King of Gas Station Scenes. Sure, North American road movies stop at them, and action movies sometimes blow them up, but in Godard's *œuvre* they are major settings, and every Godard movie has to have a scene set in a garage where cars are stolen or fights occur (*Pierrot le Fou*), fixed and cleaned (*2 or 2 Things I Know About Her*), arguments flare up (in *Passion*), where victims are killed (*Made In U.S.A.*), or, as in *Contempt*, where the two major film stars have their final conversation before dying a moment later on the highway. And even in a movie made at the age of 80, *Socialism*, there's a gas station as a major location! Godard even turns the Virgin Mary into a gas station attendant, run by her folks in *Hail Mary!*

We know J.-L. G. loves cars (big, American cars being a favourite as well as Alfa Romeos), but why the gas stations? Is it because they are in-between zones? Not home, yet not a final destination? Because of travel and motion? Because they embody global capitalism — the Arabic oil, the dependence on the petrol engine? Because they are 'watering holes', like cafés and bars, where characters can enter and leave with a legitimate dramatic reason? Because Godard had a crush on a girl whose *père* ran a gas station?! (Yes — if you go on a date with a Godard character, it won't be to the drive-in or the mall or the pizza parlour, but a gas station! Do you fancy hitting Exxon or Chevron tonight, honey?).[12]

Airports are another favourite location — appearing in Godard's first feature (*Breathless*) up to his very latest. Everyone's in transit in later Godardian works — characters are moving to the U.S.A. (*Socialism, Passion*), or hoping to escape

12 There are flirtatious asides about putting a tiger in your tank.

to Brazil (*The Little Soldier*), or to Rome (*Breathless*).

IMAGES

One of Jean-Luc Godard's recurring themes was that an image is created from two different realities; but they had to be related in order to produce a valuable or meaningful image, it couldn't be just any two realities. (But images aren't the same as words: 'Certain ministers of culture in France are saying young people should be taught how to read images and films. No. They need to learn how to see them. Learning to read is different' [2005]).

One of Jean-Luc Godard's assertions was that there are no more images, that images have been used up, that new images are required by artists, by filmmakers (Werner Herzog has similar views: one of cinema's tasks was thus to create new images for the modern age).[13] 'Chabrol is right: the important thing is not the message but the vision', Godard said in 1961.

One of Jean-Luc Godard's recurring concerns is the idea of cinema as a scientific or ethnological tool, a way of investigating the world scientifically. But it's the cinema of the spectacle that has taken over. Nothing wrong with that, Godard reckons, but it would be nice to have a cinema also of science and exploration:

> You can't spend your life saying, 'It was better in my younger days.' But at the beginning, cinema was a tool for study. It should have been a tool for study – for it is visual, and very close to science and medicine. The camera has a lens, like a microscope, to study the

13 What we lack, Herzog insists, is imagery to match the incredible advances in technology and lifestyle. Life is streaking ahead of cinema and television, for Herzog, and needs to catch up with imagery which will express the era.

infinitely small, or like a telescope, to study the infinitely distant. Having studied that, you could then convey it in a spectacular fashion. Very early on, however, audiences gave an extraordinarily warm welcome to cinema, the like of which they never bestowed on any other form of art. But what was immediately privileged was the 'spectacular', the 'commercial' aspect of it – in the worst sense of the word, for 'commerce' is also a necessary component of it all. For me, cinema is a metaphor for the world. It is image, and as such, it was an image of something. Everything is image, in the largest sense of the word. (1995)

A recurring motif in Jean-Luc Godard's cinema is signage. Godard can't resist pointing the camera at a sign if there's one in the vicinity. At the end of the gas station scene in *Pierrot le Fou*, the camera pans over to the 'Total' sign. A film like *Alphaville* is shot through with close-ups of neons and signs. Godard also loves posters (and also quotes from his own film posters). And postcards of paintings pinned to the walls. And book covers. And magazines covers and newspaper headlines.

Again, one can relate this to 1960s art, to the Pop artists in North America and Europe, who included signs and newspapers in their output (Andy Warhol, Jasper Johns, Roy Lichtenstein, Richard Hamilton, and Tom Phillips). At times, Godard's films appear as documentaries on signage in the contemporary landscape.

Another very Pop Artish element in Jean-Luc Godard's films is his use of colour, in particular the primary colours, red, blue and yellow in his 1960s films. Sometimes he has filters placed over the lens, to tint a whole shot. He has his DPs light scenes in single colours (red being the favourite). Often he has furniture or props painted in primary colours (like the red cinema seats in *Pierrot le Fou*). He likes to have bright red cars, or blue cars, or silver cars in his films (throughout *Weekend* the colours leap out of the screen).

Do the bold colours 'mean' anything, symbolically? Oh yes, sometimes they do – red, clearly, has particular ideological connotations in Godard's cinema, especially in the late 1960s (conversely, Godard states that there isn't blood in his films, just the colour red). But, often, I don't think they have much ideological or symbolic purpose beyond the cinematic[14] (i.e., all about the look and the design, rather like the way Arthur Freed and the M.G.M. art department would give a film a whole look). Indeed, although many movies of the period opted for similar graphic and Pop Art qualities, nobody used red and blue and yellow like Godard. (Similarly, altho' red is a provocative colour ideologically and politically in the late 1960s films, we have to remember that Godard never saw himself as a committed, serious Maoist or Marxist – but he loved to provoke people).

The look of Jean-Luc Godard's cinema – Pop Art, cool art, Minimal art, comicbook art – has so many affinities with the contemporary art world that it would be straightforward for curators to put on shows of material from Godard's films. His films are already like posters, billboards, graffiti, comics and TV commercials. You could take stills from 40 Godard feature films and documentaries and blow them up and there's your exhibition. Video monitors and projectors can play back iconic scenes – the Madison dance in *Bande à Part*, the traffic jam tracking shot in *Weekend*, the night of poetry in *Alphaville*, Anna Karina posing against a wall of posters in *Vivre Sa Vie*. And displays could also include props – a display case of guns, say, or J.-P. Belmondo's hat from *À Bout de Souffle*, or a Ford Galaxie or a Cadillac. And, *voilà, monsieur,* there's your *Godard-Cinéma-Godard* show for the M.O.M.A. in Gotham or Paris's Pompidou Centre.

Raul Ruiz, in *The Poetics of Cinema*, offered an intriguing view of film consumption: instead of identifying with the hero

14 But some critics have gone off on mad flights of interpretation about colour in Godard's cinema.

of a film, and living vicariously through that character,

> in any film worth seeing you should identify with the film
> itself, not with one of its characters. You should identify
> with the objects being manipulated, with the land-
> scapes, with all the characters. (119)

In this way, the film goes beyond being a spectacle, something you watch, to something you produce yourself:

> now it appears that the images are taking off from the
> airport of ourselves, and flying toward the film we are
> seeing. Suddenly we *are* all the characters of the film,
> all the objects, all the scenery.

HOW TO MAKE A GODARD FILM

> If you want to say something, there is only one solution:
> say it.
>
> Jean-Luc Godard (G, 173)

For J.-L. Godard, there was no difference between reality and the image:

> I see no difference between reality and an image of
> reality. For me they're the same. I always say, 'A picture
> is life and life is a picture'. And when I make pictures, it's
> making life. (M, 132)

Thus, there is no difference between filming or thinking about filming, between writing or filming; they are all part of the same thing, which is life. 'A novelist doesn't think that the only time he's writing a novel is when he's sitting at a table writing', Godard asserted.[15] In so many ways, Godard is 'the most writerly of filmmakers', as Raymond Bellour put it.[16] The filmmaker's a filmmaker even when the camera isn't running, or the film is in production. (That was part of Godard's notion that actors, like other artists, should work all the time, eight hours a day. They shouldn't only work when they're hired for a job, which for some actors might be for a week after three months of not working).

As an illustration, Jean-Luc Godard noted that video cameras were always running, even when the tape wasn't rolling: 'for me it's always running. To shoot is to re-run' (ib., 133). This counters the conventional view of the artist and the artistic act, or life and art, which are seen as separate. In this (traditional) view, one can't be a filmmaker unless one makes films, or a writer unless one writes. But every writer (or filmmaker or painter or whoever) knows that one spends far more time *not* writing, or *not* filmmaking or painting, than one does making the artwork. But this time is just as important, and, during it, one is still a writer or filmmaker or painter or whoever.

> Cinematographers shoot a movie [Godard commented], and then for 6 months they don't touch a camera! What makes them think they're still working when they're not looking? Images are like life. (1993, 122)

Jean-Luc Godard is the kind of filmmaker who probably can't resist picking up a camera or tape recorder if one's lying around. And to start thinking of a film to make with it. (And Godard showed that a film could be made from something as simple as a still photograph: *Letter To Jane* comprises a photograph of Jane Fonda and other pictures – the rest of the

15 If he wasn't making films, he'd be writing, Godard said. He explained to interviewers that the publication of his first film criticism article was as important to him as directing *Breathless* (G, 227). Writing, for Godard, was 'as important as anything else'. Writing 'is like filming' (G, 229).
16 In R. Bellour, 1992, 222.

film is a voiceover by Godard and Jean-Pierre Gorin in English).

Anything could be a starting-point for a Jean-Luc Godard film: the easiest thing to do would be be to pick up a book and start reading aloud from a page at random. That's two minutes, right there (it doesn't have to be Wittgenstein, Diderot or Hegel; a pulp novel will do). Then you can film a doorway, a painting, a window, or some trees. Two more minutes. Shoot anything else you like, edit the footage, and finally add a voiceover into a microphone after viewing the edited piece (or maybe without writing it – just improvize live as the film unfolds). Finally, you'd need to add some sound effects (wind noise, crows crowing, traffic sounds, and dialogue from a Hollywood movie of the Fifties)... And, lastly, some music (preferably Dvorák, Bach, Beethoven, maybe some E.C.M. artistes).

And *voilà*! – there's your Jean-Luc Godard film: it might have taken an hour to shoot (on video), two hours to edit, and two hours to add the sounds, voiceover and music. Playback is immediate, and the film can be included within a new film, adding that *frisson* of the *mise-en-âbyme* which cultural critics love.

Alternatively, if you haven't got a camera, you could construct a Jean-Luc Godard film from a collage of Godard's existing movies and upload the result onto the internet, denouncing the squeals of copyright lawyers as the fascism of corporate capitalism. Your film would be part of a radical Maoist/ Marxist/ Leninist/ Post-Everything attack on the target of your choice:

1. North America.
2. Global capitalism.
3. North America.
4. North American cinema.

5. North America.

'I'M A MAN, STILL, I LIKE TO LOOK AT WOMEN NAKED!'

Although Jean-Luc Godard's films are full of images of sex, conversations about sex, and references to sex, there are very few sex scenes in his films. Instead, Godard has characters talking/ thinking about sexual acts. Many of Godard's films centre on a romantic couple, but they are seldom seen embracing, kissing or even touching each other. Moments of tenderness occur, like dancing, but they're rare, as are happy or contented couples. 'I'm very traditional. I've always made love stories and stories of couples', Godard admitted in 1985 (1985b).

In films such as *Vivre Sa Vie*, which's about prostitution, there is an ideological and personal reason for withholding kissing (it can mean withholding some intimacy, some sense of self, of dignity and integrity, some power, from the client). And there's far less sex than kissing or embracing. In fact, there are very few images of couples simulating tupping in Godard's *œuvre*, which's unusual for a major art film director (and one who features so many couples). Many of the European *auteurs* of the 1960s and 1970s delivered sex scenes of one sort or another (Ingmar Bergman, Ken Russell, Rainer Werner Fassbinder, Volker Schlöndorff, Bernardo Bertolucci, Pier Paolo Pasolini, Walerian Borowczyk, Federico Fellini, and so on). This was the time (1960s-1970s) of increasing permissiveness, the end of the Production Code, and liberalization across popular culture, when many film-makers explored the new relaxation of censorship with more 'explicit' depictions of sexuality.

It's not that Jean-Luc Godard is puritanical or stuck-up;

he is exploring other aspects of relationships, such as emotional dependency, the relation of the lovers to art, to society, to institutions, the link between love and politics, love and ideology, love and capitalism, and so on. Godard was no prude when it came to depicting female sexuality – there are many nude women in his films (though Anna Karina does not appear nude – and I'm sure that had some impact on Godard's depictions of women and nudity in his subsequent work). The women are shown walking around apartments, or making themselves up in mirrors, or getting out of baths (tho' they are not usually portrayed in overtly sexualized poses). And if the lead actress won't disrobe, someone else can be found who'll take the thirty bucks and do it. (And the cheapest method is to pin a nude photo on a wall, or have someone leafing thru a nudie magazine). There is explicit sexuality in Godard's cinema, but it is shown in other ways. For example, in *Weekend*, there is a lengthy monologue about a threesome. In *Vivre Sa Vie*, sex occurs off-screen, suggested by dialogue.

For Claire Pajaczkowska and Elaine Meyer, the use of women in Jean-Luc Godard's later films veers on the exploitative, despite the embrace of feminism.[17] And in films such as *Contempt* and *Une Femme Mariée*, some critics see nude women being filmed with a directorial nonchalance which de-eroticizes them, while others see exploitation.[18]

For Julia Kristeva, there was something 'cold and calculating' about Jean-Luc Godard's female characters, which *Slow Motion* embodied. Kristeva wrote on Godard in *Art Press*:

> The question is whether this *beyond the pleasure principle* is a place from which they can thereby speak the truth about sexuality and male fantasy... or whether this *beyond the pleasure principle*, with its tendency towards violence, death and *jouissance* is the depth of

17 E. Meyers, in D. Holmes, 109.
18 See R. Stam, *Reflectivity In Film and Literature*, UMI Research Press, MI, 1985.

repression. (1985)

For film critics and cultural theorists, when naked women appear in Jean-Luc Godard's films they say solemnly the filmmaker is exploring issues of female representation and sexuality, or the role of women in contemporary society, or some such hi-falutin' stuff. *Oui*, sure. Godard *is* tackling those sorts of issues, but he is also staging scenes containing nude women. As he puts it, he likes to see naked women.[19]

The (European) art filmmaker, like the (N. American) film director, wants to have it both ways. They want to have scenes with lovely naked bodies in them, but they also want to be taken seriously and soberly (or it's the film critics and theorists who take them oh so seriously and literally). And the (N. American) action filmmaker also wants to be able to portray scenes of graphic violence even as they are also trying to comment upon that violence (or condemn it). So in the films of Martin Scorsese, Quentin Tarantino, Sam Peckinpah or whoever, there'll be scenes where people are blown up or shot, and the filmmakers will earnestly talk about wanting to depict the degradations of modern society, or the lengths that people will go to redeem their souls, or whatever. Yes, but they're also showing people being gunned down! (Never under-estimate how much filmmakers are like kids with cameras, filming childhood fantasies — Godard included — *viz.* the silly gun-play in Godard's films of the Sixties).

And the film critics are as guilty: they go nuts over films like *GoodFellas* or *Reservoir Dogs* or *Pulp Fiction* or *Sin City*, because they seem so 'cool', so clever, so self-conscious, so ironic, so arty. Yes, but they're also about really vicious social misfits who go around killing people! When quizzed about these dichotomies, Martin Scorsese couldn't really explain it:

---

19 And he likes to see pubic hair, too (as Eric Gill did). It was important to see pubic hair in a nude shot, Godard said, talking about the use of nudity in *British Sounds* (Mac, 284).

he said he was fascinated by gangsters even when he knew they were really ugly people.

In French cinema, important crime/ gangster movies included *Pépé le Moko* (1937), *Rififi* (1955), *Le Doulos* (1962), *Le Samouraï* (1967), *Borsalino* (1970), and *La Haine* (1995). Many of the great movies about gangsterism in France were released in the 1950s and 1960s (the golden age), and many of the classics were directed by Godard's contemporary, Jean-Pierre Melville (who played the writer in *Breathless*).

And the feminists and film critics can look at Jean-Luc Godard's films and nod wisely and write up their highly educated responses, bringing in Nietzsche or Baudrillard or Zizek (or whoever this week's trendy philosopher is; Nietzsche never goes out of fashion – especially in France), and talk about how marvellous Godard is at exploring changing social attitudes towards the representation of women or the shifting ideology of transnational capitalism. But the films also contain naked and sexualized women because, as Godard admits, 'I'm a man, still, I like to look at women naked!'

And the couples at the heart of Jean-Luc Godard's movies are not happy people. They're cranky, irritated, frustrated. As well as the unhappy couples, and love that turns out badly, there are few families in Godard's cinema. No mothers, fathers, brothers, sisters, relatives. Instead, a world of students, youths, foreigners – outsiders all.[20] As Marx said (Groucho not Karl): 'I don't want to belong to any club that will accept me as a member'.

---

20 One might have expected Jean-Luc Godard to tackle lesbian themes more often than he did. Women with women seems an ideal subject for the Maestro.

ANAL SEX.

Jean-Luc Godard has the fashionable European (and very 'French') fascination with sodomy and the anus,[21] found in the work of the Marquis de Sade, Jean Genet, Georges Bataille, Henry Miller; *The Story of O*; the Surrealists (Salvador Dali's *Virgin Autosodomized By Her Own Chastity*); in Pierro Mazoni (who sold cans of his turds for their weight in gold in 1962, a very Godardian idea); and in films such as *Last Tango in Paris, Le Grande Bouffe* and *Ai No Corrida*. In *Prénom Carmen* Godard himself talks about sticking his finger up his nurse's kiester; in *Slow Motion* the main character, Paul, discusses taking his 12 year-old daughter Cécile in the *derrière*; in *Masculin Féminin* the kids toy with different names for the butt; and in *Pierrot le Fou*, Ferdinand's wife Odile coos over her new girdle. Other Godard films, such as *Weekend* and *Hail Mary*, contain plentiful references to anal sex and fæces, playing upon the cultural links, made by the fusion of post-Freudian psychoanalysis and post-Marxist politics, forged between fæces and materialism, fæces and the art object, artistic practice and defecation, capitalism/accumulation and the anally retentive and excremental, and materialism and mysticism.

In *Je Vous Salue Marie* there are connections made between the anal and the spiritual, materialism and mysticism (writers such as Henry Miller, D.H. Lawrence, James Joyce and John Cowper Powys have spoken of 'excremental' mysticism). It's all part of what Godard dubbed, 'the civilization of the ass': the first shot of his first feature film was of a woman's ass. And in many subsequent films, Godard included images of the female *cul*.

---

21 Pierre Louÿs (1870-1925), for instance, wrote erotic fiction, and also took lots of erotic photographs (one of Louÿs' books was a study of women's behinds, entitled *La cul de la femme*).

THE WORLD OF GODARD'S CINEMA

GOD	ARD
CIN	EMA

David Shipman sarcastically summed up the typical Godard film (in *The Story of Cinema*):

> Anna Karina cavorting in a room; a montage of book jackets, postcards, advertisements; references to movies – usually bad ones (*Some Came Running, Hatari!, Viaggio in Italia*); long duologues, the camera darting to and fro, to be replaced in time with long muttered monologues to the camera, of even more stultifying banality. (1984, 1019)

Monsieur Godard's style is of course easy to parody: in addition to the above, one could include:

- scenes in cinemas, nightclubs, bars, cafés
- sudden alterations in sound, from local sound to silence
- music fading in abruptly then disappearing
- snatches of pop songs
- characters suddenly looking into the camera
- characters breaking out into dances
- characters hunched over pinball machines or juke-boxes
- characters quoting from Hollywood movies
- tracking shots along walls or traffic jams
- the camera dollying in and out unmotivated
- the background sound, in cafés for example, almost drowning out dialogue
- tracking shots from the windows of cars around Paris
- repeatetive and boring shots of streetcars
- close-ups of money changing hands
- off-screen gunshots (and birds cawing)

- philosophical, humorous and graphic intertitles
- a variety of voiceovers, including by the director
- characters undressing; nude women
- characters discussing sex and love
- shots of workers and factories
- characters eternally smoking, lighting up cigarettes, asking people for cigarettes, or a light (the Goddess Karina in *Vivre Sa Vie* smokes stacks of Gitanes)
- handheld shots of characters walking Paris's streets (the Champs Élysées being a favourite), and so on.

Put all of those elements together, and you have a cinema unlike anything else in the history of film, a cinema completely distinctive and unusual, a cinema of mastery and playfulness, of extraordinary insight and radical invention. (And if you want to spoof Godard's cinema, you could just re-stage all of the above, and doing it straight, without going for laughs, would be sufficient).

Jean-Luc Godard's world is populated by young lovers, students, gangsters, foreigners, artists, most of them outsiders. Many are lonely or isolated; many aren't particularly good at being gangsters or writers or even lovers. A world of losers, really, wannabe Humphrey Bogarts or wannabe Jean-Paul Sartres. Always talking about doing something, but never quite getting around to doing it.[22]

Jean-Luc Godard's cinema is clearly a lot of talk. As James Monaco put it in *The New Wave*: 'people in Godard's films (with very few exceptions) are paralyzed from the beginning. They may *talk* about love, about politics, but they seldom *make* either' (112). That's true: Godard's films're very French in that there is a lot of talk before, during and after anything is done.

Gangsters in Jean-Luc Godard's cinema aren't really

---

22 'If you want to say something, there is only one thing to be done: say it', Godard asserted (in J. Gerber, 116). Which's what Godard's characters *can't* do: none of them could be filmmakers. They'd like to be, but they couldn't actually carry it through.

gangsters, his political activists aren't effective activists, and his writer characters never write anything (they manage two fingers on the typewriter sometimes, but still produce nothing). Even the lovers spend more time talking about love than loving. And Godard's characters are very striking in their isolation from their families: they don't have, as noted above, fathers or mothers, or sisters or brothers, or children, or grandparents, or other relatives. They are orphans all, as Pauline Kael pointed out in *Kiss Kiss Bang Bang*,[23] cast adrift from their homes, now living in apartments in Paris or the suburbs. They live with their own kind: fellow students, or friends, or lovers. They are eternal outsiders, in the classic, Existential manner – rootless, wannabes, drifters, nomads, strangers in their own country.[24] They don't have jobs, or only part-time jobs they want to leave; they talk about escaping to somewhere exotic, but never flee; they have few possessions beyond a car, some clothes and some records; they have few ambitions or grand schemes; and all their money goes on cigarettes and magazines.

Jean-Luc Godard's characters seem disconnected from large areas of society and the world (even though they want to revolutionize it). They keep up with events (reading newspapers), but seem distanced from them. They appear alienated and introspective at times. Their love affairs never go right. They don't get to keep the ones they love. They are angry, but they don't quite know why. But all of those apparently negative aspects – the disconnection, the dissatisfaction, the depression, the disillusionment (all the 'D's') – also make them appealing.

Like other French New Wave works (and the new waves

---

23 P. Kael, 1969, 18-19.
24 As Kael put it, Godard's characters are 'most alive (and most appealing) just because they don't conceive of the day after tomorrow; they have no careers, no plans, only fantasies of roles they could play – of careers, thefts, romance, politics, adventure, pleasure, a life like in the movies.' (ib., 18)

of Germany, Eastern Europe, Russia and Italy), Jean-Luc Godard's films are narratives and dramas in themselves that also comment on themselves; on their construction, their aspirations, their cinematic devices and language. It is a very self-aware, Brechtian kind of cinema. Characters stop mid-action and turn to address the camera; the director, the camera, and the act of shooting is foregrounded. It's the essence of modernism; modernism becoming postmodernism. A cinema in which the narrative and drama is discussed on camera, a cinema constantly critiquing itself.

The received view is that Jean-Luc Godard's is very much an urban world, and very much Paris (later on it was Geneva).[25] It was the Paris of cafés, billiard halls, bars, shops, back streets, but not the Paris of the tourist route, the Eiffel Tower, Montmartre, the Louvre, or the River Seine. The countryside was often seen in relation to Paris, and usually only viewed from the perspective of a moving car or a road. *Pierrot le Fou* is unusual in taking place in the South of France, in a sunny, idyllic Mediterranean landscape (there's Capri in *Contempt* of course).

The reality is that at least half of Jean-Luc Godard's classic, urban films are set in the suburbs – *Vivre Sa Vie, Bande à Part, Made In U.S.A.*, etc – and the countryside features prominently in nearly all of Godard's films, including *À Bout de Souffle, Weekend, Nouvelle Vague, JLG/ JLG, Hail Mary, Goodbye To Language,* etc.

---

25 But it was also the Swiss capital by the time of the second film *The Little Soldier.*

CIGARETTES

Jean-Luc Godard's films are cancer films – in every pause in the action the characters are lighting up cigarettes (or the action *is* The Lighting Of The Cigarette followed by... The Smoking Of The Cigarette), and when Godard appears on screen he's usually got a cancer stick or a cigar dangling from his mouth (there are many photographs of Godard with a cigar or ciggie glued to his mouth like a baby's pacifier). If an actor asked, *what do I do in this scene?,* the answer was always: *light a cigarette* (later, cel phones took over the nervous tics of the constant stimulation of coffin nails). Maybe Godard's films were secretly sponsored by Gitanes, Gauloises, Dunhill and Marlborough. Maybe Godard, so long an anti-capitalist, anti-American protester, was secretly being financed by the tobacco companies in the United States. [26]

French actors must have training at the Cours Florent (a famous drama school in Paris) on how to keep a smoking butt glued to their mouths in the middle of action scenes or love scenes. Pretty much every actor in a Jean-Luc Godard film has to be good with gaspers. And Godard is particularly fond of having his leading men – such as Jean-Paul Belmondo, Eddie Constantine and Jean-Pierre Léaud – always seen with cigarettes and cigars. (It begins with Belmondo in *Breathless* and continues). Scenes btn lovers are played with the guy creating clouds of smoke from the Gauloise in his *bouche* – they're cheek-to-cheek, but they don't kiss, they inhale.

Fans of the marvellous British[27] comedy *Withnail and I* (1987) play a game of matching the characters in the film ordering drinks with partaking of the same stuff as they watch the film. You could play that game with a Jean-Luc Godard

[26] There's a scene in *King Lear* where a young woman (Julie Delphy) holding a tray of cigarettes yells out 'Gitanes! Lucky Strike! Philip Morris!'
[27] Yes, *British* – and far superior to any of the comedy in Godard's entire output.

film by matching the cigarette smoking – and you'd wind up in hospital.

POLITICS

> Bingo! Everyone was for sale. All you had to do was establish a price.

> Jackie Collins, *Lovers & Players*

And then there's politics. Politics and Godard, Godard and politics.

The political, ideological and social aspects of Jean-Luc Godard's cinema have been analyzed so often elsewhere. Here it's only necessary to emphasize how Godard's cinema always foregrounds political issues, how it is always dealing with politics of one sort or another (disregarding the political and ideological aspects of simply making a film in the first place, or working within the professional film industry). The point was 'not to make political films', Godard asserted, 'but to make films politically'.

> What is a rebel? A man who says no.
> (Albert Camus, *The Rebel*)

Jean-Luc Godard's direct involvement in the politics of May, 1968, and between 1967 and 1973, are well-known.[28] It was the period of the encounter with Maoism and the Cultural Revolution, with Marxist-Leninism, with anti-Vietnam War and anti-American politics, with strikes and student protests, Communism, the French Communist Party, the Russian Revolution, revolutionary politics, and so on.

To sum up: *right-wing, heap bad. Left-wing, heap good.*

---

28 Films such as *Weekend* and *La Chinoise* were seen, retrospectively, as foreshadowing the events of May, 1968.

Adding: *Amerika, heap bad. Europe, heap good.*

Godard's Maoist/ Marxist politics drew on the Great Proletarian Cultural Revolution of 1966, not long before May, 1968 – an era when the Red Guard in the People's Republic of China were at the height of their political activity. (Godard, like others in the West, feigned ignorance of the negative aspects of the Red Guard and the Cultural Revolution, such as the rampant nationalism, the demonization of foreign elements and religion, the rejection of anything Western, and the public humiliation of anybody who resisted them).

Altho' Godard and co. (such as the Dziga Vertov Group) looked to the People's Republic of China and the Soviet Union, they did not acknowledge an obvious fact: they would *not* have been allowed to make their movies within those political systems. Thousands of filmmakers in the Eastern Bloc, in Russia, and in China had projects cancelled, suppressed, and censored (and some filmmakers, such as Sergei Paradjanov, were imprisoned). Thousands left for the West; the ones who remained had to develop ways of circumventing the corrupt film production system.

Jean-Luc Godard's attacks on North America's involvement in the Vietnam War, and his sympathies with the Vietnamese, of course mirrored his own filmic practice, which opposed 'Ollywooood's domination of world cinema, as well as his own experiences with N. American producers and distributors. Godard has the romantic's empathy with rebels and oppressed peoples, the liberal's indignation, and the radical's rejection of authority. 'Every director bites the hand that lays the golden egg,' quipped Samuel Goldwyn.

Sometimes I wonder if Jean-Luc Godard were displacing his own feelings of anger and guilt about France's involvement in Algeria and Indo-China onto North America's intervention in Vietnam. Or was it because he saw N. America making the same mistakes in Asia that France had made in the Far East? Because the truth is that France's own political past in Algeria and Indo-China was just as hypocritical and violent as the U.S.A.'s in Vietnam. France had been exploiting the Asian region since the 16th century, up to 1954. (Godard had avoided the draft).

Later, Jean-Luc Godard would say that he was a late developer, and discovered revolution after everyone else. But it was always romanticized politics: 'I loved Mao as I loved Goethe. It was political romanticism'.[29]

UNMADE FILMS

Every major filmmaker has many unmade projects. There's not enough time or space to go through them all – and Jean-Luc Godard's more prolific than many filmmakers, so he'll have more unrealized films than most. 'There were a lot of projects, an awful lot of projects that never got made', Godard remarked in 1979 (M, 26). And likely just as many between 1979 and today. There were also films that were abandoned, such as *One American Movie* (*One A.M.*), which Godard made with D.A. Pennebaker and Richard Leacock,[30] and *Jusqu'à la victoire* in Palestine and Lebannon.[31]

Jean-Luc Godard, too, didn't always have final cut on his films. There are two versions of *One Plus One*, for example – Godard's cut, and the film producers' version, which included all of the song 'Sympathy For the Devil'. Godard was 37 when he made *One Plus One,* with fifteen feature films behind him, but he didn't have the power, despite being a successful, European *auteur,* to withhold the producers' version.

29 Quoted in A. Riding, 1992.
30 The existing footage was put together as *One P.M.*
31 *Jusqu'à la victoire* (*Until Victory*) was commissioned by the Arab League; Godard, Gorin, producer Jacques Perrin and DP Armand Marco visited the Middle East a no. of times in 1970.

Jean-Luc Godard agreed to make an adaptation of *Le Signe* by Guy de Maupassant for producer Anatole Dauman and Argos Films (he signed the contract on Oct 5, 1964). The production, entitled *Avec le sourire*, was to star an up-and-coming actress, Mari-Lu Tolo. But the day before principal photography, Godard cancelled the shoot. Dauman was disappointed, and Philippe Dussart was furious. (Godard finding the first days of shooting challenging recurs in his career: Godard liked to have the flexibility to shoot something else entirely from what was planned, at the last minute. Several Godard productions have had shaky starts, with the director floundering before finding his feet).

One of the most famous nearly-rans was *Bonnie and Clyde*: writers Robert Benton and David Newman have described how they really, *really* wanted Jean-Luc Godard to shoot their *Bonnie and Clyde* script, but the producers just wouldn't do it (the writers sent it to François Truffaut first, but he declined; Truffaut had shown it to Godard). Whatever Godard wanted to do, Benton and Newman would've loved it, but the producers wouldn't agree. Hell, when Godard suggested they make it in Tokyo, Newman and Benton thought, great. Godard told them he would get out of helming *Alphaville*, and come to the U.S.A. to do *Bonnie and Clyde*. The producers were saying they couldn't shoot right away for all sorts of reasons. One was the weather was bad in Texas right then. Godard's retort was classic: 'I am speaking cinema and you are speaking meteorology', Godard told the producers.[32] But when Warren Beatty heard about the project, he wanted to do it – and as film producer, too. Which meant he would be hiring the director as well – and he chose Arthur Penn after a disastrous meeting with Godard in London (B, 222). According to David Cook, the idea for *Pierrot le Fou* was inspired by the *Bonnie & Clyde* script (566). Maybe, but *Weekend* is the true

32 In S. Wake & N. Hayden, *Bonnie & Clyde*, Lorrimer, London, 1972.

continuation of the *Bonnie & Clyde* attitude.

Another unmade project was the movie about the anarchist gang headed up by Jules Bonnot, set in La France in 1911, a sort of French *Bonnie & Clyde*. Godard planned a film about the gang of robbers/ terrorists in 1967, but then decided, as usual with a period piece, that he couldn't do it justice because he hadn't lived back then.

The ambitious young Godard planned to adapt Johann Wolfgang von Goethe's *Elective Affinities*[33] into an epic project: in 1956, Godard penned a script 250 pages long. It would have been a giant production, which Godard called *Odile*, after his mother.

In the early 1960s, Godard pursued *Eva*, based on a novel by James Hadley Chase, and produced by the Hakim Brothers (they produced one of the great French thrillers, which Godard referenced, *Pépé le Moko*, dir. Julien Duvivier, 1937). It would have starred Jeanne Moreau (and Godard wanted Richard Burton; originally, Anna Karina would've appeared, but she became pregnant). But Godard disagreed with Moreau,[34] and the Hakims, about the movie. It turned up in 1962, with Moreau and Stanley Baker, as *Eva* (dir. Joseph Losey). A later Godard-directed film, *Grandeur and Decadence* (*Grandeur et Décadence d'un Petit Commerce de Cinéma*, 1986), was also based on a Chase novel.

In 1962 Godard also considered a film pairing Anna Karina with Gene Kelly;[35] her American debut, in which Karina would arrive in the U.S.A. hoping to be a star, or at least to find some sort of job; she would wind up working for novelist William Faulkner.

One of Jean-Luc Godard's favourite writers was Louis-

33 Francis Coppola planned a version of Johann Wolfgang von Goethe's *Elective Affinities* at American Zoetrope before it went bust (using Abel Gance's multi-screen technique).
34 Altho' Moreau had appeared in a cameo in *A Woman Is a Woman*.
35 Kelly worked with director Jacques Demy on the musical *The Young Girls of Rochefort*, 1966.

Ferdinand Céline: Godard planned a version of *Journey To the End of Night*, from a script by Jacques Audiard, to be filmed after *Pierrot le Fou*, with Jean-Paul Belmondo.

Lionel White's novel *Obsession* had been bought by J.-L.G. when he was making *The Band of Outsiders*: it was a *Lolita*-style crime movie, about an older man and a young woman, familiar Godard territory. Godard offered it to the young pop star Sylvie Vartan,[36] who would be teamed with Michel Piccoli. It was going to 'represent his own desperate obsession with Karina, starting from when she herself was a teenager', according to Richard Brody (B, 186).

Cuba was going to be the subject of another movie (Godard and Anne Wiazemsky had visited Cuba in 1968). Inevitably, it would have concerned the United States of Amerika and Cuba, a two-part movie filmed in the U.S.A. and Cuba (how could it be otherwise, from Godard?).

United Artists were in talks with Jean-Luc Godard to direct a film with Elliott Gould – from *Little Murders* by Jules Feiffer around 1970.[37] Godard's intention, though, was to stick it to 'Ollywooood by taking the money (his fee of $15,000) and using it to film something he wanted; it would be about a French filmmaker coming to New York to make *Little Murders* – and of course he's unable to do it.[38] That wasn't what United Artists wanted, however. Jules Feiffer had been impressed by *Weekend*, and had suggested Godard to Gould, who had bought the rights to Feiffer's play. Godard wanted Robert Benton and David Newman to script the project, which they did (in May, 1969).

Another of Jean-Luc Godard's many unmade projects

---

36 An influence on Japanese pop music idol culture.
37 The film was directed by Alan Arkin in 1970.
38 Some Hollywood studios at that time were trying out new talent, partly in response to the healthy rentals from youth-oriented pictures such as *Easy Rider*. Of the many moments when Godard might have collaborated with a major Hollywood studio, this was one. Except that Godard was also at his most politicized.

was *The Story*, which Godard worked on before making *Sauve Qui Peut*. It would be a story about stories, about the origins of narratives (B, 411). At one time, Godard had tried to persuade Robert de Niro and Diane Keaton to appear in *The Story* (and also met with Charlie Bludhorn, the head honcho at Gulf & Western, who owned Paramount; the studio wanted a conventional script, something Godard was often reluctant to deliver). The idea of Godard and de Niro is enticing (it was to have involved the making of a film about Bugsy Siegel, and early Hollywood, as well as Keaton's and de Niro's film careers; Keaton declined).[39] Godard also lost interest in the project – he felt like he'd already made it 3 times, by putting together the illustrated screenplay, with its photographs. (He would revive elements of it in *King Lear*).

In 1978 Jean-Luc Godard approached Jean-Paul Belmondo because he was interested in Jacques Mesrine's book *L'Instinct de Mort*, which Belmondo held the rights to. But Belmondo, who wanted a movie in the manner of *Pierrot le Fou*, didn't go for the Godard's idea of yet another movie about (making) movies, in which Belmondo and Godard would play an actor and a director making the film of the book.

One intriguing unmade project was Jean-Luc Godard's *Communications*, a 24-hour film with a variety of contributors, including Jean-Pierre Gorin, who was to make the Maoist section. Films along psychoanalytic lines remained unrealized, including *Moi, Je*, and a film about Sigmund Freud's Dora case.

Around 1982, Godard was thinking of adapting *The Lover* by Marguerite Duras in 1982 (it was ultimately produced by Claude Berri and directed by Jean-Jacques Annaud in 1992). A project with Marcello Mastrioanni and

39 One reason for the project languishing was Keaton's lack of interest. At this time Godard carried round a briefcase with the money in it he was going to offer Keaton. Initially, Godard had developed the idea of a movie about Hollywood and the mafia with Jean-Claude Carrière in 1978.

producer Marin Karmitz was discussed in the late 1980s. It would've been a movie about an actor (B, 520). The idea developed into *Nouvelle Vague*.[40]

Another disquisition on North America was considered in the early 1990s: it would be about Portugal, Christopher Columbus, and the historical relation between Europe and America, using *The Book of Disquiet* (1982) by Portuguese writer Fernando Pessoa as a departure point (B, 567).

Jean-Luc Godard has talked about the film he wants to make but will never make, the film about love, which recalls Raul Ruiz's concept of the 'secret film' that every film buff carries within themselves and is searching for: 'from film to film we are in pursuit of a secret film, hidden because its desire is not to be seen' (110). A secret film that will always elude the filmmaker or film lover. (*In Praise of Love* is sort of that film).

Yet there are two subjects that Godard never did produce as a feature movie: the Holocaust and the French Resistance. References to both WW2 topics crop up in numerous places in the Godard *œuvre*, and the Holocaust has much preoccupied the later Godard films. (There was an element of guilt in Godard's evocation of WW2, partly because he lived thru it but didn't actively participate in it. It's as if Godard wishes he'd been born ten years earlier, so he could've joined the French Resistance).

40 Godard had considered making *Nouvelle Vague* with Jean-Paul Belmondo and Anna Karina in 1964.

"Like a speed-freak's anticipatory vision of the political horrors to come; it's amazing"

UN FILM DE
JEAN-L...
GOD...
LA CHINOISE

PART TWO

THE POLITICAL FILMS OF
JEAN-LUC GODARD

1

THE POLITICAL FILMS
OF 1968-1973

1967-1973 was the period when Jean-Luc Godard developed a series of political films, some of which were produced by the Dziga Vertov Group with Jean-Pierre Gorin and others (during this period, he was married to Anne Wiazemsky, who appears in several of the films). The political pictures of the period tend now to be seen as Dziga Vertov Group works, but actually the Dziga Vertov Group – and Gorin – only worked on a proportion of them. According to Gorin, the group only really coalesced around the time of *Struggle In Italy* (by which time Godard had already produced several political pieces. Also, towards the end, it was really only Godard and Gorin. The name Dziga Vertov was made up by Russian filmmaker Denis Kaufman. It means 'spinning top').

The core members of the political period between 1968 and 1973 were le Maître and Gorin; Armand Marco and Jean-Henri Roger joined in 1969. Jean-Pierre Gorin was born in Paris on Apl 17, 1943. He met Godard in 1966, later advising on the script of *La Chinoise* and *La Gai Savoir*. Following the political films and Dziga Vertov Group period, which ended around 1973, Gorin taught at the University of California. He produced several film essays, such as *Poto and Cabengo* (1980), *Routine Pleasures* (1986), *My Crazy Life* (1992) and

Letter To Peter (1992).

In the Dziga Vertov Group films, collective decision-making was the order of the day – making films by lengthy group meetings. And equal collaborations (needless to say, this didn't always work in practice. Godard was opposed to directing like a dictator, but that's how it often worked out). There was also a move away from auteurism, to embrace the 'death of the author' of Roland Barthes and Structuralism. But that of course clashed on many levels with the *Cahiers du Cinéma* philosophy of enshrining directors.[1]

The political film period of 1968 to 1973 and the Dziga Vertov Group produced movies that included: *Wind From the East, Struggle In Italy, British Sounds, A Film Like the Others, Until Victory (Palestine Will Win), Vladimir and Rosa, Pravda, Tout Va Bien* and *Letter To Jane*. Some were unfinished, and some were not broadcast as planned, or released. The Dziga Vertov Group and the 1968-1973 political films were shot on Eastmancolor 16mm, with apparently everything being decided by the group, and everyone being paid equally. The money came from TV channels in Europe, with Jean-Luc Godard typically being commissioned to direct a documentary about a political topic.[2] Short *Ciné-tracts* were also produced (they were 2m 50s long, the length of a reel of 16mm film). The *Ciné-tracts*, sold for 50 Francs, were shown at universities.

Godard also visited Gotham (in Nov, 1968) to make a movie with D.A. Pennebaker and Richard Leacock: *One American Movie* (Jefferson Airplane, Tom Luddy, Rip Torn, Tom Hayden, LeRoi Jones and Eldridge Cleaver appeared). The collaboration foundered, but Leacock and Pennebaker

1 The political films of 1968-1973 and the Dziga Vertov Group
projects explore aspects of bourgeois militant practice and
theory, but never really address the issue of authorship – that
these films come from bourgeois militants, and from a bourgeois
militant culture.
2 Among the financers were Italy's R.A.I., O.R.T.F., and London
Weekend Television.

released a version of the footage in 1971 (as *One Parallel Movie*).

For the TV stations, these were niche items, to be broadcast way outside of prime time. But they were also prestige products (with a name director). Accused of dumbing down and churning out trash, TV channels could point to works like the Dziga Vertov Group films, and claim that they were upholding the broadcasting codes of being educational, inclusive and informative.

⁕

The political context of the 1968-1973 films is crucial: these works were aggressively interrogating the ideology and societies of their era. We could launch into an analysis of the politics and the ideology of the period, but noting down some key participants helps to define the time. So, here are some of the leaders continually referenced in Godard's political films:

Soviet leaders
| Nikitya Khrushchev | 1953-1964 |
| Leonid Brezhnev | 1964-1982 |

U.S. Presidents
John F. Kennedy	1961-1963	Democrat
Lyndon B. Johnson	1963-1969	Democrat
Richard Nixon	1969-1974	Republican

French Presidents
| Charles de Gaulle | 1959-1969 | Union for the New Republic |
| Georges Pompidou | 1969-1974 | Union of Democrats for the Republic |

The form of Marxism and Leninism in the movies is kind of updated to the 1960s, but Marxism as a political model is of the 19th century, and Leninism of the 1920s. For some, this form of politics was already out of date by the 1960s (the Dziga Vertov Group approach focussed on the factory system,[3] *par example*, which was a 19th century model).

The political outlook of the 1968-1973 Godard films and the Dziga Vertov Group films boils down in the main to simple oppositions, such as:

Right-wing = bad	Left-wing = good
Imperialism = bad	Socialism = good
Bourgeoisie = bad	Working class = good
Amerika = very bad	China/ Russia = very good
Hollywoood = bad	Militant cinema = good

Meanwhile, the political model is simplified to oppositions (because these are movies):

Left   Right

Or to the linear political model:

Left   Centre   Right

So the ideoloigical arguments in the political films seldom go beyond that – to, say, the circular model:

Authoritarian

Left   Centre   Right

Democratic

---

3 There are refs. to the Simca car factory in *La Chinoise*, for instance, and the meat factory in *Tout Va Bien*.

Meanwhile, two historical figures are employed as inspirations or reference points: they appear in photos, in quotations, and the voiceover actors are called Vladimir and Rosa:

Vladimir Lenin   1870-1924
Rosa Luxemburg   1871-1919

And two others:

Che Guevara   1928-1967
Mao Zedong   1893-1976

You could regard the 1968-1973 political movies as Godard's version of *The Idiot's Guide To Maoism,* or *Rioting Made Easy.*

Well-known political filmmakers of the era included Costa-Gavras, Chantal Akerman, Nagisa Oshima, Pier Paolo Pasolini, Miklos Jancso, Francesco Rosi, Marin Karmitz and Chris Marker. Groups and collectives of political filmmakers included Societé pour le Lancement des Oeuvres Nouvelles (S.L.O.N.) Group and M.K. Productions (France), Fugitive Cinema (Belgium), Band of 6 (Greece), Kartemquin (Chicago), Cinema Action and Women's Film Group (London), New Film (Sweden), Militant Cinema Collective and Feminist Film Collective (Italy), Women's Film Collective (Australia), and Workshop (Denmark).

The 1968-73 political works and the Dziga Vertov Group projects are fascinating if you admire Godard, and want to see as much of the Maestro's work as possible. But, really, only *Tout Va Bien* is essential viewing – and *La Chinoise* (though that isn't really part of the Dziga Vertov Group movies – only later did some of the political films become included under the Dziga Vertov Group banner).

It's hard to recommend most of the Dziga Vertov Group films and most of the 1968-1973 political films: there are some compelling moments (such as the tracking shot in the assembly line of a factory in *British Sounds*, and the montage of newsreel footage of Parisian riots[4] in *A Film Like the Others*), but some of the works are definitely hard-going even for dedicated admirers. I guess if you had to pick one movie of the Dziga Vertov Group in particular, that represents the works, apart from *All's Well* and *The Chinoise,* it would probably have to be *Wind From the East*.

Godard called for 'blackboard films' ('films tableaux noirs'): so we're back in school with our teacher, Monsieur Godard (he's the only *sensei* in the M.P.A. (Militant Private Academy) who's allowed to smoke in the classroom). Sit down, be quiet, get out your notebooks, and we'll begin the first lesson in the course *Marxism For Beginners*.

'Unwatchable' is the response of some film critics. James Monaco described the Dziga Vertov Group films as 'a series of difficult, tentative, experimental cinematic essays' (1977b, 323). Jean-Pierre Gorin dubbed them 'Unidentified Visual Objects', U.V.O.s. They can be tough going. Both Gorin and Godard later acknowledged that their collaboration had been valuable. 'I gave him hope when he didn't have any,' Gorin said of Godard, and Godard acknowledged that working with Gorin had helped him to keep going (Mac, 237).

But Godard must've realized he was wasting his time with this new venture. And make one shabby political film run by a collective, not not eight!

It's curious that *La Chinoise* was a hit in the U.S.A., and yet the Dziga Vertov Group and many of the political 1968-1973 films were seen by practically nobody – curious because they cover so much of the same material: young people and left-wing politics, young people getting together to

4 Godard had filmed the riots in the Latin Quarter in May, 1968.

explore political issues, in particular a group undertaking analyses of how political theory relates to social life, what a political revolution might actually mean in practical terms, and how the young generation could tackle issues such as the class struggle, self-criticism, Marxism, Maoism and Communism. But *La Chinoise* is far superior to any of the other Dziga Vertov Group works (it's obvious why).

The response to some of the political films was terrible – at the Lincoln Center in Gotham on Dec 29, 1968, when *A Film Like the Others* was screened, nearly all of the audience walked out (leaving under a hundred people); the audience also abandoned *Le Gai Savoir* when it was shown in 1969 at the New York Film Festival; and *Le Gai Savoir* had a disastrous screening at the Berlin Film Festival.

Among the topics that Godard's 1968-1973 political films and the Dziga Vertov Group films tackled were Palestine and Middle East politics in *Jusqu'à la victoire*, Chicago radicals in *Vladimir and Rosa*, revolutionary politics in *Vent d'Est*, contemporary British politics and culture in *British Sounds*, and culture and labour in Czechoslovakia in *Pravda*.

It was Dziga Vertov (Denis Kaufman, 1896-1954) not Sergei Eisenstein for Godard and his comrades for a variety of reasons. From Vertov (best-known for the remarkable *Man With a Movie Camera*, 1929, a film school favourite), Godard assimilated the idea of the camera and cinema as a scientific tool for exploring reality; an emphasis on montage; cinema as a laboratory for experiments with sound and image; a distrust of conventional narrative and scripts; and 'interval' theory, the gaps, movements and transitions between shots. [5]

They are not documentaries. They are experiments – part-essay, part-rant, part-provocation. They employ *some* elements of documentary filmmaking – such as interviews with people related to the main theme or subject; they film

5 M. Witt, in M. Temple, 2000, 36-37.

some acts and locations asssociated with the theme; and they occasionally use recreations or dramatizations. But for the rest, it is experimentation, knitted together largely by two invisible factors: 1. voices (and sounds), and 2. editing.

Sound was a vital part of the 1968-1973 political films and the Dziga Vertov Group films, for several reasons (one being economic: it was simply cheaper to mess about with sound, involving two or three people in the editing suite, than shooting with a crew).6 The late 60s/ early 70s films were more like experiments with sounds and images than straight documentaries.7 Jean-Luc Godard had of course been headed that way anyway: he began the 1960s with films composed in the classical manner (with *avant garde,* Brechtian, modernist additions), but ended the decade embracing modernism, a disjunction of sound and image. (Conventional sound was rejected on ideological grounds: it meant the dominant system, which the Dziga Vertov Group was opposed to.)

So you could argue that the 1968-1973 political films might be better suited to being radio shows. Godard and co. can do everything that they want to do in the audio format (and they often don't find decent or suitable images to go with their sounds). Sound is cheaper to disseminate, too (you hand out audio cassettes to punters at political rallies, or send open reel tapes to radio stations).

Rostrum camera material is everywhere in the political films and the Dziga Vertov Group films (or, rather, filming material pinned to a wall or handwritten on a piece of paper). It's a cheapo way of padding out the movies with captions and mantras, newspapers and photography, that're repeated many times. Sometimes the captions reduce the ideological

6 Part of the project of the political films was to make something even with very limited means and budgets, to prove that films could be made without huge resources.
7 Godard acknowledged that some of his experiments went wrong. They were bound to, he said – that was in the nature of being an experimenter.

rants to simple assertions:

strike	strike	strike	strike
workers	workers	workers	workers
union	union	union	union
struggle	struggle	struggle	struggle
politics	politics	politics	politics

Several of the captions in the '68 to '73 political films seem to come from Godard regressing to being a ten year-old boy on a rainy afternoon, playing with his coloured felt tip pens. So he writes the months of the year in black ink with October written in red ink. So he repeats the word 'blue' in blue ink and the word 'red' in red ink. It's kinda cute.

*

One of the biggest problems with the 1968-1973 political films and the Dziga Vertov Group films was finding an audience. In the idealism of the time, and with so much political unrest and revolutionary ferment bubbling away in the People's Republic of France, in Europe and in the U.S.A., it seemed the movies *should* find an audience; they *deserved* to. It didn't help that the films that Godard, Gorin and co. made were not broadcast by the TV stations that commissioned them, and few audiences got to see them (and they didn't make much money). Hence the decision to produce *Tout Va Bien*, with big name stars Jane Fonda and Yves Montand.

Making a 'militant' or 'radical' or 'Marxist' movie is one thing; getting people to see it is something else. Here's where the concept of anti-Hollywood, anti-bourgeois, Marxist/ Maoist/ militant/ radical/ socialist/ left-wing cinema runs into numerous problems. One is exhibition and distribution, where the 1968-1973 political films and the Dziga Vertov Group releases foundered. (Most distribution and exhibition networks, as young or new filmmakers soon find out, are controlled by big companies with a thoroughly capitalist agenda).

In 1970, for ex, the big films at the global box office were *Love Story, Airport, M.A.S.H., Patton, Woodstock,* and *Joe*. Faced with the choice between booking *Love Story* or *Wind From the East*, most theatre owners would plump for the Robert Evans-produced movie. A crowd pleaser. A tear-jerker. Similarly, if punters had the choice of a cheesy, all-star disaster movie like *Airport* or *British Sounds*, most would choose *Airport*. (The film industry was suffering one of its worst recessions in 1969-1970, when some pundits thought that Hollywood as it was would cease to exist).

An anti-capitalist/ anti-bourgeois/ anti-Hollywood movie could not morally take advantage of the rampant capitalism and shameless exploitation of conventional distribution and exhibition networks, nor of conventional publicity and advertizing (advertizing was fascism, according to J.-L.G.).

In order to reach an audience, then, anti-Hollywood/ militant cinema would need to develop alternative means of distribution. The films were backed by money from television stations, and not intended to be released theatrically in the conventional manner (altho' some were). Apart from television, there were other distribution possibilities in 1970 – cinema clubs, independent theatres (or chains), the college/ university circuit, etc (Gorin and Godard undertook some tours of American universities – in Feb, 1968 and in 1970).[8] It's no surprise that the television companies which financed the 1968-1973 political films and the Dziga Vertov Group films opted not to broadcast them.

The production of *All's Well* (*Tout Va Bien*) was thus an admission that the political movie project had failed – at least in terms of finding an audience. Or in developing a non-

8 Godard and Gorin took to the road to present the political films and talk about them to groups (it was exhausting and exhilarating, Gorin recalled).

bourgeois, non-capitalist, non-Western, non-Hollywood form of filmmaking in terms of production, and in terms of content. *All's Well* is a return to the bourgeois/ Hollywood/ capitalist form of film production, with big stars, a story, characters, a narrative structure, publicity, prints and advertizing, release in theatres and all. The story and the themes of *All's Well* derived from the 1968-1973 political films and the Dziga Vertov Group works – strikes, workers, factories, left-wing politics, etc – but the approach was largely jettisoned.

✻

Thompson and Bordwell sum up the Dziga Vertov Group films in *Film Art*: 'Impossible to consume as entertainment or as engaged documentary, the films carry the modernist project to an abrasive extreme' (522).

For Richard Brody, the movies of the Dziga Vertov Group period do not bear up to scrutiny in the same way that J.-L. Godard's early output does: the films are 'petrified by ideology, by doctrine, suggest hardly a glimmer of the brilliance and the vital energy that went into them' (B, 519). They are films of *process*, of ideas, but some are difficult to sit through. *British Sounds* was a project that took a lot of Godard's time and energy, but the final images 'range from neutral to vacant' in this 'absurd and failed project' which, Brody suggested, 'has the stiff and self-punishing feel of a cinematic hair shirt' (B, 345). But the period was important for Godard, not least as recuperation.

Elio Petri remarked (in 1972) that Godard's political films were interesting but too intellectual and elitist: 'when you appeal to an elite, you fall into the trap of intellectualism'. Thus, for Petri, as revolutionary cinema, Godard's 'efforts were useless. I don't believe one can make a revolution with cinema' (in D. Georgakas, 60).

Some critics found Godard's Dziga Vertov Group films too simplistic, too naïve, and too inconsiderate of the audience. As Joan Mellen put it in *Cinéaste*: 'Godard reveals singular contempt for his audience whom he believes he can politicize through the brow-beating of a steady drone of pseudo-Marxist cliché'.[9] The films 'were made for an audience that didn't exist at the time,' commented Colin MacCabe, 'and it is hard to imagine them finding a real one now. Their politics seems grotesque, if not offensive' (Mac, 237).

However, the 1968-1973 political films did receive some critical attention – they are a cinema of ideas, after all, stuffed with captions, one-liners, political rhetoric, and the sort of concepts that can be put into words, and some critics and *cinéastes* enjoy discussing ideas. So you can read film essays about film essays.

The 1968-1973 political films are very earnest and fairly humourless. Why? Why does the exploration of political and ideological concepts always have to be so serious?

✳

As they are so earnest, so desperate to take their topics seriously, the 1968-1973 political films (and the Dziga Vertov Group works in particular) are prime targets for parodies. I'd love to see the Zucker-Abrahams-Zucker team (*The Naked Gun, Airplane!*, etc) have a go at the Dziga Vertov Group films. Only they wouldn't bother, because nobody has seen them, and a primary rule of movie spoofing is that the audience has to know the original.

The 1968-1973 political films and the Dziga Vertov Group films were constructed from short scenes (and some longer rants), just like many of Jean-Luc Godard's movies. Some of the scenes were little bits of business (someone shutting a door, say), but the key factor was: they were repeated. And repeated.

Structurally, these little bits were simply put together by the editing, one after another: the editors were the orchestral

---

9 *Cinéaste*, 4, 3, Winter, 1970.

conductors of these works. The parts could be arranged in any order: devices like plot development, rising action, cause and effect, dividing films into acts, and all of the æsthetic structures deriving from literature and theatre, were not employed. The films simply started, and then they stopped. There was no Grand Beginning, and no Grand Ending or Finale. Semblances of narrative structure were suggested by the repeated use of title cards or diagrams. But not really. Some films (such as *Struggle In Italy*) were divided into topics (Family, Society, Baked Beans, Ducks, etc).

1968 was a pivotal year for Jean-Luc Godard in other ways – in his professional relationships, leaving behind (some of) his old film crews and collaborators, for instance, or the extensive travelling Godard undertook: 'I had to take a break and I left Paris,' Godard explained, 'I went to Cuba, to Canada, to the States, trying to make pictures. I knew the pictures were not successful, but it sort of broke the routine' (Mac, 213).[10] Later, Godard looked back on his ideological years and they seemed to be lost years, in which he stopped living a regular life, didn't go to the movies, and didn't read.

But more than a few folk in the cinema scene in the French Republic and elsewhere viewed Jean-Pierre Gorin with distrust: for them, Jean-Luc Godard was being lured away from his true vocation as one of the leading lights of world cinema into cul-de-sacs of extreme ideological projects.

Meanwhile, Anne Wiazemsky saw the influence of Jean-Pierre Gorin as very negative on her relationship with Godard: 'all of my problems with Jean-Luc date from his arrival', Wiazemsky asserted in 2003. They would have had a 'classic actress-director relationship', Wiazemsky maintained, 'if it hadn't been for politics, Gorin, yes' (B, 358). One wonders what Godard might've produced with Wiazemsky if Gorin hadn't been on the scene during this period of re-building in

---

10 But that's the problem with travelling: wherever you go, *you are still you*. Godard in Canada is still Godard.

Godard's life. Of course, Wiazemsky does appear in *Tout Va Bien, Struggle In Italy, Vladimir and Rosa* and *Wind From the East*.

The 1968-1973 era political films and the Dziga Vertov Group projects were examined in retrospect in *Here and Elsewhere* (1976), made by Jean-Luc Godard and Anne-Marie Miéville; but it would be fascinating to hear Anne Wiazemsky's view of those years and projects.

The Dziga Vertov Group films in particular are filmed records of the Annual Marxist-Leninist Debating Club – sometimes they have picnics, sometimes they're in cruddy colleges, or in Godard's Paris pad. Anyway, the point is, discussion is central to the concept: a good proportion of the D.-V.-G. movies is simply one debate after another, with captions, off-screen voices and newsreel or images of nude women added occasionally.

The revolutionary politics explored in the 1968-1973 film projects talked about Maoism, Marxism, Communism and socialist ideology and politics, but declined to address the issue of artists working in Communist nations. Filmmakers have been censored, had films suppressed or withheld, projects cancelled, and were even imprisoned (such as Sergei Paradjanov, a world-class film director if ever there was one – Paradjanov was making his truly astonishing films at this time, too – *The Colour of Pomegranates* and *Shadows of Our Forgotten Ancestors*). During the Communist era, filmmakers in the Soviet Union, the People's Republic of China and Eastern Bloc countries had restrictions on the subjects they could explore, and were encouraged to address socialist realist topics (as well as Paradjanov, many filmmakers suffered from political suppression, including Andrei Tarkovsky, Andrzej Wajda, and Jafar Panahi).

✳

J.-L. Godard's 68-73 political films such as *Wind From*

the East (known in Cuba as Marxism For Hippies) are careful to defend Mao Zedong and Joseph Stalin against attacks from bourgeois politicos who have accused their regimes of committing atrocities. According to Wind From the East, Mao and Stalin never put a foot wrong, never authorized repression, coercion, aggression or violence of any kind, not even a single punishment against any human (or hamster).[11] No, Mao and Stalin were saintly, kindly rulers, who gave their chiefs of staff handmade candy on their birthdays,[12] and new-born kittens along with their Christmas bonus.

According to Wind From the East and the D.V.G. films, Chairman Mao was a gentle, peace-loving philosopher who tended a Zen Buddhist garden designed with quaint, minimal simplicity in Peking. He issued orders to his underlings using Chinese calligraphy (he'd taken a 50-year vow of silence during the founding of the People's Republic of China in 1949), and he looked like Yoda from Star Wars. Everybody loved him.

Joseph Stalin was not a loathed, feared and terrifying ruler of a rotten-to-the-core government which led a superpower. No, nyet: according to Wind From the East, Stalin was a sweet, old uncle ('Uncle Joe-ski', they called him), who doted on his family, and spent most of his waking hours sorting through his beloved collection of antique music boxes in his garden shed.

Wind From the East insists that 50 million victims did not die in poverty and starvation in the Soviet Union, or were terrorized by the K.G.B.,[13] or were sent away to the Gulags — that was all a naughty lie put about by the Amerikan Imperialists. In reality, as history has shown, those 50 million souls were given all sorts of wonderful choices — a free trip to

---

11 Chickens, alas, were fair game. Very edible with noodles and chow mein.
12 Chairman Mao's intricate icing on his homemade cakes was something to behold (in red, of course).
13 K.G.B. stands for Kind, Gentle Bureaucrats.

the holiday camps in Siberia (where the All You Can Eat Buffet was a hit), and even the once-in-a-lifetime opportunity to make militant, Marxist movies on Sunday afternoons in the country! (weather permitting).

According to *Wind From the East* and the D. Vertov Group films, the Soviet Union's government had a spotless record of human rights, without the slightest hint of corruption; it never imprisoned anybody for political or ideological reasons (honest it didn't); and of course, my dear comrade, it only wanted the very best for its beloved citizens, who were completely free morally, ethically, politically, socially and ideologically to do, print, create and believe what they liked.

Thus, *Wind From the East* launches a pre-emptive creative nuclear strike against all of those Imperialist, Capitalist Pigs in the Western world who keep pointing out that the Communist regimes of the People's Republic of China and the Soviet Union (and the Eastern Bloc) from the 1920s to the Fall of the Berlin Wall) were not Paradises on Earth. They *were Paradise*, *Wind From the East* asserts. They most definitely *were* Paradises for all who were lucky enough to live there.

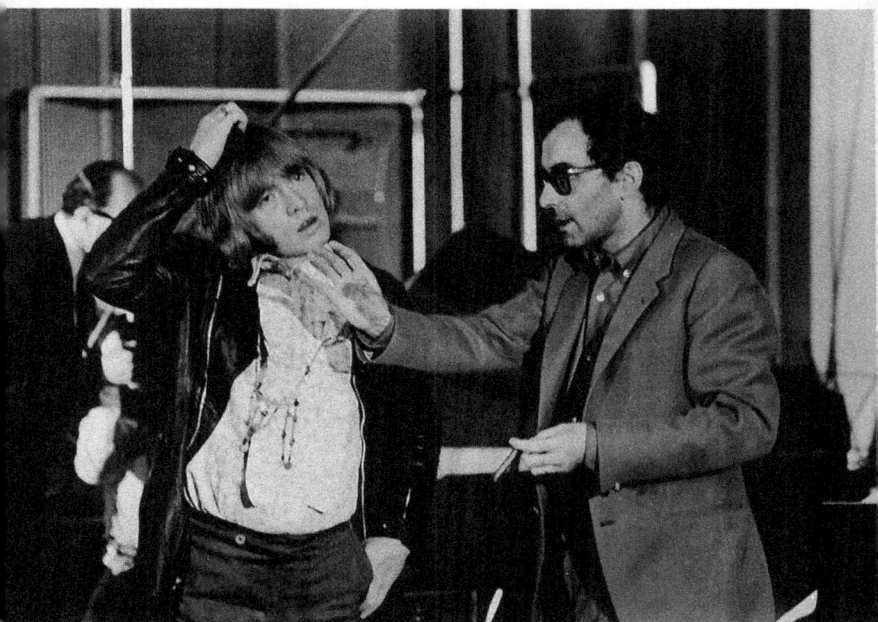

Making One Plus One (1968)

2

ONE PLUS ONE

SYMPATHY FOR THE DEVIL

INTRO.

One Plus One (a.k.a. *Sympathy For the Devil*), made in 1968, had the French New Wave director coming to the People's Republic of Great Britain to direct a film (and he would be back soon to helm *British Sounds*). Michael Pearson, Eleni Collard and Ian Quarrier produced for Cupid Productions; many in the crew were Brits: Tony Richmond (DP),[1] Arthur Bradburn and Derek Ball (sound); John Stoneman (AD), Linda DeVetta (make-up), Valerie Booth (continuity), etc.[2] Ken Rowles, Agnès Guillemot and Christiane Aya were the editors.

In the cast, apart from the Rolling Stones (the classic Stones line-up: Jagger, Jones, Richards, Watts and Wyman), were Iain Quarrier, Anne Wiazemsky, Frankie Dymon, Danny Daniels, Ilario Bisi-Pedro, Linbert Spencer, Tommy Ansah, Michael McKay, Rudi Patterson and Glenna Forster-Jones, with Sean Lynch as narrator. Also appearing were members of the Stones coterie: Marianne Faithfull, Anita Pallenberg, James Fox[3] and Nicky Hopkins. Released Nov 30, 1968. 111 minutes.

---

1 Richmond later lit *The Man Who Fell To Earth* (1975).
2 It was the first time that the Maestro had worked with a British crew.
3 Jagger, Fox and Pallenberg would soon be filming *Performance* (1970), which began principal photography on July 29, 1968 (or July 22, 1968 in some accounts), and ended on October 11, 1968.

We know what Godard thought of British cinema – very little! But Godard directed *two films* in England. He didn't make films in Spain, or Norway, or Germany, or Belgium, or Poland, or Holland – all countries with thriving film industries.

So here with *One Plus One* was the *Maître* directing a movie in the Greatest Country On Earth. But this isn't Godard's 'British' movie – *One Plus One* contains no nods whatsoever to British cinema. And no British film has ever looked like *One Plus One*! *One Plus One* simply goes its own way, like all of Godard's films (Godard's cinema has remained impressively true to itself. Fads and trends don't interest it, though of course Godard's cinema reacts continually to film culture and the movie marketplace, and Godard's cinema itself led to fads. However, it's not well-known that Godard actually directed a *Carry On* film in 1968: *Carry On Comrade* featured Kenneth Williams as a sly, stuck-up, camp factory boss and Sid James as the wily, lecherous foreman who leads a strike, with Barbara Windsor as the giggling, bouncy girl caught in the middle).

There's something outrageous about this 1968 film: to have one of the most famous pop bands in the world at your disposal, and then to film them at work in *very* long takes which reduce the fire of creativity to noodling around in a room, smoking, drinking, chatting, yawning and strumming guitars. The white-hot furance of pop music (in its finished, recorded state, heard on the radio, or in its live-on-stage state, when the Rolling Stones, at their best, were extra-ordinary), becomes as boring and everyday as typing out a film contract or delivering a crate of beer to a pub.

And then, once the 'Greatest Rock and Roll Band Ever' have been portrayed as just another bunch of guys in a recording studio (by the first ten minutes of the film) – and decidedly *not* glamorous or incendiary or revolutionary (and certainly not Their Satanic Majesties) – this genuinely eccentric film heads off in a completely different direction, cinematically – to stage lengthy disquisitions on African American music, on the blues, on race relations, and on racism.

Wow – Jean-Luc Godard had balls of steel, to have those resources (the Rolling Stones willing to appear in a feature-length movie!), and to do *this* with them!

Maybe *One Plus One* is 'a total load of crap', as Keith Richards maintained (and many Rolling Stones admirers find the political, theatrical skits silly and pretentious) – and yet this crap is also compelling, and amazing.

Perhaps the Rolling Stones were hoping for something like *Blow Up* (1966), when a Euro-art film director (Michelangelo Antonioni) explored the trendy lifestyle of Swinging London, and made the Yardbirds look cool at a concert (*Blow Up* had cars, fashionable clothing, nude women, too). Instead, *One Plus One* was the boring kind of arty movie (from a working class, rock 'n' roll perspective) – a political rant.

❂

One Plus One is known now primarily for its documentation of the Rolling Stones in their prime in the Olympic recording studio in London working out one of the anthems of the era, 'Sympathy For the Devil'. Mick, Keef, Charlie, Bill, Brian and Nicky (Hopkins) are shown rehearsing the song, trying out different grooves, and recording take after take. Sometimes they try it as a shuffle, or as a ballad, sometimes they get the bongos, shakers and tom toms out, sometimes they sit on the floor[4] in a circle, all cosy and hippyish. They try it at different tempos (i.e., they're using the studio as a rehearsal space; but if they were touring, songs would often be knocked into shape on the road).

We first hear the song in *One Plus One* in a cute circle of

4 Richards plays in bare feet – *One Plus One* is full of minor details like that.

acoustic guitars in the opening reel (with Richards, Jagger and Jones, with Jagger showing the guitar chords to Jones). Richards admitted the song (initially written by Jagger) was rhythmically dull, but became a hit when it was turned into a samba. The Rolling Stones come across as young professionals working at getting the song right, not the bad boys and rebels of Andrew Loog Oldham's slick P.R. campaigns. In between takes, they sit around and smoke (hell, who *doesn't* puff away in a Godard movie?), but they're nice, middle-class and working class lads from Dartford and Lewisham for the rest of the time.

Mick Jagger and Keith Richards are very much the ringleaders in the recording studio (it's always Richards who counts in the music – Richards was the musical director of the Stones througout their career), while Brian Jones[5] strums an acoustic guitar in his own little corner. Jones seems to be lost in his own, private world, quite apart from the rest of the band (except when Richards gives him cigarettes during breaks), and Jones's guitar is not heard on the soundtrack. Indeed, the soundtrack is markedly different from the visuals – occasionally it appears as if the sound crew are picking up

5 Brian Jones was increasingly off in his own world – it was 'his' band (originally), and Mick Jagger and Keith Richards had come to *him* (after seeing him at Alexis Korner's place). But altho' Jones was a formidable musical talent (one of those guys who can pick up any musical instrument and get a good sound out of it, according to many observers), he lost control of the direction and momentum of the band, with Jagger and Richards taking up centre stage. Jagger in particular was simply too ambitious and too focussed (and too much of a control freak) to allow anything to upset the artistic or professional equilibrium (and the money-making machine that the band became).
What's striking about Brian Jones's role in the Rolling Stones is just how long the rest of the band tolerated him. For months, and even years, it seems that Jones was in a psychological freefall: apart from taking plenty of drugs and drink, he was messing about on stage, hardly playing anything, and baiting the audience. In the recording studio, he contributed little, being out of his head or simply not bothered. At band meetings, he would be asleep on the table.
When Jones died in July, 1969, a U.S.A. tour was organized only a few days later; it was the first American tour for over three years, so that Jones's condition was probably one cause for the delays.

sound with the filmmakers' own mike – which un-professionally swings into the shot from time to time – or, most of the time, they're getting a feed from the control room. (Which goes against the grain of what fans would prefer: a fly-on-the-wall documentary where we hear the Stones' banter. Instead, we hear a selective mix, which doesn't include all of the instruments, and often we can't hear what the band're saying off-mike, or even the sounds from the instruments being played right in front of us. That derives partly from Godard's unique approach to sound in cinema).

'Sympathy For the Devil' comes from the era at the end of the 1960s when the Rolling Stones fooled around with supposedly 'Satanic'/ occult material (during the *Their Satanic Majesties* album).[6]

> Pleased to meet you,
> Hope you guessed my name, oh yeah.
> But what's confusing you
> Is just the nature of my game.
>
> Just as every cop is a criminal
> And all the sinners saints
> As heads is tails
> Just call me Lucifer,
> 'Cause I'm in need of some restraint.
>
> So if you meet me
> Have some courtesy,
> Have some sympathy, and some taste.
> Use all your well-learned politesse
> Or I'll lay your soul to waste, oh yeah.

'Sympathy For the Devil' has become somewhat notorious: rock critics always seem to cite the fact that Meredith Hunter was murdered at the famous Altamont Speedway concert during the Stones' song 'Sympathy For the Devil', as if this is a terribly poignant, ironic event (actually, as

---

6 Actually, Mick Jagger's dalliance with Satanic/ occult material was fairly superficial (and was soon dropped). Rock stars such as Jimmy Page (of Led Zeppelin) were much more into it. Page was a well-known Aleister Crowley fanatic.

the movie *Gimme Shelter* shows, it was during 'Under Your Thumb'). Like *wow*, the youth died while Mick Jagger sang about having 'sympathy for the Devil'. So someone's death becomes food for a journalist's story, as if the stabbing and the murder wasn't enough. (The Altamont concert (Dec 6, 1969, with 300,000 souls) is often referred to as 'The Day The Sixties Died': 'America at Altamont could only muster one common response. Everybody grooved on fear. One communal terror of fascist repression.'[7] Altamont is seen by critics as the End of the Era of free love and hippy-dippy ideals. But it's far from the most dangerous pop concert ever — 100s have died at many gigs and nightclubs since then, during sets by Pearl Jam, the Who, Great White, etc, from falling structures such as scaffolding and seats, from crushes at the stage, and, deadliest of all, from fires. Some concerts have claimed over a hundred lives).

The filmmakers cover the recording session with lengthy, slow tracking shots. The camera not only captures the musicians, but also the engineers and people hanging about in the wings (several movies could be made of the Stones' colourful entourage during this period, like Andy Warhol's Factory).

One Plus One is a curious document of a rock 'n' roll band in the studio — not at all like the average rockumentary (the band are not interviewed, for a start, nor do they or the filmmakers provide a commentary, or even basic contextual information, and nobody acts as a narrator or M.C. There's no indication of where we are, or why, or how (no exterior images of the recording studio, for example). The movie simply dives straight away into the band rehearsing the song).

And the 1968 film contains many pauses and halts which many other documentaries or films of a rock band would cut out. Moments where musicians fiddle around with

7 George Paul Csicsery, "Altamont, California", *The New York Daily News*, December 8, 1969.

guitars, where Keef solos, where Charlie tries out rhythms. The film dwells on pauses when 'nothing happens' (and yet these moments are part of life, and part of being in a pop band. *One Plus One* is precious partly because it does include those unfaked, unglamorous, everyday moments, like Charlie yawning, or Keef asking for an adjustment to his guitar sound). The camera tracks around the standing flats to show friends of the band who aren't identified, and just seem to be hanging out. The picture doesn't, for instance, go into the control room, where much of the real action in a recording session occurs. So the producers, the engineers and the liggers in the control room aren't heard or seen, except as vague figures behind the big pane of glass.8 Instead, the film stays resolutely on the floor of Olympic Studios. (In the light of Godard's highly politicized cinema of the late 1960s, you might see this tactic as deliberately staying on the factory floor,9 and not venturing into the managers' offices or the front of house offices. When Godard filmed people at work (such as in the Dziga Vertov Group films, including a car plant in Cowley, Oxford), it was *always* the working class folk on the floor of the factory, doing the actual work).

A typical filmed account of a music recording session would automatically include the producers, maybe an engineer, usually someone from the record company, maybe a journalist hanging around, maybe a publicist, maybe fans waiting outside the studio for a glimpse of the stars, and maybe several journos to contextualize the pop music scene, the band's history, etc. But *One Plus One* does none of that. It doesn't interview the band, either.10 Yet it still works (it helps, of course, that this is a world-famous rock 'n' roll act – it

8 In one scene, there are over a dozen faces palely peering out of the control room window.
9 It's not only an account of the Rolling Stones in the recording studio, it's a glimpse behind the scenes of how pop music is constructed.
10 We don't see the Stones on their breaks, or eating – we are always on the factory floor of the recording studio.

wouldn't have quite the same resonance if it was a bunch of unknowns. But because it's Mick and Keef and the boys, it's fascinating. And the 1960s fashions are terrific in *One Plus One* – bright yellow, green and red pants, pink and purple shirts, scarlet boots).

Garry Mulholland found *One Plus One* 'an incredibly strange film':

> I love the clothes. Everyone in this film looks heart-breakingly cool... Most of all, I love the way Godard's camera prowls slowly, around the Stones, around its actors and locations. It lingers on something interesting, gets bored, moves on, and takes in every detail of its surroundings on its way to the next thing worth linger-ing upon. Godard's camera is as great an art thing as the Rolling Stones were in 1968, and that is a very good thing indeed. (76-77)

Gathered in a circle around a mic, late in the *One Plus One* movie, members of the Rolling Stones entourage croon the 'woo-woo' backing vox for 'Sympathy For the Devil', now sounding more like the final result (while Mick Jagger sings on the other side of a baffle). Anita Pallenberg and Marianne Faithfull, two icons of the British pop scene, add some glamour to the proceedings (check out those fab glad rags!). However, alas, we don't see any close-ups – the camera stays back as it dollies around them (and they have their backs to the camera).

Again, this can seem like squandering the potential of the participants. Anita Pallenberg, for example, is a stunning screen presence, the equal of any of the celebrated actresses in the Godard film catalogue, including even Brigitte Bardot and Anna Karina.[11] (Pallenberg could've essayed the Wiaz-emsky role in *One Plus One*, for example, with potentially amazing results).

Some of the footage of the Rolling Stones at work depicts

11 With Pallenberg visiting for the day, it's a pity that a scene wasn't developed for her.

them producing some not especially spectacular music. The second visit to the recording studio, for example (the second 10-minute scene, beginning around 20 minutes into the 1968 movie), shows a fidgety, lacklustre version of 'Sympathy For the Devil' being rehearsed. This sequence begins with a shot of the back of Brian Jones' head – for 70 seconds! And the song continues with stops and starts, while the camera drifts over to Old Rubber Lips, or Richards (playing bass), to Watts and Wyman (on percussion), then back again. And again. Jagger looks up at the camera sourly – as if daring the viewer to comment on this shabby interpretation of his new song. Or perhaps His Jaggness is now seriously regretting allowing cameras in the recording studio. (Jagger had an ambivalent attitude towards the media and documentaries. Essentially, he liked to be in control, and here he isn't).

THE ROLLING STONES.

The Rolling Stones,[12] with their self-conscious, contrived 'tough', sneering image (entirely manufactured), were often trumpeted, like many other bands, as 'the greatest rock 'n' roll band ever' (every band has been lauded thus: Led Zeppelin, the Who, the Beatles, Nirvana, Abba, the Spice Girls, etc). Somehow, the Rolling Stones roll on – like Jean-Luc Godard himself – outlasting all of their contemporaries: as Philip Norman remarked in his Mick Jagger biography of 2012:

> Only the Stones, once seemingly the most unstable of all, have kept rolling continuously from decade to decade, then century to century, weathering the sensational death of one member and the embittered resignation of two others (plus ongoing internal politics that would impress the Medicis); leaving behind gener- ations of wives and lovers; outlasting two managers, nine British prime ministers and the same number of American presidents; impervious to changing musical fads, gender politics and social mores; as sexagenarians

12 The name comes from a Muddy Water's song, and it was Brian Jones who named the band.

still somehow retaining the same sulphurous whiff of sin and rebellion they had in their twenties. (4)

Like Jean-Luc Godard, the Rolling Stones have enjoyed a remarkably long career[13] in showbiz: even well into the 21st century, you could still see the Stone live,[14] and in the 2010s, Godard was still releasing new movies!

THE ROLLING STONES IN CINEMA.

Here's a note on some of the movies/ TV shows featuring the Stones of the era of *One Plus One: Gimme Shelter* (the Maysles Brothers,[15] and Charlotte Zwerin, 1970) is one of the classic rock concert movies, featuring the Rolling Stones at their peak on tour in the Land of the Free (yet again). Famous for its footage of the infamous Altamont Speedway gig, *Gimme Shelter* also includes many scenes backstage, in recording studios, in dressing rooms, at press conferences, doing press interviews, managers and lawyers arranging the Altamont gig (minus the band), the band fooling about (tho' they're pretty sedate, and far from being heavy duty party animals), plus live turns from Ike and Tina Turner and Jefferson Airplane.

Although the Rolling Stones became linked in legend to Altamont, the event was in fact originally planned by the Grateful Dead. It wasn't the Stones who put on the show, or invited the Hell's Angels to do the security (some have questioned the notion of 'security'). Mick Jagger was keen to do a concert in the U.S.A. as big as Woodstock, and to recreate the Hyde Park[16] experience on the other side of the Atlantic

13 Charlie Watts, tho', griped that it was only ten years work out of fifty years.
14 The Stones toured every three years or so through the 1970s, 1980s and 1990s (such as the *Steel Wheels, Licks, A Bigger Bang* and *Voodoo Lounge* tours), which celebrated the ageing rockers who reckoned they could still cut it live (and audiences thought they could).
15 Albert Maysles had filmed Godard's episode in *Paris Vu Par*.
16 Hyde Park was the biggest concert of its kind, with around 250,000 punters turning out to see the Rolling Stones (150,000 had attended not long before, for Blind Faith).

Ocean (and to do a free gig – the Stones were already famous at this point for over-charging for tickets. In later years, a Stones ticket could cost hundreds of dollars, and one of your fingers).

The concert footage in *Gimme Shelter* is of course incendiary – even when the photography is as abysmal, under-lit, out of focus and cock-eyed as in *Cocksucker Blues*, and the sound's grainy mono. You can't fail with a band this white-hot, and music this good (even the most cack-handed film crew could come up with something interesting – and a lot of crews were technically incompetent in this era).

Meanwhile, *Cocksucker Blues* (1972) was a tour documentary directed by Robert Frank, at the invitation of the Rolling Stones[17] (during their *Exile On Main Street* tour of North America of 1972).[18] *Cocksucker Blues* (great title!)[19] became a notorious movie when it was withheld from release, due, apparently, to some of the scenes in it.[20] The movie became the subject of conflict between Robert Frank and the filmmakers and the Rolling Stones (to the point where Frank wasn't allowed to release it, and could only screen it if there was a topless groupie with big boobs, lines of cocaine, a bottle of Remy, and an irate road manager in the room at the same time).

Cocksucker Blues is a terrific document of a rock band on tour in the 1970s, partly because it features many

17 It was Charlie Watts who asked Robert Frank to photograph the Stones' next album cover, and to shoot the documentary.
18 Among the authors covering the U.S.A. tour for magazines like *Saturday Review* and *Rolling Stone* were Terry Southern and Truman Capote. But their 'combined literary talents would contrive not one sensible or original word about the tour in print', according to Philip Norman (1984, 361).
19 You hear a bit of Mick Jagger's crude cocksucker blues song on the soundtrack: 'where can I get my cock sucked?/ Where can I get my ass fucked?' Written with Keith Richards, it was intended as a middle finger to record label Decca, which the Rolling Stones had recently left for Atlantic (they owed Decca a final song, and this was their parting gesture).
20 *Ladies and Gentlemen: The Rolling Stones* was released instead (filmed by Butterfly, John Lennon's company).

unguarded moments[21] (tho' some are staged), partly because it's Jagger, Richards and the lads (a legendary ensemble in rock music), and partly because it has some classic incidents which you associate with Seventies rock excess (groupies, drugs, silly pranks, and of course some highly combustible rock music).[22] *Cocksucker Blues* does feature so many ingredients of the rock 'n' roll tour – the jet hired for the tour, the limos, the scenes by the swimming pool in L.A., some fooling around with naked groupies, and of course some drug use.

The Rolling Stones Rock and Roll Circus (1968, prod. Sandy Lieberson, dir. Michael Lindsay-Hogg), made the same year as *One Plus One,* was conceived partly to give the Stones something substantial to do performance-wise, and to heal rifts within the band and its entourage (Mick Jagger was travelling to Australia to appear in *Ned Kelly*, which meant the band couldn't tour). It was Jagger who conceived the idea (but the legal ramifications of the TV show were still being debated by lawyers into the mid-1990s).[23]

The accounts of the recording of that ill-fated TV show have become legendary – how, for instance, everything was running late, there were technical problems, and the audience was getting tired, and Mick Jagger rallied everybody in the early hours to get the recording done (in his excellent biography of Jagger, Philip Norman reckons it was one of Jagger's finer moments, rallying the troops, and whipping up the energy when everyone was flagging).

THE PRODUCTION.

One Plus One had a troubled production history. Jean-

---

21 Certainly few major rock acts have allowed such access or such scenes to be included in the final cut. Most bands would veto much of the material.

22 After some concerts, the band were already on their way from the venue after the encores, and with a radio mic Mick Jagger was able to talk to the audience.

23 The 66-minute show was released in 1996.

Luc Godard said he hadn't wanted to come to England to make a picture,24 but he would if he could have either the Beatles or the Rolling Stones to film.25 The deal for *One Plus One* was brokered by Greek film producer Eleni Collard, via the British talent agent Mimi Scala, whom Godard had met in a Parisian nightclub (B, 326). Collard produced the movie with her partners Iain Quarrier and Michael Pearson. The Rolling Stones agreed to do it, and the Maestro came to Blighty on May 30, 1968, with a budget of £180,000 ($270,000, which is $2.5 million in 2025).26 The Stones were filmed at Olympic Studios in Barnes, South London (one of the regular haunts of numerous pop acts of the era – pretty much everybody recorded there), over three or four days at the start of June.27 (Olympic Studios, at 117, Church Road, was a former sound stage in the 1950s, a cinema before that, and also a theatre, with the space separated by baffle boards, and the windows shuttered against daylight.28 Legendary producer Glyn Johns was the house engineer. Among the pop acts who recorded as Olympic were Jimi Hendrix, David Bowie, Led Zep, the Who, Eric Clapton, Queen, Ray Charles and the Beatles).

The initial idea for *One Plus One* was to interweave two stories: one of the Rolling Stones in the recording studio (a story of construction), the other about a white woman (played by Anne Wiazemsky, Jean-Luc Godard's young wife) who commits suicide when her black lover leaves her to join a Black Power group (it would also have involved a love triangle

24 Apparently, initially Godard was due to make a film in England about abortion. The change in the law led to the idea of doing *One Plus One*.
25 Keith Richards couldn't understand why a director like Godard would be interested in the hippy scene in England; in his biography, Richards summed up the movie as 'a total load of crap' (252).
26 The budget was £250,000 ($390,000) according to the producers (B, 341).
27 As with the rest of *One Plus One*, the camera dollies constantly, on tracks set out in a figure 8 in the studio.
28 Today it has reverted to cinema status again (re-opening in 2013), though there is a small recording studio in the building.

– the French woman would've been involved with a right-wing guy from Texas, then hooks up with a left-wing black guy). Actually, altho' the Rolling Stones have been linked to the political upheavals and the radical politics of the late 1960s, they simply weren't interested in politics.

In the end, *One Plus One* does not link the two main components of the 1968 film directly (the recording studio and the theatre scenes), or in an expected manner, but thematically. The notion of white, British musicians taking up black, American musical forms (the blues, soul) is employed as a point of departure for lengthy, agitprop-theatrical sequences which explore notions of race, of racial tension, of blues music, of the cultural migration (appropriation) of musical forms, and of the role of ethnicities in a predominantly white society. Typically for Jean-Luc Godard, some of the explorations take on the incendiary aspects of race relations – the demonization of black guys as threats to white society, stealing white women and raping them. *One Plus One* knows it is being deliberately provocative (and downright offensive in its racial caricatures. But that is often Godard's mode of operation (to prod, to push, to provoke).

✪

Problems Jean-Luc Godard encountered while shooting in London included the arrest of Brian Jones, and replacing Terence Stamp[29] (who would have played Iain Quarrier's part – and he would have been far better; Quarrier doesn't seem to quite fit into a Godard film, or into this film). The Black Power scenes were disrupted by rain.[30] The studio roof in Barnes caught fire.[31]

---

29 Stamp was arrested.
30 The weather threatens to scupper the shoot at Camber Sands: it's often very windy on the beach, and the day the production was there was another blowy one.
31 It was the heat from the lights that caused the fire at Olympic Studios; according to engineer Glyn Johns, Godard was standing to one side and filming the efforts of the Rolling Stones and co. to get their gear out of the studio on a 16mm camera.

In the footage of Godard filming *One Plus One*, he is directing in English. He's very patient: if an actor flubs, he'll use the mantra of all directors everywhere in any media: *let's do it again*. He isn't sitting behind a bank of monitors (well, video assist and video villages didn't exist then) – he's in the midst of the cast and crew. There's no question of who's boss on the set.

One Plus One seems to have been one of Jean-Luc Godard's less than happy productions, and he was glad to return to France (it was May, 1968 when Godard left for Britain, and he might have preferred to stay in Paris, with so many things going on politically).[32] In July, 1968, Godard returned to Blighty to complete the film ('always complete what you start,' says Fritz Lang in *Contempt,* and Godard usually does). Godard later said that 'the whole thing was a mistake', which's too harsh, though there is something in Wheeler Dixon's complaint (in *The Films of Jean-Luc Godard*) about 'a thinness of material' and Quarrier's interference (I don't agree at all though about Dixon's view of the 'timidity of execution' of *One Plus One*. 'Timid' isn't a word you could apply to *any* of Jean-Luc Godard's films, even the failures like *King Lear*).[33]

Iain Quarrier, one of the producers, didn't see eye to eye with Jean-Luc Godard. When the Rolling Stones' manager and Quarrier added the completed version of the song 'Sympathy For the Devil' onto the end of his film, Godard attacked him at a public screening at the London Film Festival. You don't do that kind of thing to a Great Artist like Godard! (Quarrier was determined that a complete rendition of 'Sympathy For the Devil' would appear in the picture). Godard subsequently

32 1968 was of course a year of political unrest, riots, assass-inations, etc; it was the year of May, 1968 in Paris, of anti-Vietnam War protests, of civil unrest, and the assassination of Bobby Kennedy.
33 Dixon called *One Plus Ones* 'boring, didactic, and commerc-ially compromised' (W. Dixon, 1997, 107; M. Goodwin, 28).

disowned Quarrier's version. The point was, Godard contended, that art and politics took years to develop, and the audience should only know a little of the song. The song was still developing, Godard said, and shouldn't be seen at the end. It was unfair to emphasize the Stones more than the group of black people. They were both as important as each other.[34]

In the producers' version of *One Plus One*, the song 'Sympathy For the Devil' is heard at the end, over the final parts of the beach scene. To extend the movie while the song plays (because it isn't long enough for the length of the song), the producers had the film freeze (and change into the psychedelic colours popular the time).

One aspect of *One Plus One* that critics drew attention to, apart from its collage, non-narrative structure, its troubled production, and its account of the Rolling Stones in action, was that Jean-Luc Godard was shooting the film in English. Nearly all of Godard's films have been made in French (with English as the main secondary language). English has been used in many films (such as *Tout Va Bien, King Lear* and *JLG/JLG*), but Godard was clearly much happier writing and filming in French (yet he directed the actors and crew quite competently in English. Indeed, Godard had already directed English-speaking actors, and he was OK with conducting interviews in English). Maybe shooting in English altered the way Godard presented his polemics (even though they were often aimed at North Amerika). Godard tended to use 'American English' in his films, rather than 'British English' (which goes back to the Fifties and Godard's love-hate relationship with Americana and North American movies).

REVOLUTION IS SEXY.

One Plus One is a collage of other Jean-Luc Godardian

---

34 Godard, in J. Cott, *Rolling Stone*, June, 1969.

concerns: politics being number one, of course – this being 1968 and the height of Godard's political cinema, and politicization of cinema.[35] There are references to J.F. Kennedy, Mao Zedong, Communism, the Federal Bureau of Intelligence, the Central Intelligence Agency, airlines, liberalism, democracy, and trade unionism, all the usual Godardian, political obsessions and *bête noirs.* Godard adds his political histories, of course, but slants them in some instances towards British history (citing Trafalgar and El Alamein). Race and ethnic issues are also foregrounded.

Anne Wiazemsky is seen spraying graffiti on cars, shops, walls, sidewalks, fences, billboards, embankments, doors and hotel windows around London. The words include 'Stalin', 'Freudemocracy', 'Cinemarxism', and '(SO)VIETCONG'. (She's playing the part of a Godardian political activist in a long coat and hat: a woman who's cute *and* into politics: it's the ultimate, Godardian fantasy!).[36] Her character isn't explained until halfway through the movie. *One Plus One* is a pæan to graffiti, the film as readymade art, 20 years b4 it became fashionable. Some of the graffiti is wordplay and acrostics, which Jean-Luc Godard has always loved:

```
          M
          A
          R
  S   E   X


  M       A   O
          R
          T
```

If a bunch of media or film or drama or Eng. Lit. students

35 At Cannes in 1968, which was famously politicized, taking place in the midst of unrest, Godard delivered a classic quip: 'I'm talking to you about solidarity with the students and the workers, and you're talking to me about tracking shots and close-ups!'
36 Expanding on the lads painting slogans in *Masculine Feminine.*

went out and filmed themselves graffitying walls and doors with revolutionary word puzzles, a tutor might send them out again to do something *interesting*. But Jean-Luc Godard can get away with it. Not because he 'means it', not because he 'believes' in this leftist, Maoist, Marxist, Freudian revolutionary politics, but because... well, he's *Godard*.

Jean-Luc Godard makes revolution *sexy*. Or at least *fun*. Soviet and Russian propaganda films can be so solemn, so serious. But Godard adds *humour* to revolutionary politics, which is extraordinary – and still extraordinary decades later. The world may be very different in the 21st century (is it, though?), but the additions of humour and verve mean that Godard's films don't appear as didactic, sombre, po-faced treatises. If you put Anne Wiazemsky or Anna Karina into a piece on pro-left-wing, anti-right-wing politics you have something automatically appealing.

One Plus One, along with *La Chinoise* and *Weekend*, are Jean-Luc Godard's form of political cinema at its best. Unfortunately, the humour and satire didn't carry over into the Dziga Vertov Group films, which are tiresomely earnest. *One Plus One* demonstrated that the same points about left-wing/socialist politics could be delivered within an experimental cinematic framework that also included humour.

❂

One Plus One seems to have been conceived in terms of takes as long as a ten-minute reel of celluloid. The camera was fitted with long, 10-minute magazines. Thus, we are in the woods with 'Eve Democracy (in 'All About Eve') for about ten minutes; and just before that, we saw the Stones at work for ten minutes in the studio.

There are some extraordinary, very long takes in *One Plus One* (a master of montage, Jean-Luc Godard also features more long takes than most filmmakers). One of the most amazing sequence shots (in the first section) lasts some

10 minutes and thirty seconds,[37] filmed in a car scrapyard, beside the River Thames (and a railroad bridge), which appears to be the base of a Black Power group (all black, and all male). The camera tracks and pans constantly (it's one of Godard's 360° track-and-pans): past individuals reading from political texts, and newspapers, and a book about the history of popular music (in particular about the blues, which the Rolling Stones, like many other white bands of the time, happily raided); another guy who hands out rifles to his comrades and later on in the shot fires his gun; a group of three white women in white dresses are brought into the compound in a red Mini car; the women are prisoners and victims; a man strokes one woman who lies on the ground, while another guy next to him talks about black men's desire for white women; the other women are taken somewhere off-camera (one appears to be raped, in the back of a car, another is shot dead; both are bloody). Sometimes jets overhead, or passing trains, or horns from boats on the Thames River drown out the people reading aloud; and sometimes the narration by Sean Lynch is faded up over the direct sound.[38] At the end of the sequence shot, the revolutionary leader says, 'it's not a question of left or right, it's a question of black'.

In the second black militant scene (the 'black syntax' scene), again at the junkyard by the River Thames, again covered in a track-and-pan shot around 360 degrees, the men are now arranged around the compound on cars, and throw the rifles and guns from one to another repeating phrases such as 'kill them!' or 'this is a stick-up!' Slogans such as 'Malcolm X' are sprayed on the cars and the walls. A Black Power leader is interviewed by two black, female journalists, voicing many of Jean-Luc Godard's revolutionary concerns.

37 The shot may be continuous, but there are cuts to other shots.
38 Sometimes the long sequence shots threaten to come unstuck – when actors nearly forget their lines, or botch up their readings from texts. Some of the actors were clearly not used to Godard's challenging way of filmmaking.

Near the Mini car a man lays the guns on the corpses of two white women – the symbolism of war and death needs no gloss. During this sequence, the film sets up a series of actions and rhetorical motifs which it returns to (the rifles, for instance, are thrown back the other way between the guys). Here the actors are at the edge – either of corpsing, or of forgetting their lines.

This is very typical, Godardian cinema, a slice of prime, Sixties Godardania, with added interest for a British audience because it was filmed in the mythical nation of Albion. In amongst the Marxist/ radical polemics are parts of contemporary Britain, which give *One Plus One* a particular flavour, quite different from Godard's French or Swiss films.

The British setting is endlessly fascinating for me – it's something to do with the way that Jean-Luc Godard and his team have filmed Britain. It's not the London of films made by Brits in London – the *Carry On* films, or *James Bond*, or 1960s musicals like *Oliver* or *Mary Poppins*. Godard is in London, but he avoids every single major landmark, the ones that crop up in every film set in London: Big Ben, Buckingham Palace, Tower Bridge, the British Museum, red London buses,[39] etc. Only the River Thames and parts of the river bridges are present.[40] But it's still very much London: Godard's film provincializes London, turns it into a series of small roads... grey corrugated fences that hide industrial plants... a junkyard... a row of small shops... In short, he Godardizes Britain, turning London into Godardland.[41] (He did the same thing in *British Sounds*, two years later).

And this London, this Britain, in *One Plus One* hasn't changed one bit in four decades or more. Only the cars are

39 Actually, red buses do pop up in *One Plus One* (try filming during the day on main roads in London and avoiding red buses).
40 Hyde Park, the Embankment and the Hilton Hotel also feature.
41 Which he does wherever he films.

different, and a little of the street furniture. Somehow Jean-Luc Godard and his collaborators have filmed Britain in 1968 and made it timeless and unchanging, whereas the comedies, the musicals, the spy thrillers and the 'Swinging London' films look incredibly dated, very much fixed in their time.

❂

Another long take in *One Plus One* (entitled 'All About Eve') has Eve Democracy[42] (Anne Wiazemsky) being interviewed by Iain Quarrier and a film crew in a sunny, leafy, English wood. As Wiazemsky/ Eve and Quarrier wander around the trees, bushes and grass, Quarrier fires questions at Eve, who replies to everything with a one-word answer, yes or no (though it's mostly 'yes' – how can you say 'no' to Godard's barrage of rhetoric? And what could Democracy answer, Godard said, but yes *and* no).

Tony Richmond's camera tracks back and forth, capturing this extended piece of comico-political schtick in a single take. The shot is kept visually interesting by having the actors walk slowly back and forth, with Eve in front, and Quarrier directing his camera team to follow her. The sound guy captures the real sound for the film (as in other scenes, which enhances the reality).

Godard's questions[43] include classic Godard gems such as:

- 'do you have a theory about who killed Kennedy?'
- 'do you feel exploited by interviews?'
- 'orgasm is the only moment when you can't cheat life'
- 'is taking drugs a form of spiritual gambling?'

The questions do not require an answer, and they all come from Jean-Luc Godard. You could take all of those questions and publish them as a political pamphlet. (It's London, 1968, and it's pop music and the Stones, so there are

42 David A. Cook calls this character 'a lobotomized fairy godmother' (1996, 569). Eh?
43 Apparently some of them came from a *Playboy* interview with Norman Mailer.

more questions about drugs than in any other Godard flick. Godard said he didn't use drugs because they had too strong an effect on him. He did partake of tobacco, of course, and chain-smoked).

Maybe it's Eve from the *Bible* in Paradise, a young woman in a lemon yellow dress in a sunny, green woodland. That relates to the original concept for *One Plus One*, which was to have been a film about creation (the Rolling Stones at work in the studio), and destruction (the suicide of a young, white woman when her lover joins a Black Power group). And it's Eve because one of Godard's concerns at the time was the notion of starting from zero.

Critics have complained that Jean-Luc Godard's cinema doesn't provide answers, but only asks questions. Of course. Godard loves to ask questions, and he doesn't have all the answers (or any answers). He wants to ask – he can't stop himself from asking – but he can't deliver pat answers to his own questions. (Pier Paolo Pasolini said the same: his films are questions. And Rainer Werner Fassbinder remarked that he didn't want to describe utopia for the audience, but to let them work it out for themselves).[44]

The narration of *One Plus One* (read by Sean Lynch) was typical Jean-Luc Godard: descriptions of scenes of sex, *film noir* thriller, political observations, counter-culture activism, pop culture references, ruminations about revolution, plus allusions to Communism, Joseph Stalin, Mao Zedong, Russia, J.F. Kennedy, the Central Intelligence Agency, the Federal Bureau of Investigation, Walt Disney, etc. It sounded like a Burroughsian cut-up of counter-culture faves such as Terry Southern (*Candy, Dr Strangelove, Blue Movie*), William Burroughs (*The Naked Lunch*), J.G. Ballard (*The Atrocity Exhibition*), Tom Wolfe (self-consciously cool Americana),

44 Pier Paolo Pasolini insisted that his films were not finished works: rather, they were questions. 'My films are not supposed to have a finished sense, they always end with a question. I always intend them to remain suspended' (1969, 56-57).

Norman Mailer and Henry Miller. The voiceover is heard all of the way through the film, including the final shot (the narration is also inserted into the Olympic Studios scenes, sometimes mixed above the music, which no doubt irks Rolling Stones fans even further). I would love to see Godard make a film of the book of the narration, though! It would be the Ultimate Godard Movie – a twenty million dollar revolutionary call to arms (or a hundred and thirty million dollars at today's prices).

❂

The most amusing scene in *One Plus One*, and one of the funniest in Jean-Luc Godard's output, was constructed from more lengthy takes, set in a small bookstore that sold paperback novels, comicbooks and magazines. Iain Quarrier (clad nattily in bright purple), reads aloud from *Mein Kampf* as he walked round the room, while a female secretary called Jackie typed (maybe taking down Quarrier's words, or maybe not – but why would you re-type *Mein Kampf*?), and customers perused the merchandize.

The camera zoomed in and out of the rack of pornographic and lifestyle magazines, the comicbooks and the pulp softbacks. While Adolf Hitler's famous tract was read aloud, the camera panned slowly along images of magazine covers showing half-naked women and coverlines like 'see Sophia Loren nude!', or North American superheroes. This was, again, pure Godard. *8mm Magazine, Slaves To Sin, The Body,* Agatha Christie, Mickey Spillaine, *Perry Mason, Conan, Mayfair, Penthouse, Playboy, Duke* and *I Gave My Body To Hitler...* Plus magazines of motoring, celebrities, true stories... Were these book and magazine covers made up for the movie? No! This is all real stuff. Remarkably lurid imagery – many covers (no doubt personally selected by the Master, to tie in with the right-wing theme), featured Nazis torturing women in cages, a Nazi dominatrix punishing a man, in pulpy scenarios.

No other commentary was needed: this display of late 1960s publishing was bizarro enough (the way the camera crawls across those wonderfully sensational book and magazine covers was like a history lesson or museum display in itself: it was Godard's own *Guide To Book Publishing In Late 1960s Britain*).[45]

Talking about museums – Jean-Luc Godard would make one of the best guest curators you could imagine for a blockbuster museum show. In *Jean-Luc Godard's Century of Cinema*, there would be displays devoted to 'War', 'Image', 'Politics', 'Maoism', 'Resistance', 'Vietnam', 'Paris', and 'Amerika', of course, and visitors would be invited to create their own political interviews live, as their friends read out a list of Godardian questions and an assistant would mix the cameras and intercut red and blue captions such as 'WAR OR TERRORISM?' or 'IRAQ/ IRAN').

If this wasn't silly enough, Jean-Luc Godard had each of the customers *seig heil* to Iain Quarrier after they'd selected their books. An old man with a young girl, a young woman, and a balding, middle-aged man in a suit were among the extras invited to be part of this highly unorthodox scene.

The customers also got to slap two hippy peaceniks sitting on one side (presumably meant to be some kind of political dissidents or activists – one has a head wound and a bloody bandage). They yelled out slogans: 'long live Mao!' + 'Peace in Vietnam!'. The scene was a pantomime of counter-culture discourse, very silly, very irritating, very didactic, very amusing, and very Godard.

It's the kind of scene that the Monty Python team might have made a year or so later in their TV shows at the Beeb:

45 Decades on, nothing has changed in dear, old Britain – there's simply loads more – the same book and magazine publishing, the same bookstores – those that haven't been squeezed out by the cultural imperialism of Smith's or Waterstone's.

Adolf Hitler in his retirement running a porn-mag-and-pulp-paperback emporium, loudly declaiming from his own *Mein Kampf* while customers happily *seig heil* him. It might run like this:

Hitler (John Cleese of course): Ah, guten morgen.
Customer (Michael Palin): Morning. *(Peruses display, chooses a magazine)* How much is this one?
Hitler: Ten and six. *Aber, mein freund*, how about zis? My own komposition: *Mein Kampf (Begins reading aloud)* 'ze Third Reich will come about –'
Customer: No, no. This will do, thank you very much.
Hitler: *(snatching the magazine and peering at the title)* '*Slaves To Zin'?* Vot is zis rubbish? *Amerikan.*
Customer: Yes, but –
Hitler *(getting crazier)*: Now, zis is ze good stuff! Listen: 'ze Third Reich will start by –'

And so on.[46] Thing is, many of Jean-Luc Godard's films are already humorous, and so close to parody, that very little is required to make them more comical. You wouldn't call Godard a comic genius, but the comedy in Godard's cinema is overlooked far too much – especially by those film critics who solemnly discuss his films in the hallowed tones of the court or the church.

❂

One Plus One closes with two scenes: one is another visit to Barnes, to Olympic Studios, where the Rolling Stones are sitting on the floor and jamming (Charlie plays a drum, Mick a small djembe, Keef an electric axe, Bill a bass, and Nicky an electric piano).[47] It's a bluesy jam that goes nowhere, and shows the Stones in a poor light, musically (if they'd had final cut on this movie, this scene would be dropped).

The second scene is a bizarre sequence staged on the

---

46 In fact, the Monty Python team delivered a similar scene in a store selling porno in their TV series.
47 Brian seems absent – but he might be behind that baffle, where an engineer adjusts a mike.

beach at Camber Sands in Sussex[48] (a small resort in Southern England). More guns, terrorists, films-within-films, self-conscious cinematic referencing, and Anne Wiazemsky as Eva Democracy racing around, stumbling a few times in the soft sand, doused in fake blood (by the director himself, a job he liked to do), before winding up on a camera crane, slumped beside a camera, and two flags (one red, one black).

The final image of *One Plus One* has Eva D. on the camera crane raised in the air and framed against the sky and the sun behind clouds. It's an arresting image, certainly – the camera, the crane, the woman, the flags, the sky and the sun – tho' *of what*? Of anything you like – it's multi-purpose. Godard can be seen in a long coat and hat, running about directing the scene in high wind.[49]

✪

One Plus One is more a series of Godardian skits and sketches and essays with only the Rolling Stones sessions offering a through-line (the graffiti scenes are graphic punctuation, without a developing narrative).[50] And the dramatic blocks of the film don't meld (but that was partly Godard's point, of course, and one reason why the completed song 'Sympathy For the Devil' isn't heard – this is a film that the viewer has to put together themselves). For that and other reasons, some Godardians find it a minor and not very satisfying work, and some barely mention it. Maybe. I really like it – for its British settings, its sense of fun, and its music and studio sessions. And, let's not forget, this is the Rolling Stones!

48 Several Stones had places in Sussex (such as Watts and Richards). Redlands, site of the famous drugs bust, was in Sussex.
49 I've used Camber Sands as a location, too – as have the *Carry On* team. I filmed a big scene for my movie *Ritual Magic* there.
50 Fredric Jameson wasn't impressed by *One Plus One,* complaining about: 'the low budget look of amateur actors, staged tableaux, and vaudeville-type numbers, essentially static and strung together' (1990).

The producers adding the complete song over the frozen image of Anne Wiazemsky on the camera crane doesn't really alter the film that much. *One Plus One* is not a film one could re-edit too many different ways without it coming out either very different or still quite close to Godard's conception. One reason, of course, is the use of the long take. As with Orson Welles and Andrei Tarkovsky, Godard knows that long takes are harder to re-work than montages of short shots.

There's also the pleasure of seeing Anne Wiazemsky skittering thru London trying to whip up revolutionary fervour with her slogans. Somehow, Marxist, Maoist Revolution and Quaint, Shabby, Provincial England don't go together. Yes, I know some of 1968's political demonstrations occurred in G.B, but, somehow, desolate Essex not quite the same as Paris or North America.[51]

---

51 Godard was depressed by the apathy among the students he met at the University of Essex. Another French radical visited Britain in the late 1960s (Guy Debord, of the Situationists), hoping to find revolutionary fervour, but Debord was similarly disappointed.

However, Britian's radical Angry Brigade, the university drop-outs from Essex and Cambridge, inspired by Guy Debord and the Situationists and theorist Raoul Vanelgem, attacked 123 targets (including Miss World, the Biba store, London police, banks, embassies, politicians and the Territorial Army). Mendelson, Creek, Barker, Greenfield *et al* were arrested and, after a long and controversial trial, given long sentences.

EAN-LUC
GODARD
ONE
PLUS
ONE
THE ROLLING
STONES

ID PRODUCTIONS PRESENT a Jean-Luc GODARD film. STARRING ; "The ROLLING STONES"
a JAGGER/Keith RICHARD/Brian JONES/Charlie WATTS/BIll WYMAN, Anne WIAZEMSKI.
ICTOR of PHOTOGRAPHY; Tony RICHMOND. PRODUCED by Michael PEAHON & Iain QUARRIER.
ECTED by Jean-Luc GODARD, © CUPID Productions Ltd. 1970

One Plus One (1968),
this page and over.

3

UN FILM COMME LES AUTRES

A FILM LIKE THE OTHERS

A Film Like the Others[1] (*Un Film Comme les Autres*, 1968) was one of the early political Love-Ins from Godard (this is 1968, *camarades*, a year after the Summer of Love – 1967 – but it's still Love and Peace For All!), in this laugh riot with an average of six big belly laughs per minute (*six*! – not even Bob Hope or Jerry Lewis achieved that level!).

This movie is *really* funny – it's one of the funniest movies you'll ever see.

No, not really.

Not at all, actually.

It's not the Summer of Love.

It never *was* the Summer of Love.[2]

It's 1968, it's soon after the tumultuous, you-had-to-be-there events of May, 1968, when Paris and then the whole of the People's Republic of France erupted in rev–o–lu–tion.

Or something.

With *A Film Like the Others* (also known as *The Marxist Guide To Tax Evasion – Film Director's Edition*), the politicized Herr Godard was just warming up: he hadn't reached the wacky heights of *Wind From the East* yet, but he was getting

1 Or *A Film Like All the Others*.
2 The Summer of Love is a bourgeois, imperialist lie!

there. Just think, ladies and gentlemen – after *A Film Like the Others* you've got *Wind From the East* to look forward to! Followed by – get this! – *Struggle In Italia, British Sounds, Palestine Will Win, Vladimir and Rosa, Pravda, All's Well* and *Letter To Jane*. (*A Film Like the Others* was a Godard film, however, financed by the man himself; it was not a Godard-Gorin collaboration. But it set the structural template in every important aspect for the subsequent Godard-and-Gorin collaboratons. It reminds us that much of the content and the approach of the political films came from Godard, not Gorin).

∗

Oi, comrade! we're going to sit in the fields and debate Marxism, are you in? We're gonna make a movie with Godard! Yeah, him! (Free packs of Gitanes included!). Of course, you're up for it? OK!

As in later Dziga Vertov Group films, part of *A Film Like the Others* features seven or so young(ish) people sitting about on the grass and conversing (at Flins, near the Renault car factory). The open-air format for the Annual Marxist-Leninist Debating Club Picnic would be revived in *Wind From the East* and other Godard-Gorin films. (Presumably, Godard (and later with Gorin) selected open-air spots because they were (1) free [*all locations should be free! Permits should never be required to film anywhere on Earth! It's our Planet, too!*], (2) didn't need any lighting [*lamps, trucks and cables are bourgeois!*], (3) were relatively devoid of disturbances [*cops are not welcome on Marxist-Leninist film sets. Go home, pigs!*], and (4) were quiet enough for a discussion to be recorded (compared to the noisy cafés favoured by Godard's movies).

From the outset, *A Film Like the Others* slyly alienates the audience in the familiar, Brechtian manner of late Sixties Godard: with, for instance, very lengthy shots of the back of a person sitting in a field and part of the body of another person, while the voices we hear are (presumably but not necessarily) of someone else in the group discussion (tho' not the two people we see). And there are other voices on the soundtrack, too, spouting the familiar Marxist/ Leninist/ left-wing ideology. The people are white and seem to be French; there's only one female. (For a long time we don't see their faces. Sometimes in documentaries that's because the participants wish to remain anonymous, or because the filmmakers want us to listen and not be distracted by identities. Or maybe it's an æsthetic choice: these are just anybody, not particular people.)

The third element in *A Film Like the Others* is slinkier and less in-your-face than the debate in a field or the newsreel footage: the voiceover. Multiple voices are heard, but two predominate: a man and a woman, performing the familiar double act of a Godardian rant.

The narration has been written after the filming, and often it's allowed to overwhelm the group discussion (sometimes cutting into it rudely). In fact, it's striking how Godard's political films use voiceovers: if the on-screen discussions are flagging or veering off into what are deemed uninteresting areas, the voiceovers muscle in with more pertinent material. So if someone's talking about topics the filmmakers don't go for, they simply replace the voices with their own verbiage. It's a kind of live dubbing, but instead of accurately syncing the voices up with the actors on screen, the narration just says what it wants to say.

The *very* long debate featuring young people in *A Movie Like Every Other Movie You've Ever Seen* runs on and on: we aren't shown faces, or close-ups, or reaction shots, and we're not introduced to any of them in a conventional manner. No names. No identity. Maybe the camera pans a little (but not too much). We peer thru grass and bushes. Who are these people? Some are apparently students,[3] but they don't want to be recognized as students, because in 1968 students, according to this film, were scorned as bourgeois and privileged (actually, they were from Nanterre University). One guy claims he's always worked for a living (two of the participants worked in the nearby Renault plant); the only woman in the group apologetically and guiltily admits that she is a student (her views come from a different ideological place from the rest of the group, and she often has to talk loudly and firmly to get her views across).

The unmistakable hoarse, lipsy tones of Jean-Luc Godard himself are heard, but he, too, isn't seen (is he even there? Is he standing near the camera, throwing out questions, as he often did? (The debaters do seem to be responding to him). Or are his comments added later, in the dubbing studio, as with so much of *A Film Like the Others*?). Godard's questions are wry and off-centre, as usual.

Not much of this group debate is clarified at a personal level, because it's the speeches that count, what the youths are debating: strikes, general strikes, unions, the Renault car factory, industrial action, how workers slave for bosses, the exploitation of the labour force, and how intellectuals and students relate to these fractious topics.

There are other elements in this first section of *A Film Like the Others*, however: newsreel footage (mostly in b/w) of civil unrest on the streets of Paris and other cities. Like the voices heard off-screen, the newsreel footage is cut into the sunlit debate (it was recorded by a film collective). There's no faking now, this is the real deal: the imagery of riots, of mass demonstrations, of angry take-overs of factories, of burning cars, of tear gas and smoke, of protestors lobbing rocks at the cops, and of people running for safety from water cannons retain their raw power (even tho' the quality of the

3 Very few of the students or participants in the Dziga Vertov films are non-white.

camerawork is appalling – why could nobody hold a camera steadily in the 1960s?). So that when we cut back to a small group of people talking in the sunlight in grassy Flins, it reveals just how dull much of *A Film Like Any Other Political Film* is (you have two works here that could be split apart – one a montage of newsreel footage, the other the group debate. I suppose it is mildly interesting that the events of May, 1968 in Paris, as seen in the newsreel footage, are set within a debate about them some time later).

✳

A Film Like the Others tests the determination and endurance of any radical, left-wing, Marxist-Leninist revolutionary firebrand, including a super-cool political anarchist like myself. *A Film Like the Others* is one hour and forty-five minutes long. That's the same length as an average movie like *Raiders of the Lost Ark* or a *James Bond* flick. But for a political debate it seems interminable.

Just when you thought the bunch of youths sitting in the grass had surely – *by the Gods!* – said everything they want to say, and everything that *could* be said, and everything that *will ever* be said about strikes and unions and students and class struggles, they start up again (or they never stop – every time we cut back to them, they are prattling on and on).

✳

We can see, can't we, ladies and gents, that this film has been *edited*. We can see that someone has sat at a Movieola and sliced this baby.[4] We can see that the footage of the group debate has had newsreel footage cut into it, and newspaper photos, and posters, and several voices have been added to it.

But it runs on for too long, it repeats points (several times) that have already made, and it dissipates its impact by out-staying its welcome. So it *isn't* 'edited', as in trimmed into

4 Probably in Godard's apartment.

a satisfactory state, it's filled with repetitions and padding (like, actually, many of Godard's movies).

Thus, *A Film Like the Others* becomes what it tries hard *not* to be: a boring lecture. We've all sat through them. We've all listened to dull lectures. And we've all sat in group discussions in cafés or college bars where one or two people (and it's always the *same* darn one or two people) dominate the debate. We have listened to them going on and on, providing one example after another to illustrate this or that ideological point. Sure, they're smart and well-read and all, but enough already!

For those who dislike the cinema of Jean-Luc Godard, the political films of the late 1960s and after are exactly like that: lectures which soon become boring delivered by a very clever, highly educated but ultimately domineering and obsessive tyrant.

You might stand up and begin your opposition to the Ciné-Genius's harangue with a 'but –', or a 'wait a minute –', but you won't get any further than that. Godard silences all. Not when the Master is on a roll. And even when what he's on clearly *isn't* a roll, when he's obviously not on an express train of cinematic energy, you still can't stop him!

With the Dziga Vertov Group films, your job is simple:

Shut up and listen.

And after you've seen a Dziga Vertov Group film, your job is simple:

Change your life/
start a strike/
organize a political cell/
bomb a newspaper/
intimidate the bourgeoisie/
overthrow the government/
travel to a new planet and colonize it with Marxists and cinéastes, etc.

＊

The debates in *A Film Like the Others* waffle and wiffle on for what seems like centuries. Even after 20 minutes there's no let-up.

Then 30 minutes.

Then 40 minutes.

You can be reincarnated through several lifetimes (once as a Marxist firebrand in 1930s Spain, once as the Executioner guillotining Marie Antoinette in 1793, etc), and come back here, and *still* the kids are talking about strikes and class struggles and how to make political action. (You won't believe this, but the debate rages (or dribbles) on and on until the very final minutes of *A Film Like the Others* – a whole one hour and forty-five minutes!).

Thus, *If Only All Other Films Were Like This* is only *in part* a radical film from Jean-Luc Godard, with its intercutting of newsreel footage of May, 1968 in Paris with offscreen voices outlining key events in the history of left-wing/ Marxist political life, and class struggle, and political activism.

But much of the time, *A Film Like the Others* is *actually* a group debate featuring seven or so youngish people (who seem to be French, or living in France, and some are possibly students). Thus, *A Film Like the Others* resembles a television debate, one of those 'worthy', 'serious' programmes that public service TV channels put on regularly (to show that they are following the government-imposed guidelines on what should be broadcast. Yes, television is State-controlled – or it's the mouthpiece of all governments. The Dziga Vertov Groups films remind us of that fact, but some of us have never forgotten it).

Usually, debates of this kind are staged in a TV studio in Paris or wherever (Godard has participated in many). Someone will be leading the discussion. Sometimes the format includes a live audience, with questions, etc.

True, the TV debate format is wryly subverted by the political films of 1968-1973 – with voices-off competing with the direct sound, with the camera pointedly *not* including close-ups and reaction shots, and allowing the ten-minute roll of 16mm celluloid to focus on bits of bodies seen from awkward angles (no one else has filmed people's backs so often). But it's still basically a television discussion intercut with amazing newsreel footage of May, 1968.

And, like so many television round table shows, this baby keeps repeating the same material, the same points-of-view, the same political whinges. Let's face it, folks, if you keep the same group of contributors in a TV studio (or on a patch of grass near Paris) on screen for more than ten or so minutes, they start repeating themselves. You have to be as incredible a talker as, say, Orson Welles (or Jean-Luc Godard himself), to maintain the energy and the interest beyond, say, 20 minutes. (That's partly why TV shows are based around questions-and-answers, to keep the flow of chat going, and to guide it in certain directions. There *are* people who can talk for lengthy periods without needing prompts or questions, but television *doesn't want that*, either! Television doesn't want to give an individual an unlimited and unplanned (i.e., unagreed) and unrehearsed platform).

This isn't a TV chat show, with an interviewer feeding questions (which have been decided beforehand) to an interviewee so that the celebrity can trot out their favourite stories. And it's not a political interview, where a politico continually avoids questions and keep repeating what he really wants to say, regardless of whatever the stern, serious interviewer asks (politicians, as we know, are slippery customers, and bend any question round to what they want to say).

No: *A Film Like the Others* is essentially a television debate format but without complying to the standard schedules of TV (30 minutes, 45 minutes or 60 minutes tops for a round table discussion). Rather, *A Film Like the Others* flounders past the usual time slots (just as Godard's fiction movies do). Where you might expect a summing up, or the introduction of a new element, *A Film Like the Others* chunters on.

Another issue, related to the seemingly unstoppable political gasbagging, is that these youngsters are – how to put it politely? – not as engaging as their equivalents among professional performers of the period (Terence Stamp, say, or James Fox, or Anna Karina, or Jean-Paul Belmondo, and of course Jean-Pierre Léaud). The adorable Léaud, bless him, could make this kind of radical, left-wing whingeing compelling (as he does in *La Chinoise*). Léaud could be comical, and goofy, and irritating – but *the same political points would have been made*.

The domineering, 'I know better than you' attitude emerges in the group debate in *A Film Like the Others* – one guy (such as the older, beardy guy) treats the others like they are know-nothings; the younger, idealist guy splutters in response that *he* knows best. The young woman tries to compete with the guys, but her opinions are rather small-minded (she's only concerned, it seems, with how things affect students). And on and on it goes.

✳

Towards the end of this *extremely* long film, the group discussion among the youths in the sunny, Flinsian fields of 1968 is still going strong. However, like many round table conflabs, it is always the same people talking (how often have we joined discussions or Q. and A.s which are advertized as 'open to all', only to find the same two or three people dominating the proceedings?). Here, only three people have managed to endure: the older, bearded guy, the younger, idealistic guy, and the young woman. The others are listening and playing with grass stalks (and sawing off their legs to alleviate their boredom).

As the debate continues in *A Pill Like the Others*, it gets narrower and narrower, until all that the youths are talking about is workers vs. students, and factories vs. universities. As if these are the only areas of human activity anywhere on the planet (or anywhere in La France).

The end comes with a final newsreel selection, culminating in a shot which pans around the protestors on the street, and a silly image of the camera wavering 'tween the word 'blue' and the word 'rouge' (that's the only option here: blue or red, right-wing or Gauchist).

✳

Seen as a whole, there is far less in *A Film Like the Others* to enjoy, in general, as cinema, as an experience, as data sliding past our eyes and ears, compared to some of the other Dziggy Stardust films. Even mostly rubbishy films like *Wind From the East* or *Struggle In Italy* have more moments which lift us out of the muddy, murky trenches of the Marxist-Leninist World War Three.

4

BRITISH SOUNDS

SEE YOU AT MAO

British Sounds (a.k.a. *See You At Mao,* 1969) was directed by Godard,[5] written by Godard and Jean-Henri Roger and prod. by Kenith Trodd and Ivan Teitelbaum for Kestrel Productions. DP: Charles Stewart, editing: Elizabeth Kozmian, sound: Fred Sharp. It was filmed in Feb, 1969. 52 mins.

Godard may've bitched about British cinema in his film criticism, but he made one significant movie in Albion which's still viewed today: *One Plus One* (largely due to the presence of the genuinely legendary Rolling Stones). *British Sounds* was the second 'British' film produced by the Maestro in England.

British Sounds was commissioned by London Weekend Television, the regional commercial television station for the capital (1968-2002, when it was replaced by I.T.V. (Independent Television) London), along with Thames Television (1968-1992, when it was replaced by Carlton Television). Once London Weekend Television saw what the French Genius and his team had produced, they refused to broadcast it. What a surprise! (And two years later, the TV station criticized *British Sounds* on its talk show *Aquarius*).

Because in *British Sounds*, Jean-Luc Godard and company are being gleefully, childishly (and intelligently)

---

5 Some say it was co-helmed by Godard and Roger.

provocative. They know which panic buttons to press, they know how to annoy audiences, they know what images and what statements will angrify people (broadcasters, producers, TV critics and TV audiences). There is plenty in *British Sounds* to wind up viewers, TV producers and their bosses in the TV centre on London's South Bank: the multiple offscreen voices; the ridiculously over-the-top statements from the British establishment; the repeated attacks on the bourgeoisie and capitalist societies; the shots of a naked woman drifting about (plus a two-minute shot of said woman's naked torso); while the voiceovers contemplate feminism and women's rights, etc.

Like the other 1968-1973 political films and the Dziga Vertov Group films, *British Sounds* is a rant – an ideological, political rant which romanticizes the workers and left-wing politics like Mao/ism and Marx/ism, and despises the bosses and the bourgeoisie and of course the social system – capitalism – which benefits the Haves and scorns the Have-nots. Much of the film's voiceover is condensed down to slogans (*solitary pleasure and fascism,* for example). Similarly with the scribbled captions (*Hitler and Hollywood,* for instance, or the months of the year written in black ink with October in red ink).

As with the other 1968-1973 political films and the Dziga Vertov Group films, *A Britful of Mao* contains the full compliment of Godardisms – the double voiceovers (male and female, a man and a boy, a woman and a boy), the very lengthy shots, the self-conscious camerawork, the grabbed images of people at work on the streets, the pithy-political captions, the pseudo-documentary approach, and the en-shrinement of Marxist-Leninist politics and ideology.

It's all here in *British Sounds* – segments about the class struggle, about struggling on two fronts, about encouraging a political revolution which would overthrow the dominant ideology of capitalism, anti-Amerikanisms, and the idealized hope for turning a social system on its head, so that the workers would be in the ascendant and the bourgeoisie would be reduced to peeling potatoes in a dingy basement (or, if you're in a *Weekend*-style rage, set on fire).

✳

British Sounds opens with a classical Godardian scene, which is definitely the finest segment of the film:[6] a very lengthy tracking shot along the assembly lines of a car factory (filmed at Cowley at the British Motor Car factory in Oxfordshire). Like the similar shot in *Tout Va Bien* along the rows of cashiers and shoppers in a hypermarket, this shot says it all. There's no need for the voiceover which contextualizes the images in a pro-Marxist, anti-bourgeois philosophy. The image says everything (as with the supermarket scene in *Tout Va Bien*).

It's something to do with the way that Godard and the team set up the shot, with the way that they film the workers putting together the shiny, new cars[7] that consumers buy in their millions, with the way that the shot operates within the context of the film.

British Sounds could've selected more degrading, filthier jobs (cleaning public toilets, for instance), but this shot performs the role of evoking the robotic, dehumanizing reality of mass labour, where people are reduced to acting as a cog in a giant machine. They're producing items for a capitalist market, for consumers today.

Yes, this is what people are doing everyday, day in, day out. It's part of Godard's view of labour in a capitalist social system as slavery or prostitution. As the narration puts it, the workers are not invested in the final product (new cars), but in earning money to live; the voiceover asserts that labourers are

6 At least the best comes first – after it, you can slip out of the theatre via the exit marked 'Workers'.
7 M.G. cars in tame, conservative Racing Green colours and flashy Phallic Red colours.

sacrificing their lives in order to survive; and they have no say in the system of production they are part of, where the whole enterprise is controlled and run by the bourgeois bosses. (The round table discussion in Dagenham brings out some of these issues, of ownership and having a stake in a business; one guy points out that the workers can't afford to buy the cars they are putting together in the factory).

*

Like some of the other 1968-1973 political films and the Dziga Vertov Group films, *British Sounds* is several films in one package. The images are only one of the filimc levels here – the voiceovers add at least two more levels. The voiceovers often feature two people – a classic Godardian device, which Godard has employed more effectively (and more often) than anybody else. (Godard used the ploy throughout his career – in later films such as *Socialism*, voices are panned to the left and the right of the stereo spectrum). Some of the voice pairings in *British Sounds* have an adult coaxing a child to repeat their ideological rants and their potted histories[8] – a great touch, which somehow makes the rants and the history lessons even more disburbing (that is, when a child speaks of political injustice and coercion).

Among the topics discussed in the many narrations in *British Sounds* are trade union movements; famous left-leaning movements in British history such as the Tolpuddle Martyrs and the Levellers; Oliver Cromwell; the British Government's suppression of the working class; feminism and women's rights; condemnations of capitalism and the bourgeoisie; political revolution, and so on.

The captions in *British Sounds* are cheapo – written by the Maestro in his familar script on pieces of paper (rather than the printed, optically-achieved captions of the feature films). The handcrafted captions help to give the Dziga Vertov

---

8 References to the Levellers, for instance.

Group output its homemade feel (charming for some, scrappy for others. Anyway, you'd better get used to it – Godard is a filmmaker dedicated to putting his own handwriting in film after film).

The 16-millimetre footage is horrible in places, as in all of the other Dzviga Vertov Group films (nobody as talented as Raoul Coutard was operating the camera, which is a pity). The filmmakers refuse to employ anything as bourgeois as a movie lamp, so the lighting is often flat and just frail.

An intriguing sequence captures a bunch of car factory workers (from the Dagenham plant, which had recently seen some political unrest) as they discuss the politics of labour, capitalism vs. socialism, unions, the recent British 'socialist' government (Harold Wilson was Prime Minister), etc. This scene allows the British factory workers to voice their own feelings, rather than have the filmmakers impose their ideology on them.

This may be the most valuable episode in the whole Dziga Vertov Group works, where we hear employees voicing their gripes with the factory-based system. And it seems more authentic than the gatherings of students and one or two workers in the French political films.

Unfortunately, it's spoilt by the camera performing whip-pans between the participants. So instead of the usual round table conflab, we are looking at a bunch of guys, with the camera only occasionally settling on the one who's speaking. The silly, self-conscious camera movement is countered, however, by the sound, which captures the people in the room clearly (so at least, this time, the viewer can follow the flow of the conversation). But of course more voiceovers were added.

Like the other Dziga Vertov Group and late 1960s political works, *British Sounds* has a charming, amateur texture at its best (when the mix of ideological ranting and documentary imagery fuses). Tho' at its worst it comes across as a shoddy piece (such as the endless images of road crews fixing the highways and byways of England, which are padding. Here, *British Sounds* stumbles when it tries to film people at work, one of Godard's key aims in this period).

✳

The weakest section of *British Sounds* comes near the end, with some youths (who were students at Essex University) playing at being radicals and revolutionaries. They are depicted painting posters and trying (very feebly) to alter the lyrics of songs by the Beatles to reflect trendy Maoist, revolutionary politics (they come across as hippies sitting around with an acoustic guitar in their funky, 1960s clothing, and they're about as radical as a used teabag).

If you want to take on the Beatles, once again John Lennon had already done it all in his song 'Revolution' – which the students attempt to rewrite.

You say you'll change the constitution.
Well, you know we all want to change your head.
You tell me it's the institution.
Well, you know you better free your mind instead.

They also have a go at 'Honey Pie' and 'Hello Goodbye'. (Had London Weekend Television broadcast *British Sounds* they would've needed to clear the rights to the songs we hear by the Beatles, including 'Revolution', 'Hello Goodbye' and 'Honey Pie'. It's likely that the Beatles would have been happy to be part of a Godard movie – Paul McCartney, particularly – he was by far the most *avant garde* and experimental of the Beatles, and they had met Godard).

The near-incoherent, decidely unremarkable conversations of the Essex Uni. students are occasionally superceded by more voiceover from Brits pinpointing significant events in the history of British trade unions, general strikes and workers' movements. (If the discussions on-screen dip below a certain level of interest, the film simply fades them down and puts on a voiceover, a device employed in all of the Dziga Vertov Group pieces).

There's an upper-class twit in a suit and tie at a desk satiriziing a TV news presenter[9] declaiming about long-haired, work-shy oiks and Indian foreigners who live in squalor and should be deported or killed.

Another element of *British Sounds* that would offend the head honchos at London Weekend Television was the full nudity. The shots of a naked woman (of course she's young and slender – Godard very seldom films large or older women – except in *Passion*, when recreating famous paintings) wandering around a house (coming right after the opening salvo of factory workers), and then standing there while the camera captures a very prolonged view of the Centre of the Cosmos (the naked pubis and torso) – were not only completely gratuitous (and beside the point – any point!), they were also guaranteed to scandalize radical feminist viewers in a section of the film which supposedly voiced pro-feminist politics. The feminist discourse appeared in the voiceover (feminist writer Shiela Rowbotham collaborated on this section). The views expressed in the female voiceover are classic, second wave feminism, an assertion of women's rights to be on equal terms with men in contemporary, British society.

Once again, Jean-Luc Godard happily outrages his audience: by this time, in 1969, he was a Super-Class-A Genius at surprising and confronting viewers (Godard specialized in cinematic confrontation). And by this time, after so many feature films, it was getting harder to surprise and disturb audiences, as he knew well (but *Weekend* has a good

9 This has the feel of a *Monty Python* or Spike Milligan skit (tho' nowhere near as accomplished). But even in jest the Pythons or Milligan wouldn't have been able to get away with some of the vitriol ladled out here.

go at it).

✳

British Sounds is a kind of of portrait of contemporary Britain which continued the visual approach of *One Plus One*, which followed Anne Wiazemsky painting slogans around London. Vignettes in *British Sounds* feature workers in a park, on roads, on building sites, and street scenes of London and elsewhere. The muddy, poor quality footage helps to make parts of England look squalid and drearily suburban. This is not the England of myth and legend, or of artists and writers, but a shabby nation still recovering from World War Two.

But Jean-Luc Godard has a fondness for filming out-of-the-way locales, spots that no one else would bother to film, little corners where nothing is happening.

What's striking in contemplating Godard's two British films is how little the country has changed in 50 years. It's still tatty and mediocre, still hopelessly provincial and miserable... yet it's still the Greatest Country In the World, and London is still the most wonderful city of all cities (and more people visit London than any other city in the West – including, yes, Los Angeles, Roma, Berlin, Madrid, Rio, Paris or even Noo Yoik).

5

PRAVDA

PRAVDA

And so to *Pravda* (1970), filmed in Czechoslovakia in 1969, and dir., ed. and wr. by Jean-Luc Godard, Paul Burron and Jean-Henri Roger. Claude Nedjar produced for Centre Européen Cinéma-Radio-Television. Vera Chytilova and Godard were in the cast. Eastmancolor 16mm. Screened: May 21,1970 (New York). 58 mins.

Some recent events in Czechoslovakia's history which are part of the context of the *Pravda* film include:

1918	Czechoslovakia founded.
1939	Germany took control of the nation.
1945	Russia moves into Czechoslovakia.
1948	A coup is staged by the Communists.
1968	The Prague Spring is suppressed by the Russian military.

(The Prague Spring, overseen by Alexander Dubeck (leader of the Czechoslovak Communist Party), lasted from January to August).

The U.S.S.R., Nikita Khrushchev, Marx, Mao, Lenin, Engels and others are continually referenced. (Yet *Pravda* omits plenty of the recent history of Czechoslovakia, such as the formation of the Czechoslovakia Republic after WWI, in 1918, and the Nazi invasion in 1939).

✳

The structure of *Pravda* comprised filming in contemporary Czechoslovakia (including Bratislava and Praha) combined with voiceovers. As usual with the other political films of Godard of the period, it's the voiceover that knits the whole thing together, that provides the contextual framework, and that makes numerous political points. You could regard *Pravda* as a voiceover illustrated with images, rather than a narration commenting on images. (Once again, the voiceover isn't a single voice explaining everything, as in the usual TV documentary. Instead, it's two voices (male and female), engaged in a dialogue. Yes, it's Vladimir and Rosa once again).

Pravda looks as if Jean-Luc Godard gathered two or three cohorts to visit Czechoslovakia and make a documentary about it. They flew in with their 16mm cameras (sounds and voices could be added later), hired a car or two at Prague Ruzyne International Airport, and began driving around and filming whatever took their fancy.

Pravda is not a State-sponsored work: it's the sort of warts-and-all portrait that Communist authorities wouldn't like to see shown in the West.

As usual in the political films, Uncle Godard and company concentrated on scenes of people at work, often grabbed from afar (and perhaps without permission): women in a field, labourers outside a factory, and one of the Godardian stand-bys, road-mending crews.

Among the many images and scenes featured in *Pravda* are:

- people at work in factories;
- guys fixing roads;
- a farm labourer on a farm;

- women working in the fields;

- images of fields, of farms;

- two people working at a haystack;

- an architect working in an office;

- a blast furnace;

- a classroom of students at a college;

- university students in Prague in a discussion;

- students outside their Prague university;

- an interview with workers in a factory;

- streetcars (lots of streetcars!);

- the colour red (of those streetcars);

- the car rented by the filmmakers at the airport (of course it's red);[10]

- big cars (the upper class) and small cars (the working class);

- waspish comments about Skoda cars;

- soldiers marching;

- military folk filmed secretly, from cars;

- propaganda posters and art;

- hotels;

- TV shows – news;

- television sets re-filmed;

- political rallies (in newsreels);

- a cinema[11] seen from outside;

- photos of films screened in said cinema;

- the covers of boxes of Airfix model kits (!);

- magazine articles and ads (some with Godard's writing over them);

- a red rose in a puddle;

- red wine being poured into a glass;

- pornographic photographs;

- a crowded tea dance;

- youths playing soccer in a local park;

10 But it's not a Maserati, alas.
11 Kino Orlik.

- street signs and graffiti;

- advertizing hoardings and logos at night.

Godard returned to the same sorts of images when he filmed in Sarajevo 36 years later for *Our Music* (2004) – the streetcars again, the signage again.[12]

Pravda carefully avoids the famous sights of Czechoslovakia and Prague. No tourist spots, no Charles Bridge or St Vitus Cathedral or Old Town Square, no castles and ski resorts, no beautiful forests and mountains. Rather, *Pravda* focusses on regular, suburban streets, on factories, on parks. It's everyday Eastern Europe, where real people live and work.

Pravda is filmed in a seemingly socialist or Communist nation, but this time Godard and company are sceptical and critical. Czechoslovakia is not portrayed as a Marxian Paradise. It is compared with the West (and France in particular), but it's not seen as a Socialist Utopia. If you listened to the youths debating politics in Dziga Vertov Group films such as *A Film Like the Others,* you'd imagine that a visit to a Communist country would be a Dream Trip. What could be more exciting than seeing how Marxist, socialist political theory works in practice, in a real community?

But no. *Pravda* sees similar social differences between the bosses and the workers to those in the French Republic, and exposes the flaws in putting Communist theory into practice.

Pravda features the usual Godardian pops at Americana – *Playboy* pin-ups, U.S rental firms (Hertz, Avis), and the American military. (None of Godard's political films miss out the chance to abuse the U.S.A. And forty years later, Godard was still kicking Uncle Sam).

A red rose held up to the camera and later looking sad and forlorn in a puddle is a symbolic motif in *Pravda* (can the

12 The score includes workers' songs and folk songs (and some are in French, not Czech).

movie get away with such an overtly sentimental device?).
Indeed, the colour is rhymed many times in cars, streetcars,
walls, blood, clothing, wine, etc (red's also deployed throughout Godard's 1960s movies).

There's a long account featuring Vladimir Lenin,
blacksmiths, plows, peasants and the land, evoking notions of
labour, collectivism, ownership, and Communism. Rosa, the
female voice, speaks rapidly, urging the audience to action –
to fight Imperialism, the authorities, the class system, etc.

For whom? against whom? is a recurring question in the
voiceover, along with the usual encouragements to resist
oppression, to fight the system, to be critical, to continue the
class struggle, etc.

The most powerful shot in *Pravda* is of a guy working at
a giant machine (a lathe?) in a metalworks factory. The
beginning of the shot has handwritten captions intercut with
it. But then the shot continues – the narration has died away,
the captions are left aside, and there's no music, but the man
keeps working.

The shot says it all about the tedium and numbing
repetition of labour, the mindlessness of work, the de-
humanization of work, the exploitation of work. It also captures
the troubled relationship between humans and technology,
how people are slaves to machines (rather than vice versa).

Jean-Luc Godard was certainly brilliant when it came to
filming people working. And these scenes are often the most
striking of all of the material in the political films of the 1968
to 1973 period. Godard often remarked that you don't see
people working in movies, so he rectified that.

The 1970 film about Eastern Europe closes with workers
leaving a factory after a day's work: accompanied by a rousing
workers' song, this scene forms a sentimental tribute to
labourers everywhere. The red rose pops up again. And the
final image of *Pravda* is of a small, red flag attached to the

front of a truck trundling thru the countryside, filmed from a car driving alongside (it's reminiscent of the flags attached to the camera crane at the end of *One Plus One*).

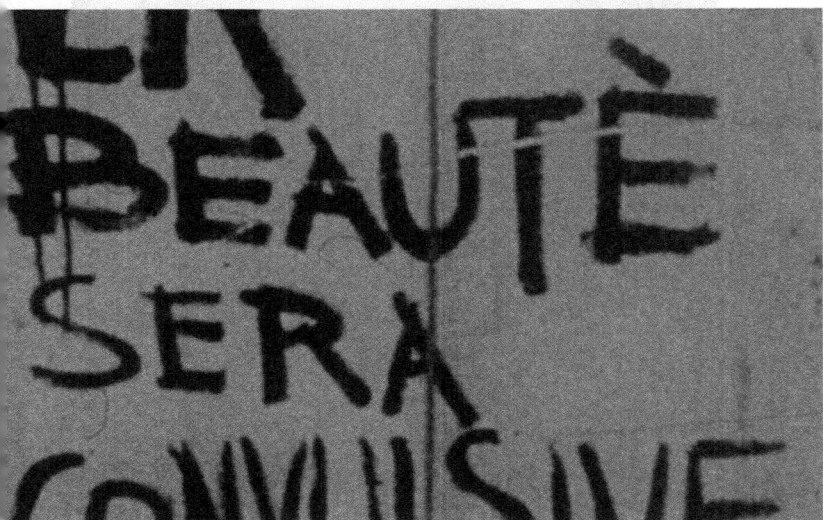

A Film Like the Others (1968).

British Sounds (1969), this page and over.

WHAT IS WORK ?

Pravda (1970).

6

VENT D'EST

WIND FROM THE EAST

Wind From the East (*Vent d'Est*, 1970) was:

A disgruntled, irritated film.

A self-conscious, defiant, wilfully eccentric rant.

A litany of personal and political disappointments which have been disguised by an off-screen, puritannical political lecture, which has only partially digested Marx, Mao and Lenin, which is accompanied by captions, quotations from Lenin, Eisenstein, Vertov, Althusser *et al*, plus insert images of Stalin, Mao *et al*, and illustrated with irrelevant, repetitious bits of boring actorly business (Actor A wanders over there, with a rifle; Actors B and C lie in the grass; Actor D does something else equally nothingy).

Here be the credits for *Wind From the East*: co.-wr. by Godard, Jean-Pierre Gorin, Sergio Bazzini, Gianni Barcelloni, and Daniel Cohn-Bendit ('Danny the Red') – the largest number of writers credited on any Godard movie. It was co-dir. by Godard, Gorin and Gérard Martin. DP: Mario Vulpiani, editing: Gorin and Godard, sound: Carlo Diotalleri and Antonio Ventura. The cast: Gian Maria Volonté, Anne Wiazemsky, Christiana Tullio-Altan, Allan Midgette,[1] Vanessa Redgrave, Glauber Rocha, Palo Pozzesi, José Varela and Götz George. Released: Aug 19, 1970. 95 mins.

---

1 An Andy Warhol impersonator.

Cineriz put up some of the money (Cineriz had been founded by Federico Fellini and Angelo Rizzoli in the early 1960s, initially to back Fellini's projects).[2] Money also came from Polifilm (Rome), Film Kunst and C.C.C. Studios (Berlin), and Georges du Beauregard (Paris).

The initial idea was for a 'Left-Wing Spaghetti Western' to be filmed by Jean-Luc Godard. The concept sounds great — and it's the best thing about *Wind From the East* (known in the People's Republic of China as *Cooking With Chairman Mao* — available on VCDs in the backstreets of Beijing).

Gian Volonté was familiar from the Spaghetti Westerns (you'll recognize him from gun fights with Clint Eastwood in the *Fistful of Dollars* series). Volonté harboured passionate left-wing politics.

Anne Wiazemsky is the other well-known face in *A Fistful of Marxism* (tho' at the time — 1970 — only known to those who'd seen her appearances in the films of Godard and Robert Bresson and one or two others. She was only 23). Vanessa Redgrave (known for her leftie politics) appeared, too — but where? With her long, swishy, gypsy dresses, Wiazemsky looks like a Haight-Ashbury flower child,[3] and about as non-revolutionary and non-militant as possible (altho' she's called Miss Althusser, and is sort of supposed to be one of the radicals/ activists).

The filmmakers gathered in the countryside outside Roma (interiors were filmed at De Paoli Studios in Rome, and exteriors at Elios Studios). But the production rapidly became messy. The shooting wound on for three months (*far* too long for Godard, as we know), during Spring, 1969. Godard considered ankling (it's amazing that he stayed that long).

2 When Federico Fellini established the Cineriz company with Angelo Rizzoli in the 1960s, with the aim of taking on other projects as well as Fellini's own, it soon became apparent that Fellini wasn't that bothered. He liked to immerse himself in his own productions.

3 She even has a flower in her hair and a white, cotton dress.

Much of the film was re-shot in and around Paris (consequently, some of the cast didn't appear in the re-filmed version).

There was a substantial budget for *Blow-Out From the East* – rumoured to be $220,000 = $1.8 million in 2025. That can't be accurate – *Weekend*'s budget was $250,000, for instance (a much bigger movie in every way). If there really was $220,000 in the coffers, it was likely spent on other things, like cigarettes or purple flared pants. (The budget was big enough, however, for some of the film collective to decamp to the Eternal City, where the production was going to be made. In the end, much of the Italian footage was scrapped, and the film was re-staged back in France. Rumours developed of the money paid to the crew (handed out each week by Uncle Godard himself) finding its way into buying a Ferrari, or paying off debts to the Mafia, or for running guns to Israel. Not really. That's a lie! Whatever).

❧

Like the other 1968-1973 political films from the Maestro and his chums, *Wind From the East* attracted some interest from critics – it's a film essay that's perfect for discussing in film essays (such as Peter Wollen's "Godard and Counter Cinema: *Vent d'est*", Julia Lesage's "Godard-Gorin's *Wind from the East*: Looking at a film politically", and Jacques Derrida's "How I Learned To Love *Vent d'est*").

The 1968-1973 agitprop films raise the question: can a successful film director subsume themselves in a filmmaking co-operative, and be just one of the gang? Answer: No – not when they are a superstar *auteur* who has genuinely invented and re-invented cinema (which nobody else in the collective had achieved – not then and not since. Let's face it, fellow *cinéastes,* we are only thinking of maybe possibly one day contemplating these movies because God-Art was involved).

So the notion of the *auteur*, the film director as Herr

Dicktator, is rejected – because they are bosses, like the bosses who run car factories – in favour of the collective, where all pigs (ooops, I mean all dogs) are equal (why does *Animal Farm* come to mind here?).[4]

Wind From the East draws attention to its manufacture, and how the collective of filmmakers worked: decisions were made by the group (Down With the Boss! Kill Herr Direktor!); film conventions like proper sound and editing were rejected (too mainstream, too bourgeois); the films were made cheaply, with small crews, on 16 millimetre; and in the end it's about (the) process (very 1960s – linking the films with Process/ Systems/ Serial Art, where artworks were based on simple processes or principles).

Wind From the East does come across in parts (the parts which exhibit Jean-Luc Godard's input) as if the Maestro was worrying over his committment to political issues, and how to produce political cinema. Yet we also know that Godard insisted many times (at the time and later), that he was a *superficial* follower or believer in Maoist and Marxist politics. He loved to wind people up. He loved to take the opposing theoretical position (no matter what it was), just for the hell of it – and because that's how he's put together as a person. (You think that Godard is extremely left-wing and Maoist-Marxist-Leninist, but then he'll deliberately annoy everybody with jokes about Adolf Hitler or fascism).

J.-L. Godard asserted that he had never read *Das Kapital* or Karl Marx's other trashy novels about jet-setting, coke-addled supermodels. Godard used Marx 'only as a provocation, mixing Mao and Coca-Cola and so forth'. Godard said it was a 'political romanticism': 'I loved Mao as I loved Goethe'. Yet many intellectuals and critics (including some who should've known better), bought it wholesale (at the time *and* since). They really did find the racist, right-wing skit in

4 *Animal Farm* – now there's a novel that's perfect for late 1960s Godard!

British Sounds disturbing. They really did think (or some of them seemed to think) that this very bourgeois, Swiss-French film director (son of a doctor, from a thoroughly bourgeois background), had become a Left-Wing Rebel Artiste, the Che Guervara of Political Cinema.

※

Did Jean-Pierre Gorin lead Jean-Luc Godard astray, into collective filmmaking and over-zealous ideological rants? Anne Wiazemsky, the chief female presence in *Wind From the East*, thought so. For Wiazemsky, it all started to go wrong for her and Godard when he became involved with Gorin and the co-operative approach to filmmaking. (In some scenes, Wiazemsky does not look happy to be there).[5]

Many of the meetings of the political film collective in this late Sixties era took place at Jean-Luc Godard's Paris apartment, where he lived with Anne Wiazemsky; some of the group stayed over or lived there. Maybe those meetings and discussions got a little uncomfortable for Wiazemsky.

However, Jean-Pierre Gorin only joined the production of *Wind From the East* late in the shooting; his contribution, rather, was to the editing and the sound. But after *Wind From the Crease*, in films such as *Muggles In Italy*, Gorin's input was considerable.

※

The left-wing politics in *Wind From the East* is Marxist and Leninist – in line with women's lifestyle magazines such as *Marxist Marie-Claire* and *Leninist Elle* (J.-P. Gorin worked for the *Cahiers Marxistes-Leninistes* magazine).

Wind From the Priest is also a teaching aid, a guide for militant filmmakers, Godard 'n' Gorin's *Handbook of Radical Cinema*. There are numerous exhortations to the audience (and to the filmmakers themselves – this is Godard's encouragement to himself and to like-minded souls).

5 Possibly in the scenes directed by Gorin.

Wind From the East begs you to start making militant/ radical/ left-wing films. *Wind From the Lease* reminds you:

- It's OK to rebel.
- Don't be abstract. Be clear.
- Read the Marxist and Leninist texts.
- Be socialist (but not a bourgeois socialist).
- Avoid 'Ollywooood, the West, capitalists, bosses, Swiss cheese.
- Go on strike. Cause trouble. Throw bombs. Terrorize.

Visually, *Wind From the Fleas* is a patchwork of Godardisms, poked and prodded into some kind of simulcrum of life by the process of film editing (cut back to a shot of Stalin, cut to a caption, cut to a shot of the crew sitting about, cut to a shot of Mao, cut to a shot of a tree)... Without the editing chopping up this mess of images (i.e., thankfully shortening the shots), *Wind From the Squeeze* would be unbearable. (This is one of many Godard productions which was largely created in post-production).

This time, in *Wind From the East*, the attempts at dramatization were decidedly lukewarm at best, and came across in the main as silly home movies. A bunch of filmmakers (scarily looking like hippies and as bourgeois and non-radical as you can imagine), go into the countryside in Summer to film some actors doing nothing in particular. Oh, all right, they *are* some activities or attempts at some such – they graffiti slogans on walls ('U' or 'UNION' in red paint), they run down a hill (no, this isn't *Jules et Jim*), they climb thru a barbed wire fence and pin a piece of paper on it containing the phrase: 'WHERE'S MY MONEY?' (no, no, it's 'UNION' again), and they... oh, *who cares*?!

Maybe the weedy efforts at dramatizations in *Wind From the East* (known in Nebraska as *How To Start a Revolution – On 20 Dollars a Day*) are what emerge from the fllm co-operative approach, the let's-all-be-equal decision process. In which case, the committee failed many times: images of people walking in fields and trees such as these are hollow. There's simply nothing here. (J.-L. Godard would later call such shots 'empty').

✳

Wind From the Unease opens with a single shot of two people lying on the ground for four minutes – as if the movie has already given up and collapsed from over-indulgence due to ideological ranting even before it's begun. And so by 8 minutes into *Wind From the East* (i.e., a *long* time in movie terms), we've thrilled and gasped at only *four shots*: another angle of the couple on the grass, and two fantastically empty shots of a guy (Gian Volonté) with a rifle walking on a wall (instead of stopping the camera, the guy repeats the action, so we get several takes of absolutely nothing). Will the movie get better than this? *Hmmm*. Don't be on that. (As an opening sequence, it's among the lamest in *das kino*).

Over these scenes several voices off-screen evoke strikes, factories, workers and bosses; the chief voice (female) anchors the movie within a Marxist-Leninist rhetoric; other voices include unionists and a union delegate, in relation to a strike. The narration of the *Windy East* movie thus dramatizes a recent strike (and it sounds more compelling than the images we're shown).

Wind From the Geese admits to all that it hasn't found or developed the images to visualize or dramatize whatever the film purports to be about. A more honest (or more accurate) approach would be to ditch the stupid scenes of actors wandering about in fields and trees completely.

These scenes look like someone is doing a pastiche of Jean-Luc Godard's form of cinema but without any punch-lines or jokes or even a solid point-of-view. The material is so feeble, we wouldn't be discussing it today if we didn't know that Godard was linked to it (without Godard's name, this 1970 film would be dumped in the pile marked 'Might Watch Later' (knowing damn well we'd never watch it later), and never see the light of day again).

The voiceover in *Wind From the Hades* urges us to:

Think. Read. Look. Wait.

And I would add:

Itch. Yawn. Sleep.

The voiceover castigates you, me, everybody – complaining that you/ me/ all of us aren't making the right sort of movie, that we/ you/ us haven't understood the class struggle or Marxism or revolution properly. This is Godard and Gorin criticizing themselves.

Ingmar Bergman found Godard a 'fucking bore' – that was in relation to the wonderful movie *Masculin Féminin*. Lordy knows what the Big Berg-Man of Sweden would've made of *Wind From the Grease*! (Bergman can't have seen it – very few people have).

The images of young and middle-aged people sitting about in the sunshine somewhere in the country while a debate rages on the soundtrack are wilfully clumsy (these seem to be filmed during the meetings in the morning where the group decided What To Do). The political arguments we hear are not linked to the images we see. Better to simply use black leader, and have the screen go dark (it's cheaper).[6]

The black leader and the red leader in Godard's cinema make themselves known in force in the 68-73 politicized films. The movies' voiceovers sometimes refer to the use of the leader, fumbling around with analyses without coming clean about the chief reason: *padding*.

So the group discussion is filmed, but it's all *faked*: all of the voices we hear on the soundtrack are *not* spoken by the figures we see on the screen. We might see people looking as

6 This occurs later on.

if they are sitting on the grass and yabbering (and smoking cigs like chimneys), but we don't hear their speech, we hear other voices. And we also hear the female narrator, who's talking about something else entirely (strikes and such). The movie thus imposes a single voice of authority on top of what was supposed to be a democratic group discussion. (The cutting also fakes the notion of the democratic discussion by bringing in images of Chairman Mao and Josef Stalin and the captions. But the political regimes overseen by Stalin and Mao were not democratic!).

There's another group discussion scene towards the end of the 1970 movie (you can see Godard sitting on the grass with the youths). But it's sabotaged by being cut into uselessly tiny portions, has a different voiceover plastered over it, and then visual noise is superimposed on it (or maybe the footage was wrecked in the lab, but the filmmakers had to use it anyway to make up the running time).

✳

Wait a second — maybe the fooling around by these bourgeois hippies in *Wind From the Purleeze* is actually meant to be a Western? The diatribe in the voiceover suggests so: it makes the link between the West and one of Hollywood's famous film genres, the cowboy movie. Get it? The West and the Western. (Let's forget for the mo' that Godard absolutely adores many Westerns, and regarded directors like Anthony Mann and Howard Hawks as gods).

So the horse, the rifle, the Capitalist, the Yankee, and the 'Native American' guy are kind of sort of maybe supposed to be evocations of elements of cowboy flicks?[7] OK. But why spend so much of the movie with a lame send-up/ political satire of a film genre which is detested for what it represents — bourgeois cinema *à la* Hollywood (or "Ollywooood" as it's pronounced in French by the off-screen voice). These scenes

7 Or maybe a Spaghetti Western.

are the remnants of the 'left-wing Spaghetti Western' concept, filmed in Italy.

We get the point from five minutes of satire/ spoof/ parody — there's no need for more'n that. The more screen time that *Wind From the Cheat* spends laying into its loathed forms of imperialist cinema means *less* time for putting forward the kind of cinema the filmmakers would like to see. (Sure, it makes sense to clear out the Old before setting up the New (like super-villains in action movies who want to destroy the world), but we already know what the Old is).

Why spend so much time sending up bourgeois, 'Ollywooood cinema? It's a waste of effort: tell us what you really want to film, instead. Or better yet, *show* us. Anybody can send up cowboy flicks.8 (Besides, 'Ollywooood and cowboy pictures are too easy targets for radical/ political/ activist filmmakers. An attack on such targets is like shooting fish in a barrel — with a Colt 1855 pistol, of course)

One wonders if a cowboy movie was selected as the subject of parody in *Wind From the Jeez* because there had been a brief rivival of Westerns around this time: in 1969, the top-grossing movie globally was *Butch Cassidy and the Sundance Kid* ($97.7 million gross in the U.S. of A.), while *True Grit* had also been a hit. (And maybe the bizarre religious/ hippy Western *El Topo* (1970), directed by Alejandro Jodorowsky, which started the craze for midnight movies, is another reference point, plus *The Wild Bunch* and some of the bleaker Spaghetti Westerns).

The truth is, *Wind From the East* and the other 68-73 political films and the Dziga Vertov Group films happily *attack* Hollywood, or institutions, or political systems, or bourgeois ideologies, but they have *nothing of their own* to put in their place, nothing to replace them with, nothing for us to focus

8 Besides, to be really picky, Spaghetti Western are *European* pastiches of North American film forms. The target should be John Wayne movies, not Sergio Leone movies.

on.

Yes, we understand the bile and hatred for the Western world, for capitalism, for 'Ollywooood, for bosses, for repression, for the ruling classes. *We're with you, comrade!* But what is going to replace it? Where is the utopian project which outlines a new art, a new cinema, a new politics, a new world, a new life? Where is the flood of thrilling ideas for new forms of existence, new political systems? Are we just going to watch people attacking something without suggesting what might work instead? Anyone can destroy stuff – humans are brilliant at it (it's something they find very easy to do, something they learn how to do very young).

Rainer Werner Fassbinder had a get-out clause: he wouldn't cook up a utopia for you; instead, his view of formulating a utopia was to leave it to the viewer's imagination:

> I don't want to formulate this utopia for you because if I do, it ceases to exist as a utopia. It's an idea and that can be struggled for. (in D. Georgakas, 183)
> ✳

A bourgeois woman reads aloud from Marcel Proust while people wielding a hammer and sickle attack her – it's the embodiment of 'death to the bourgeoisie' issue, of traditional, comfortable culture. (Don't yawn – stay awake! Think! Read! Be self-critical!).

A table of books set up in a field is the stage for several weedy skits in *Puff of a Breeze From the Orient*. Anne Wiazemsky holds forth (reading from a tract). The Capitalist holds forth (reading from a book). A guy plays a recorder incredibly badly.[9] People heckle from behind the camera (it might be the film crew (we hear the Maestro), or it might be a passing busload of drunk Japanese tourists looking for the Eiffel Tower).

9 Reminding us that unless the plastic recorder, staple of music lessons in schools, is played properly, it always sounds horrible.

Near the end of *Wind From the Lefties*, close-ups of how to make bombs or weapons were included – a provocation to political activism. (These scenes were added later, as were many of the skits).

There's lots of red in *Wind From the Knees* – it's splashed over actors during scenes (even over Anne Wiazemsky – as at the end of *One Plus One*), evoking political repression, and the screen is tinted red (it makes a change from black).

By the mid-1960s, the films of Jean-Luc Godard included repeated takes of the same action. Oh, it wasn't padding, you understand, fellow radicals, because all of Godard's movies fell short of the expected 80-90 mins for a feature film. *Mais non*, it was a brilliant deconstruction of bourgeois, imperialist cinema. *Wind From the Piste* performs the feat several times (Godard's films only did it once or twice). So we have several takes of a guy (Mr Soldier) on a horse leading a guy (the 'Native American') on a rope; and more shots of the guy on the horse leading the guy on a rope; and several takes of the Yankee strangling Miss Althusser (while someone (likely Godard) off-camera throws red paint over her), etc.

An hour into the 1970 movie, and the shrill woman[10] on the soundtrack is *still* prattling on about strikes and factories and workers and bosses. Eh? Weren't those points (*worthy, to be sure, my donkey-jacketed comrade*) already made by the twelfth minute of the movie? Why are the *same messages* being delivered in the narration 50 minutes later? In case those of us remaining in the audience forgot? We didn't forget! We're right here, watching the fucking movie! (Or is it, like the repeated inserts of 'Comrade Stalin' earlier, more padding?).

Wind From the Sleaze isn't all images of young radicals

---

10 She never identifies herself.

gathered for their Annual Marxist-Leninist Picnic in Rome or the Bois de Boulogne: there *are* images of Other Things: a Parisian street. Workers outside a car factory. The River Seine. Farm labourers. (And immediately, the stern voiceover slaps the film's fingers: you train a camera on people at work and think you're a radical filmmaker?).

✳

Much of *Wind From the Tease* is actually a harrangue like a radio broadcast – not national radio, but college radio, amateur, student radio beamed out over the campus with only eleven people tuning in (and that's only after they've been leafleted on their way to the Student Union bar). Yes – we are preaching to the *converted*, my duffel-coated comrades. It doesn't introduce ideas about revolutionary politics, and about revolution and ideology, or contextualize them, or relate them to other political concepts; it assumes that the audience is already there, with them, manning the imaginary barricades of this imaginary debate.

In case you don't have a brain, and have forgotten something that was intoned on the soundtrack, *Wind From the East* repeats itself:

Bourgeois = bad	Left-wing = good
'Ollywoood = bad	Militant cinema = good
Nixon & Johnson = bad	Stalin & Mao = good
America = very bad	China = very good
Cheese after 8 p.m. = bad	Cheese on toast before 2 p.m. = good

These simplistic oppositions resemble a list of likes and dislikes of 'What's New' or 'What's Cool' in lifestyle magazines.[11] These are regular features, published when

11 Hey, what a surprise, my beauties, black is 'in' this month again! Like wearing black ever went out of fashion in Paris, Milan, Tokyo or New York!

journos are out of ideas: a list of current cool fashion, say, or current tastes. The Dziga Vertov Group films and 68>73 politi-films are Godard's versions of lists – with the 'dislikes' far out-numbering the 'likes'. Big G.'s political works assert what they *don't* like all the time: the bourgeoisie, bosses, factories, Amerika, capitalism, fake tans, pencil skirts, John Wayne, the colour blue, slow drivers, old men who wear baseball caps, people who don't ever pick up the tab at lunch, and filmmakers who won't shut up.

Don't worry if you've forgotten what the voiceover just said, it'll be repeated ten minutes down the line, in the next pseudo-quasi-meta-para scene. That old voiceover keeps coming up with juicy nuggets from the Class Struggle. Like:

It's right to rebel.[12]
Think about the civil war between labour and capital.
Death to the bourgeoisie.

One thing is very obvious looking at *Wind From the Feast*: this is *not* all Godard-Godard-Godard. For a start, it was co-written with Jean-Pierre Gorin, Sergeio Bazzini and Daniel Cohn-Bendit, and it was co-dir. by Godard, Gorin and Gérard Martin. Many scenes are clearly not directed by Godard (we can tell by the use of the camera, the camera angles (and even the choice of lenses), the blocking of the actors, the movement within the frame – Godard has a very distinctive cinematographic style, and *Wind From the Least* was not all overseen by the Maestro). Some of the editing and the sound editing of voices off was also not by Godard. (However, Gorin, recovering from an accident, only joined the production towards the end of the schedule. So maybe it was more Godard and Martin).

✳

12 Damn straight 'it's right to rebel'! It's the most sacred act of being human.

And it's humourless.[13]

Wind From the Beast is hard-going, even for dedicated Godard worshippers like us. I mean, even his most passionate admirers have found the Maoist-Marxist works of post-May, 1968 difficult.

(But then, *Wind From the East* doesn't make things easy for the viewer! It opens with a four-minute shot of two people lying on the ground! Is this a spoof of Andy Warhol[14] and his films of people sleeping or doing nothing? Is it a satirical commentary on political activism? (i.e., *non*-activity?). Is it two people embarking on their own political revolution, their fervent class struggle and self-criticism, by doing nothing and resting? Are these people conducting their own strike – a strike from themselves? or a strike against life itself?).

*

The meat[15] of *Wind From the East* is found in the voiceover: *Wind From the East* presents a collage of (1) rants, (2) several voices off, and (3) found sounds (including extracts from news footage). It's in the off-screen, invisible element of sound that *Wind From the East* delivers its true subject – which is politics in general, ideology in general, and Communist/ left-wing/ socialist politics in particular, and cinema/ media/ representation in particular. (That is, *Wind From the East* was largely created after pre-production and after filming, in post-production).

The 1970 film assumes a good deal – for example, that the audience is already well-informed of the social-political context of the topics it's raising. You do know all about Stalinism in the 1930s, don't you? Of course you do. You know about Sergei Eisenstein's unmade film projects in the '30s? Of

13 Even though Godard in *Vent d'est* is certainly at his jokiest and most playful.
14 And you thought *Chelsea Girls* (1966) was challenging to endure for even 15 minutes.
15 It's not prime steak, of course, but, for the hippies in the audience, a veggie substitute.

course. You know the key dates of revolution (1789, 1871, 1937, 1968)? Yes, you do. You know about the political allegiances of long-gone journals such as the *Humanist*, don't you? *Bien sûr*.

Wind From the Wheeze comes across like a personal film project of a small group of filmmakers (Ye Olde Collective or Co-operative or Workshoppe — very 1970), who have bravely and nobly produced a film. But it's created primarily (maybe solely) for themselves. (Well, they do say that you have to please yourself first as an artist, otherwise you can't expect to thrill anybody else. Unfortunately, it didn't work here).

The impassioned ranting in the voiceover of *Wind From the East* evokes all of the usual motifs of socialist/ left-wing political activism:

Strikes	Workers	Unions
Bosses	Capitalists	Governments

In the gimmicky parlance of the voiceover, Nixon-Paramount is pitted against Brezhnev-Mosfilm (that bit is definitely written by Godard). The narration also points out that they're pretty much the same, a Nixon-Paramount-Brezhnev-Mosfilm conglomerate. And, *tch,* they're bourgeois anyway.

✳

Jean-Luc G. and company had done it all before — in *Weekend, One Plus One* and *La Chinoise, par example* (the latter also starred Anne Wiazemsky, like *Wind From the East*). All of the points delivered in *Wind From the Cheese* in that angry but awkward manner, about Communism under Lenin, under Stalin, under Mao • about how Stalinism, Leninism and Maoism relate to the present day • about political filmmaking (here dubbed 'militant filmmaking') • about how very bourgeois and repressive 'Ollywooood cinema is • about the significance of Sergei Eisenstein and Dziga Vertov to today's cinematic practice • about what students, young people, and activists should be doing in contemporary society in the political arena...... *all* of these issues had already been raised and debated in movies such as *One Plus One, La Chinoise* and *Weekend* (and, many would agree, much more successfully. Or, at least, much funnier).

You want an anti-bourgeois film? *Weekend* is that – and *Weekend* is not a polite, well-mannered anti-bourgeois, anti-decadent film, it's violently angry.

But the fictional structure of the feature-length movies helmed by Jean-Luc Godard prior to the politicized pieces of post-1968 doesn't negate or weaken any of the ideological/political material delivered within stories. On the contrary, the fiction films are far more accomplished at making the same points. (For the political films and for the Dziga Vertov Group project, fiction was deemed bourgeois, imperialist – documentary or 'realism' was the thing).

Well, you could argue (if you could be bothered) that *Wind From the Ease* is a kind of like a look back at 1968, and at Godard's involvement in political cinema, and revolutionary politics, and at the impact of the civil unrest of 1968 two years down the line.

But *Wind From the Freeze* has not dated well, and seems too niche, too self-enclosed, and too snobbish about its political, ideological approach. It doesn't invite you in – hell, it doesn't really want you to watch it at all (why? Because you're *too bourgeois*! Because audiences are *bourgeois*! Because the very notion of films playing to audiences is *bourgeois*![16] Because if you've paid for a ticket or for a DVD disc, you are *bourgeois*! And if you're watching this on a television set you bought, you are *bourgeois*!).

16 Even Eisenstein is *bourgeois!*

John Lennon (not Lenin) did all of this in a three-minute pop song, 'Revolution' (first recorded by the Beatles at the end of May, 1968). Yes – *Wind From the East* has already said all it has to say by – what? – ten minutes into the piece? 20 minutes? After that, it's repetition all the way.

That's common in a lecture in a theatre. We've all sat thru lectures – in colleges, universities, art museums, cinemas, etc – where the speaker has only one thing to say. Maybe two, tops. But they spend 45 minutes, or 75 minutes, repeating it, and providing variations on it.

The best lectures are entertaining *as well as* informative/ provocative/ knowledgable. The worst lectures think it's enough to simply deliver information, like a machine, from mouth to ear, from mind to mind.

It's a sin to be given an audience of 200 people and then to bore them. But what the viewer thinks of the D.V.G. movies isn't really much of a consideration for the filmmakers, it seems. They seem to be making these movies for a small circle of friends and colleagues.

✳

I don't buy this movie.[17]

I also reckon that *Wind From the Keys* was a mere footnote to material and issues that Godard and company had presented far more significantly and skilfully elsewhere. *Wind From the Bees* is like an amateur, Sunday afternoon painter's version of what a political film might be: *grab a camera! call your friends! bring your air guns! jump in the VW camper! let's go and make a movie!* (Or maybe it's the Godardian/ Marxist/ Activist equivalent of a Hollywood musical movie like *The Band Wagon* or *Summer Stock*, where Fred Astaire or Gene Kelly or Mickey Rooney lead a bunch of rosy-cheeked, red-checked-shirt-wearing, eager youngsters: *hey kids, let's put on a show!* And they all pile into the barn to do just that).

---

17 But I *did* buy this movie! Or the DVD, at least.

Hollywood cinema is the sublimest expression of the Great American Dream, right? (Along with pop music, cars, Coca Cola, etc). So what is *Wind From the East* and the political 1968-1973 films? The Great Marxist Revolution?

Not hardly.

7

LUTTES EN ITALIE

STRUGGLE IN ITALY

Luttes en Italie (*Lotte en Italia/ Struggle In Italy*,[18] 1971) was another of Zen Master Godard's politicized, post-1968 all-action, all-star spectacles. A blockbuster epic filmed on four continents with a cast of thousands, *Struggle In Italy* told the story of the rise and fall of the Roman Empire from its origins in the mists of time to the height of the Caesars and the subsequent invasion by Barbarians, Vandals and Goths – but from the point-of-view of a slave girl called Lottie (who, incredibly, was a Marxist activist two thousand years before that pretentious pose became fashionable among white, bourgeois intellectuals in late 1960s Paris).

You remember *Spartacus* (1960), of course? – a famously left-leaning film starring Kirk Douglas – the team behind it (including the blacklisted writer, the star/ producer and the director) espoused left-wing political views (and not too long after the witch-hunts of the early 1950s). Well, *Struggle In Italy* built on the example of *Spartacus*: yes, my red-flag-waving, wannabe working-class comrades, you *could* make a giant movie in the Hollywood system which delivered action, romance, comedy, spectacle and thrills *and*

18 The title comes from a supremely bourgeois film, one of Godard's very favourites: *Voyage In Italy* (one of the Top 100 Best Films on many critics' lists. (I haven't been able to get through even half of it).

clear and provocative left-wing politics. Thus, *Struggle In Italy* makes *Spartacus* look like a shabby political rant filmed in an apartment two two actors.

The credits for *Struggle In Italy*: dir. and ed. by Dziga Vertov Group, Godard and Gorin; and prod. by Cosmoseion for R.A.I. TV. The cast: Cristina Tullio-Altan, Anne Wiazemsky, Paolo Pozzesi and Jerome Hinstin. Godard said that Gorin was responsible for much of the film. Most of it was filmed in Godard's Paris apartment, with the odd trip to the *tabac* for a newspaper and packet of cigarettes. (Godard did the same in his later works, which included scenes filmed in his digs, or out of his office window, or on the street just outside. Why bother to trek to distant locales when you can do it all from your home? Godard is brilliant (and bold) enough to be able to pull that off. *Detective,* for example, was set enitrely in a swanky Paris hotel. The budget for these Dziggy Fartoff films didn't stretch to that. And anyway, hotels were too imperialist, comrade, too nationalist and bourgeois for that).

Scenes From the Class Struggle In Italy was centred around a young woman (Paola Taviani, played by Cristina Tullio-Altan);[19] her political activity formed the loose structure of *Struggle In Italy*, but the film was the usual left-wing rant disguised as a pseudo-*avant garde* film which hoped to be a call to arms. (So it's a remake of *La Chinoise* – a girl and radical politics).

These are films of ideas, of processes, of the relationship between the filmmakers and the audience – they are not finished, glossy products (!). *Struggle In Italy* was not intended, either, to be released in theatres alongside *Billy Jack, Fiddler On the Roof, Carnal Knowledge* or *Diamonds Are Forever* (the top-grossing movies of 1971). *Struggle In Italy* was commissioned by German television (where it was shown on February 27, 1971).

---

19 She was in *Wind From the East*

✳

This is just miserable.

Struggle In Italy (known in Cuba as *Everything You Never Really Wanted To Know About Marxism*) has no reality, no juice, no *oomph*, no nothing. *Struggle In Italy* is so tough-going, it makes you long for Godard-directed turkeys like *King Lear* (1987)! Everybody is free to make mistakes, sure, but nobody watching the dailies of this movie could've imagined that it would make for compelling viewing.

Richard Brody suggested that *British Sounds* 'has the stiff and self-punishing feel of a cinematic hair shirt' (B, 345). Yes, watching the 1968-1973 political films, it does feel as if you've been kidnapped in the night, bundled into a truck (with a smelly sack over your head and your hands bound), driven into the mountains, and told to sit on the freezing ground and wait. [20] After an hour, the hood is roughly removed, you blink, you look round: *oh shit!* – you're one of 300 people making up the audience of an open-air cinema and what's on the screen? *Sunrise*? *The Magnificent Ambersons*? *The Seven Samurai*? *Airplane*? *Star Wars*? Nope: it's *Struggle In Italy*!

✳

The main character/ figure/ lifeform in *Struggle In Italy* is Paola Taviani (named after one of the Taviani film director brothers, b. 1931). Perhaps Cristina Tullio-Altan was cast for her very ordinariness, a regular Italian woman. But Tullio-Altan doesn't make this film any easier to get through. (So it wasn't, alas, Anne Wiazemsky or Juliet Berto. [21] Maybe Wiazemsky was deemed too glamorous for this part – she had already essayed the same sort of role in *La Chinoise*. And the film wanted an Italian actress).

Lotte en Italia doesn't mean *Lottie In Italy* in English – this isn't a sequel to *Roman Holiday*, charting the adventures

20 Remember, you must: Wait. Think. Read. Practice. Wait.
21 Anne Wiazemsky, bless her, appears in the role of a sales-woman in a clothing store (!), helping our young activist try on clothes (and speaking in Italian, too).

of a cute starlet in the Land of Passion and Opera!

Hell, no. *Lotte/ Lutte* means *struggle*, folks. Struggle (I repeat this because the film repeats essential items, too – because the film repeats essential things, too).

In a typical piece of Godardian eccentricity, Cristina Tullio-Altan speaks in Italian but is translated by a female voiceover into French. Television prefers this kind of dubbing, instead of subtitles (TV typically uses live dubbing for news interviews), but it always comes across as clunky, and, in the ethical terms of the approach of Godard's political films of 68-73, it's ideologically dubious. Yet we know that Godard preferred dubbing for his own movies, which he thought was more honest than subtitles)

Struggle In Italy is sort of divided into sections: 'Society', 'Identity', 'Family', 'Sex', 'Shopping', 'Plumbing', etc. But the way that these topics are evoked is rather patchy – 'Family' doesn't particularly evoke the family of the young woman Taviani, but suggests parental figures with off-screen voices[22] (and a close-up of soup being eaten).[23] The parents berate the girl for continuing to live at home, exploiting them.

Struggle In Italy is itself an artefact that questions itself: who is this film for? Who is this film against? Self-criticism is a key practice in the Dziga Vertov Group comedy epics.

*

I watched *Struggle In Italy* immediately after *Wind From the East*. it's the same movie! No, OK, not exactly – but it's the same left-wing diatribe! It's the same political-ideological-social rant from a left-leaning perspective – the only difference is that the bunch of dopey hippies in the countryside have been replaced by a very boring young woman in an apartment.

Watching the two films gives you the scary, depressing

22 Talk about low budget! Where's Dad? Oh, he's an off-screen voice!
23 The fancy bowl and the formal-ish dinner suggests Taviani's bourgeois background. See, this film *is* thought out!

notion that this group of politicized filmmakers actually had only a few things to say. Or they repeated the same things many times. (And they padded out their meagre works with black leader or red leader or they recycled the footage).

This is political, ideological claustrophobia. It feels like being trapped, it's torture in the form of being force-fed rhetoric.

You want to laugh but that has been outlawed.

You want to cry but that has been outlawed.

You want to leave the room but that has been outlawed.

You want to dematerialize to another dimension of space and time but that has been outlawed.

✳

Sound was one of the preoccupations of the political films of the post-1968 era and the Dziga Vertov Group works (handily, it was also one of the cheapest components – a voiceover is much cheaper than 25 nights for 30 crew at even a modestly priced hotel). The 1968-1973 political films are, literally, sounds and images, pieces which draw attention to their construction as sounds and images. James Monaco noted that for Godard, sound 'suffers under the tyranny of image; there should be an equal relationship between the two' (1977b, 324). Maybe – but Godard got his own back by including black or red leader, thus negating the image with a sledgehammer. Or he recycled the images, anæthetizing the viewer.

At a budgetary level, some of the 68-to-73 politics films impress with their clever use of off-screen voices and sounds to suggest things that they don't have the $$$$ or the FFFFF to show. A police officer (or some such) asking to see the papers of the young woman Taviani in *Bungles In Italy* is merely an off-screen voice and the hand/ arm of a crew member (no need for even a police uniform). Ditto with the store owner who orders a shop assistant back to work, or even parents (Daddy can just be an off-screen voice). One guy — Paolo Pozzesi — plays those off-screen embodiments of patriarchy (cops, fathers, bosses).

Altho' the film is entitled *Struggle In Italy*, it might've been filmed anywhere in the Solar System[24] (most of the scenes are interiors). There are shots of Italy which might come from a film library, or maybe someone was sent to Italia with a 16mm camera to grab some exterior shots. (But there is no feeling whatsoever that this is Italy, no contextualization, and there's nothing particularly Italian about the movie). In fact, most of it was filmed in Godard's pad in Paree.

Struggle In Italy ignores contextualization by, say, looking at the Partito Comunista Italiano,[25] or conducting interviews with left-wing activists. If you take *Struggle In Italy* at face value, the only person pursuing Communist politics in Italy is this one woman, Taviani (and one cohort).

⁂

Like other Dziga Vertov Group films, *Struggle In Italy* admits shamelessly that it does *not* have enough material to stretch to an hour of running time. The black leader already appears within minutes of the start (sometimes it's red), so that the screen goes dark for a few seconds, while nothing is said, nothing is heard, and nothing is seen (in other sections, the voiceover and the dialogue continue over the black leader). In addition, the movie's title card — an ugly, handwritten note on white paper (costing 20 centimes) — is repeated. (Towards the close of the 1971 movie, the red leader lasts for eons — enough time to stage a two-hour, sit-down strike at Pirelli, grab a coffee in your favourite café afterwards, be interviewed for the R.A.I. News at six, and get back to the movie in time for more red leader).

Is it an arty statement-non-statement? Is the black

24 Pluto and Neptune have reasonable rates for visiting film productions (but the food's terrible).
25 There's a shot of a building with an Italian Communist Party sign outside.

screen symbolizing the Cosmic Void? Is it a low-budget version of Samuel Beckett?

And then there's the vexed issue of repetition (of repetition… of repetition). Pretty much all television documentaries repeat material, often when they hope to make a point. OK. We let that slide. But *Struggle In Italy* takes the concept of repetition to ridiculous lengths:

A shot of someone closing a door.

A shot of the young woman Taviani writing at a table.

A shot of said woman eating soup.

A shot of a factory exerior.

In an outrageous move, the third part of the *Snuggles In Italy* film ('the third part of the film', 'the third part of the film', 'the third part of the film')[26] repeats many of the shots of the first section of the film, but justifies that in the voiceover, because now Ms Taviani is analyzing how she was presented earlier, how the topics were explored. (Yes, it's Maoist/Marxist self-criticism taken to the limit: part two critiques part one, and part three critiques parts one and two. Handily, the auto-critique format allows filmmakers to recycle what they've already presented).

But the critiques are, it has to be said, meagre, unconvincing and obvious: • meagre because they don't have much to say, • unconvincing because the weak arguments they make are not justified by the images (an image of a factory does *not* illustrate the link between bourgeois ideology and revolutionary militant action!), and • obvious because all of the points being made are woefully simplistic.

And of course there's a voiceover, to make sense of this mess (or to try to make sense of the mess). In typically eccentric Godardian style, it's spoken in Italian (by a guy), then translated into French (by a woman – but in a hesitant, awkward manner). Later, Taviani's Italian is translated into

26 Are these repetitions annoying you as much as me?

French. Repetition infects the narration like a deadly virus, *comme ça*:

> Reflections.
> Reflections.
> Reflections.
> Reflections.

> Practice. Practice.
> Practice. Theory. Practice.

> The class struggle.
> The class struggle.

> The third part of the film.
> The third part of the film.
> The third part of the film.

Oooh là là! It looks like a Gertrude Stein poem when you print it like that! I wish! Stein's famous 'Lifting Belly' poem, this ain't.

You will want to shoot the voiceover itself – plus the stupid French woman reading it out – and the idiot Italian man.

By the way, the phrase 'the third part of the film' is repeated *nine times* – just in case you total nutjobs in the audience didn't hear it the first time (didn't hear it the first time).

If you thought watching the Dziga Vertov Group films was like going back to a crummy school, you are right (you are right):

Come on, pay attention! Quieten down! *Shhh!* Listen! This is your education we're dealing with here! Listen! Think! Sit up straight! Take notes! What did I just say? I said, <u>TAKE</u>

NOTES! Write down what I'm saying! Your red pen has run out, Comrade Fritz? Here, use mine!

By the way, you bourgeois morons, we will be having a test on the political ideas outlined in the film at the end of the session. Anybody who gets less than 10/10 will be taken outside and shot. Failure is not an option! Now *shut up and listen*!

Buggles In Italy is Gorin and Godard at their school teacherest worst (or, if you're a masochist, their teasingly best). When the Master-Of-All-Cinema talks, you listen, if you value your life.

✳

The politicized films take the form of political leaflets handed out to your co-workers at a factory. Alas, the films last a *lot* longer than the time it takes to glance at a leaflet and toss it away. [27]

This is certainly one reason why the 1968-1973 political films found it difficult to find an audience, or were rejected by audiences. Any decent political-ideological-sociological film-maker could make their points in a much shorter time, or at least in a much more compelling fashion.

The Dziga Vertov Group films and the 1968-1973 political works refuse to sweeten the deal, to candy dust their messages, to embellish the contract between the artwork and the audience. So there are no car chases, no gun fights, no girls in bikinis, and no explosions.

You get the political messages straight, and repeated, too, as if we're at college, taking notes in a lecture, and the teacher repeats the key phrases for us: class struggle... Marxist critique... workers on strike... (Indeed, *Strangle In Italy* shows us what we should be doing: sitting at a table and writing notes; and later, handing out leaflets in a factory,[28]

[27] Happily, we see one of the workers in the textiles factory doing just that.
[28] Filmed in Roubaix.

which is what Paola Taviani does).

Theory and practice.

(A) Theory in *Straggle In Italy* means reading lots of stodgy political tracts, and regurgitating them to camera against a wall[29] (often by reading aloud from them).

(B) Practice means writing out quotes from said treatises and cobbling together leaflets to hand out to co-workers in factories.

(C) And self-critique means going over the whole shebang and analyzing it (which means, in the tradition of all French films, talking about it).

✳

Sections of *Struggle In Italy* (known in Wisconsin as *Cooking Cabbage the Marxist Way*) are offensively simplistic — like the nods to a quasi-second wave feminism expressed in the form of stereotypical evocations of the young couple in the film making love in the afternoon. How this exploration of the class struggle in Italy brings in a romantic couple is really clunky and chauvinist. (Similarly, works such as *British Sounds* bungle the womanist/ feminist issue).

There's a suggestion in *Luggage In Italy* that romance and love are bourgeois and indulgent, and that proper left-wing militants and activists wouldn't waste time lovemaking — there's too much studying and leafleting to be done. In the view of the Dziga Vertov Group and Godard in his 1968-1973 political films, sex and love are best left to others (you'll feel guilty afterwards anyway, like a Catholic sinner, and we can't have that, because religion is also bourgeois). Anway, Marxists and Leninists don't procreate (it's the wrong kind of production!): instead, babies are hatched on an assembly line at the Fiat factory in Turin (but there's a Chinese Communist Party-imposed quota — only one child per household).[30]

✳

29 Lacking sets, the film simply puts actors against a wall.
30 And you better hope it's male.

So in the third part of the film ('the third part of the film', 'the third part of the film', 'the third part of the film', 'the third part of the film', 'the third part of the film', 'the third part of the film', 'the third part of the film', 'the third part of the film', 'the third part of the film'– *nine times*, remember?), *Struggle In Italy* reviews the first and second sections. It's the summing up section of a lecture which is always intolerably boring, *because we've just heard the damn lecture*! We don't need it to be summarized!

But this is Godard 'n' Gorin in their stern, teacherly mode: you <u>will</u> sit quietly and <u>listen</u> to the summing up (and <u>keep</u> taking notes). The summary is important, you see, sickle-wielding comrades, because of the test that will follow the film (Question 1: Who made the film? Question 2: What is the film about? Question 3: Who is the film for and against?).

One aspect of *Struggle In Italy* is intriguing: the focus on editing in the third part of the movie ('the third part of the film', 'the third part of the film', 'the third part of the film'). The voiceover explains how shots of the young woman (taken from 'the first part of the film', 'the first part of the film', 'the first part of the film') are now intercut with shots of production (i.e., a factory) on either side. It's one of the instances where Godard/ Gorin contemplate the manufacture of cinema in the form of montage. It's clumsy, and certainly not the finest example of analyzing how cinema works in Godard's *œuvre*, but it does lift *Struggle In Italy* above being another left-wing rant.

✳

It's too long.

It's a familiar complaint that has been made about millions of films. Television demands products built around time slots of 30 minutes and 60 minutes. If there isn't enough news that day, a news show will still have to stretch the material to fit a half-hour slot. I reckon that on Slow News

Days, when nothing is happening, TV news shows should broadcast black screens – exactly as Godard's 1968-1973 political films do. Or admit that there isn't enough news to broadcast, and shorten the news show appropriately (or allow other shows to take over the time slot. So on a Boring News Day, the six o'clock news would run for three minutes, with 27 minutes of black. Or three minutes of news followed by 27 minutes of commercials).

The television industry won't agree to that. A half-hour news show has to be half-an-hour. With the 1968-1973 political works, the pressure of stretching material to 60 minutes was too great: *Noodles In Italy* demonstrates this vividly. You can see that the film editors (Godard and Gorin) sat at the K.E.M. in the editing suite (set up, no doubt, in Godard's front room), and kept reaching for more black leader and more red leader, and spliced it into the film as it was being cut. And the editors snipped off another three feet of the long roll of the title card of *Struggle In Italy* and cut that into the movie, too (the 68-73 politicized works are very much celluloid films, cut with scissors and razors; they're not digital, not using computers).31 Then the editors kept adding and adding – more padding and repetitions and black leader – until they got close to the target of the all-important sixty minutes. (Each 1968 to 1973 political film certainly hits the skids in their final sections. But that's also true of many Godard movies).

✳

Question: Why didn't Jean-Luc Godard use his considerable influence in film circles and invite Pier Paolo Pasolini to appear in *Struggle In Italy*? A movie from a left-wing perspective exploring the class struggle in modern-day Italia (and with references to the Italian Communist Party) is right up Pasolini's street. Godard had contributed a short film

31 And not yet the video experiments that Godard undertook in the Seventies.

to *RoGoPaG* (1963), which featured Pasolini's satirical skit *Curd Cheese*. And for sure the firebrand filmmaker would be an infinitely more compelling presence than anything we see in *Struggle In Italy*. (At the time – 1970-71 – Pasolini was at work on his African *Oresteia* documentary (*Appunti per un'Orestiade Africana*) and shooting *The Decameron,* plus short works such as *Appunti per un romanzo dell'immondizia* and *Le Mura di Sana'a*).

Maybe Pier Palo Pasolini could've been brought in for the Discussion With a Philosopher section which Godard inserted in several of his 1960s films (usually in the final act, where the philosopher chats with the main character). We might've seen a truly mind-boggling idea:

Pasolini and Godard debating on-screen.

8

VLADIMIR ET ROSA

VLADIMIR AND ROSA

INTRO.

Vladimir and Rosa (Grove Press/ Evergreen Films/ Telepool,32 1971) was in part another political rant (in the guise of an essay/ documentary about the Chicago Eight and other right-on topics) • in part another lecture about political theory and practice • in part a whinge about contemporary society in the Capitalist Republic of France • in part another disquisition on the media and representation • and in part a home movie in which Godard and Gorin horse around with their friends in Godard's Paris apartment. *Vladimir and Rosa* raises the issue of putting political views and ideas into a practical form (theory and practice, theory and practice, as the narration waspishly informs us).

When you look at the 1968-1973 political movie output of G. 'n' G., you can't help wondering: what the hell was the Gangster Genius of French Cinema playing at? Why was a hyper-intelligent filmmaker like Godard, who had *already* re-invented cinema several times in films such as *Vivre Sa Vie* and *Breathless*, doing with these amateurish film projects? Surely not to explore other ways of discussing all of the topics (politics included) that his movies had already covered?

32 The backing was from New York and Munich.

Surely not to re-invent forms of filmmaking? Surely not to argue and analyze ideology and politics, including left-wing forms, in such a juvenile manner?

The cinema of Jean-Luc Godard was far in advance of this group of filmmakers – indeed, far in advance of pretty much every other filmmaker on the Planet. Was it the lure or the pleasure of getting involved with some younger filmmakers, to explore the same things again, but with fresh faces and new talent? (It sure wasn't the lure of money – these projects were produced on tiny budgets, and the Maestro financed some of them himself).

If you thought *Wind From the East* was hard-going, wait until you see *Blowing Bubbles In Italy* or *Vladimir and Rosie Get Laid*.

＊

THE CAST.

Everybody in *Vladimir and Rosa* looks ugly – even glamorous figures like Anne Wiazemsky and Juliet Berto (the cinematography is truly horrible – it was filmed on 16 millimetre Kodak scraps left in the trash behind the film processing labs at Joinville, which the filmmakers scavenged after dark). Absolutely, definitely *no* make-up artists were hired for this production (make-up is too capitalist! No actor or actress should partake of Max Factor, it's bourgeois! Only 'Ollywooood uses make-up – not militant-political guerilla filmmakers).

Many in the cast of *Vladimir and Rosa* were culled from the Godard Circus of the 1960s. Often, however, they are called on to pose in flat *tableaux*, which conspicuously lack the zing of similar scenes in, say, *Weekend* or *Masculine/Feminine*. (The cast is truly squandered in *Vladimir and Rosa*).

In the 1968-1973 political films of Monsieur Godard, it's considered too bourgeois to have performers learning their lines, so dialogue is read from scraps of paper (resulting in some very ropey performances). Eh? How about a Bertholt Brecht play? Is every Brecht play performed with the actors holding scripts as they walk about the stage? No.

Vladimir and Rosa has a shoddy, stingy look that undermines its mission (it seems to relish in its low budget status — it's cool (no, it's militantly radical) to look rubbish! it's cool to look as bad as *The Blair Witch Project* 30 years ahead of its time). To compensate for its lack of visual punch, the soundtrack is busy with information, from multiple voice-overs, sudden eruptions of pop music, and sound effects.

THE CHICAGO EIGHT.

The events of the Chicago Eight (later the Chicago Seven) have been made into documentaries, plays, radio plays, and films (including contemporary accounts). If you want a straight documentary account of the Chicago Eight, there are several possibilities available. *Vladimir and Rosa* is, as you'd expect from a filmmaker as unusual and wilfully eccentric as Jean-Luc Godard, not a typical documentary. It takes up the issue of the Chicago Eight as a pretext for exploring other issues, such as revolutionary politics, seen from a left-wing perspective.

Thus, aspects of the Chicago Eight events are referred to, and even jokily dramatized (in a thoroughly cheapo manner, such as the trial, where a scuzzy room stands in for a courthouse), but much of *Vladimir and Rosa* is about other things (i.e., what the Two G.s really wanted to explore, which was *their* form of revolutionary politics).

That is of course one of Godard's chief approaches to cinema and television: give him a subject, or hire him to make a documentary about a topic, and (*if* he agrees to do it) the project might start out close to the contracted subject. But pretty soon it'll be what Godard wanted to make anyway.

Another ideological tension in *Vladimir and Rosa* is that

the Chicago Eight issue is in part an *Amerikan* story, a narrative of resistance and revolt within the North Amerikan social system. Godard, Gorin and the Dziga Vertov Group had already explored the French and the European aspects of the events of 1968 and political activism in films such as *Wind From the East* (and Godard had examined some of the political events which led to 1968 in films such as *One Plus One*, *Weekend* and *La Chinoise*). Turning their gaze on North Amerikan society in *Vladimir and Rosa* inevitably raised the problematic issue of the political stance of the 1968-1973 political film projects and the Dziga Vertov Group film projects, which were at times virulently anti-Amerikan. To be Amerikan was intolerable, according to the Dziga Vertov Group.

THE GODARD AND GORIN SHOW.

Vladimir and Rosa was another laugh riot from the comedy team of Godard and Gorin – and in this film, they appear on-screen, wryly commenting on the movie as it unfolds. But the Two G.s are no Martin and Lewis, no Hope and Crosby, no Groucho and Chico, no Laurel and Hardy.

A photograph of the Marx Brothers in *Vlady and Rosy* reminds us who the Great Marx is in film history. If only Groucho had been called on to crack wise in *Vladimir and Rosa* (he already has the cigar permanently attached to his maw – and Groucho can act better with a cigar than either Godard or Gorin).

(The title – *Vladimir and Rosa* – refers to Vladimir Lenin (not Lennon) and Rosa Luxembourg. They are played by Godard and Gorin. So the film is a kind of double act, the comedy duo of the Dziga Vertov Group).

The only people laughing among the cast, the crew and the audience are the directors, Godard and Gorin. (The laugh-out-loud political diatribes of Gorin and Godard continue in the voiceovers, too, with commentaries that escalate to yelling matches.)

Jean-Luc Godard's turn in *Vladimir and Rosa* sees him putting on one of his stupid voices (as does Jean-Pierre Gorin), which he did from time to time in his cameos. It doesn't really work, and neither does the staging of the would-be humorous banter in the middle of a tennis court (Godard was a keen tennis player). Two teams of doubles bat balls back and forth while Gorin 'n' Godard walk on the tennis court beside the net, pontificating into microphones and a portable tape recorder. In the voiceover, Godard uses a different, equally stupid accent.

Why didn't Jean-Luc Godard hire someone to do an impression of him? (which every comedian in France could do). Or a Godard lookalike? Why didn't he have Anne Wiazemsky or Juliet Berto impersonate him? (Godard in drag?). Or why didn't he cast someone who is genuinely funny, like Raymond Devos in *Pierrot le Fou*?

✳

As it continues, *Vladimir and Rosa* comes across as an indulgent home movie for an audience of two – Godard and Gorin (just like a home movie of, say, a family picnic in Provence, is only of interest to the family). It's not a film about politics, or about a legal trial in the U.S.A. which concerned politics and political activism, or about the class struggle, or about Marxist-Leninist-Maoist ideology. No, *Vladimir and Rosa* is a film in which the Two G.s indulge themselves in adolescent capers which sort of relate to political inquiry.

We're back with the assumptions that *Wind From the East* makes of its audience is that they (we) are all in agreement that:

Communism = heap good	Capitalism = heap bad.
Left-wing = good	Right-wing = bad.
Stalin & Mao = good	Nixon & Johnson = bad.

Militant cinema = good   Hollywood = bad.

THE SKITS,

And so to the sketches... *Vladimir and Rosa* contains would-be humorous ingredients,[33] but it begins with a stern, moralizing lecture, reminding us that we're back at school, and are we taking notes?, and are we listening carefully? In case some of us *aren't* listening closely, the teacherly narration repeats itself (theory and practice, theory and practice, coffee and cigarettes, coffee and cigarettes). If a movie could stretch out a wooden ruler from the movie screen and rap us on the knuckles, it would. (This is not how to start a movie which later has some witty, comical ingredients).

The off-putting opening scene in *Vladimir and Rosa* (focussing on two photographs of Comrade Vladimir Lenin at his most Communist-ish and working-class-ish, complete with mandatory proletarian cap), sets up the film as an irritable, irritated object.

In one skit, both Gorin and Godard have cigars in their mouths as they evoke nations (France, Israel, Germany, the U.S.A.) and *seig heil* and threaten with batons. During a break in the trial, they fool around with footballs and a chair (oh my, that chair! It's red! Whoopie! A red chair! Hey, kids, let's see another shot of that fucking chair! And another! It's a chair! It's red! A chair, a chair, a chair!).

One of the skits in the *Vlad an' Rosy Show* tackles feminism and women's liberation (judging from previous outings from the Dziga Vertov Group and Godard's political 68-73 films, we know this won't be good). This is a clunky episode where second wave feminist philosophy has been inadequately digested by the film, and regurgitated in a series of clichés.

The episode centres on Anne Wiazemsky, hard at work

33 *Vladimir and Rosa* attempted to use humour to tackle political issues, but it was rather shabbily delivered.

in her militant-hippy apartment screenprinting Tee shirts with right-on images. Yves Afonso plays her boyfriend who's struggling (class-struggling, I should say) to understand the modern woman's form of gender politics (Afonso is a superb example of a loutish, crude Frenchman who's attempting to be reborn as a sensitive New Man. The idea that a radical, politically-active feminist (and played by the dainty, prim princess-like Wiazemsky) would date such a Neanderthal oik isn't addressed).

As in much of the rest of the 1968-1973 political films, Anne Wiazemsky appears grumpy and dissatisfied, flicking back her lovely, amber locks to print some more Tee shirts, while Yves Afonso loons about, reading from feminists' texts. (Is she secretly thinking, *I wish my husband had never met that fool Gorin, and can't these smelly, would-be revolutionary idiots get out of my apartment?*).

Jean-Luc Godard would return to this territory many times subsequently (and more successfully), using the battle of the sexes in a heterosexual relationship as the setting for disquisitions on gender politics.

Being provocative comes naturally to Jean-Luc Godard – he just can't help himself. If he stumbles into a situation where authority or rules can be subverted or satirized, he does it. *Vladimir and Rosa* features many prods and teases from the French-Swiss ruffian genius – like characters seig heiling, like using images from porn magazines and having suggestive phrases scrawled over them (so we see 'revolution', 'fascism', 'enculer' and 'merde merde' written over a (picture of a) woman's naked ass).

A lengthy riff on race relations in the U.S.A. is focussed on the figure of Bobby X. (Frankie Dymon), seen in court during the trial with his hands cuffed and a pistol held to his head (and he's in prison earlier). As in films such as *Masculin Féminin* and *One Plus One*, Godard's method of portraying race issues is bold and hysterical (some would say regressive and objectionable).

REPETITIONS.

As with the other 1968-1973 political films, *Vladimir and Rosa* doesn't develop the images and/ or scenes it needs to match its aims, its political deconstructions (or even its voiceover). The telltale black leader appears early on, and continues throughout the piece. (Black leader – it's just rolls of black plastic – is cheaper than raw film stock!). The black leader bulks out the movie. And then we have white leader. And cuts between black leader and white leader. Only Godard would have the guts to create a scene from white and black screens – and use the voiceover to talk about race relations. Only Godard would have the guts to draw attention to the black screen in the voiceover: *Coming up next, folks, another section of black leader!* (Could Godard make an entire movie from black leader? Yes. In fact, Godard and Gorin produced *Letter To Jane* using one photograph. And it's 52 minutes long!). *Vladimir and Rosa*, like the other 1968-1973 political films, would work as well (or better) as a radio show.

Incredibly, the filmmakers draw attention to the black screen *again*, later in the 1971 film – this time to further excuse it or explain it. So now, according to the so-droll voiceover from Herr Direcktor, the screen is black because: (1) Columbia Broadcasting System and Gaumont would not permit the filmmakers to include certain images; (2) the filmmakers could not think of shots to fit the material (such as to demonstrate what bourgeois and imperialist cinema is).

What rubbish! That Godard would be put off by copyright threats from companies like C.B.S. is ridiculous (look at *Stor/ies of Cinema*! He includes material from all over the place); or that Godard couldn't develop a way of representing bourgeois cinema (he could insert images from his own *Contempt*! *Le Mépris* is a movie about a disintegrating marriage! And about making a film – talk about bourgeois!).

At one point, Godard even suggests that the black leader is included to dramatize the absence of Bobby X. (following his disappearance from the trail). And he links the black screen with black people in race relations.

Note to Godard: don't show this movie in Brooklyn or Inglewood!

Repetitions occur throughout *Vladimir and Rosa*, too – another admission that the 1971 production doesn't have sufficient material. Shots are repeated, and phrases in the voiceover are repeated (cheese and pickle, cheese and pickle, cheese and pickle • where's my coffee? where's my coffee? where's my coffee? • did you buy my cigarettes? did you buy my cigarettes? did you buy my cigarettes?). If you don't like (don't like) repetition (repetition), don't watch (don't watch) *Vladimir and Rosa* (*Vladimir and Rosa*).

∗

In the last section of *Vlad an' Rosa*, the filmmakers have given up: there are so many repetitions of shots we've already seen it goes beyond a joke. *Vladimir and Rosa* looks like a film where the editors ordered up ten reprints of the same takes, so they could cut the same junk into the movie over and over. (Another shot of the jury; another shot of a TV screen; another shot of the apopleptic judge; another shot of that stupid red chair; another slice of black leader).

Vladimir and Rosa includes, for example, surefire shots which demonstrate that a filmmaker is totally out of ideas: shots of a tape recorder. And later, the same shot (or the same tape recorder but on a TV monitor). And shots of a flatbed editing machine. Well, folks, if that's all you can think of to show in a movie, the enterprise is creatively bankrupt.

EVENTUALLY, EVEN THIS FILM ENDS.

Like all of the other political film projects of the late 60s and early 70s epoch, *Vladimir and Rosa* has made all of the points it wants to make early on, using the rest of the film to repeat them with variations (or, to hell with variations, to repeat them straight. To repeat them straight. To repeat them straight. And to excuse that repetition by calling it Marxist/ Maoist self-analysis. And to excuse that repetition by calling it Marxist/ Maoist self-analysis. And to excuse that repetition by calling it Marxist/ Maoist self-analysis.)

Well, if Godard can (if Godard can) make a film (make a film) by repeating sh¡t (by repeating sh¡t), then maybe I (then maybe I) can write a book (can write a book) by repeating sh¡t (by repeating sh¡t).

The repetitions³⁴ (meaning, the repetitions – that is, in French, the repetitions – and in English, the repetitions) of the already unappealing material helps to render *Vladimir and Rosa* hard-going. There simply isn't enough content in *Vladimir and Rosa* for a feature-length work. The reptitions (plus that stupid black screen) turn *Vladimir and Rosa* into the very thing it is denouncing: it's like *work*, it's like being on the factory floor, doing those demeaning jobs for Renault or Mercedes or Ford or Audi or Volkeswagen or General Motors or Fiat.

Vladimir and Rosa is keen to deride mindless, repetitious work in factories which exploit the workers – *yeah! we're with you, comrade! fight the power! strike! strike!* – but watching this movie is itself drudgery!

∗

34 It's like the joke in *A Night At the Opera* by the Marx Brothers – 'the party of the first part shall be known as the party of the first part'. As Groucho and Chico run thru this marvellous send-up of cretinous contracts and legalese, they tear up the sections of the contract they don't-a like. Maybe we should-a do that with this film.

PALESTINE WILL WIN.

Lastly, the Palestinian trip produced an abandoned film project, *Palestine Will Win* (a.k.a. *Until Victory*, 1970). Jean-Pierre Gorin and Jean-Luc Godard had visited Palestine in Feb, 1970, to work with the political organization Al Fatah. The ideological approach of *Palestine Will Win* comprised the familiar Godardian political rebellion once again – Palestine versus Israel (and, by extension, Amerika). So it was another cinematic rant against Imperialism, against the West, and against Amerika.

The project was about two-thirds complete before it was shelved. The footage was re-edited by Godard and Miéville in 1974, as *Here and Elsewhere* (*Ici et Ailleurs*).

＊

For many artists, the group of films produced by Jean-Luc Godard between 1968 and 1973 would be a huge committment creatively and personally, and a significant achievement cinematically. Yet the 1968 to 1973 period is just *one* item in Godard's truly remarkable career in cinema.

Le Vent
d'est

Jean-Luc Godard
(Gruppo Dziga Vertov)

VENTO DELL`EST

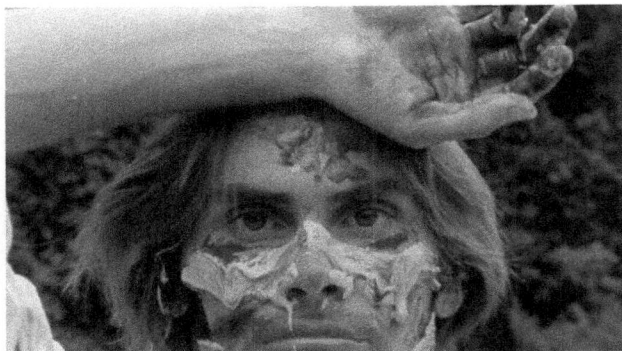

Wind From the East (1970).

Struggle In Italy (1971),
this page and over.

ROSSO ROSSO ROSSO ROSSO ROSSO
OSSO ROSSO ROSSO ROSSO ROSSO
SSO ROSSO ROSSO ROSSO ROSSO
SSO RO SSO ROSSO ROSSO ROSSO
SSO ROSSO ROSSO ROSSO ROSSO
SSO ROSSO ROSSO ROSSO ROSSO
SSO ROSSO ROSSO ROSSO ROSSO

LOTTE
IN
ITALIA

Vladimir and Rosa (1971).

9

TOUT VA BIEN

ALL'S WELL

The wickedness of the world is so great you have to run your legs off to avoid having them stolen from under you.

Bertholt Brecht, *The Threepenny Opera*

Tout Va Bien (*All's Well* a.k.a. *Just Great,* 1972) was an attempt at making a feature film version of the 1968 to 1973 political films and the Dziga Vertov Group projects which would get seen by actual, real, living audiences.[1] Hence the casting of two big stars of the era, Jane Fonda and Yves Montand. The budget was just over $1 million (= $8 million in 2025). Unfortunately, the film wasn't a success economic-ally or critically,[2] and was a difficult shoot.

Jean-Pierre Rassam produced for Anouchka Films/ Vieco Films/ Empire Films; Alain Coiffier was assoc. prod.; Jean-Luc Godard and Jean-Pierre Gorin wrote and directed; Jacques Dugied, Olivier Girard and Jean-Luc Dugied designed the sets; music was by Eric Charden; Thomas Rivat and Paul Beuscher; Isabelle Pons was A.D.; Antoine Bonfanti and Bernard Ortion did the sound; and Kenout Peltier and Claudine Merlin edited

1 Initially *Tout Va Bien* was set up with the Xerox Corporation, and then with Paramount (B, 359).
2 The Paris cinema run was short.

the film. The DPs were Armand Marco, Yves Agostini and Edouard Burgess (filmed on Eastmancolor stock in 1.66 ratio). Principal photography ran from Dec, 1971 to Jan, 1972. Released: 1972.4.28 (in La France). 95 mins.

In the cast were Vittorio Caprioli, Elizabeth Chauvin, Castel Casti, Éric Chartier, Louis Bugette, Yves Gabrielli, Pierre Oudrey, Jean Pignol, Anne Wiazemsky, Didier Gaudron, Hugette Mieville and Cristiana Tullio-Altan (some of the actors had appeared in the previous Dziga Vertov Group films).

Jane Fonda disagreed about some of the movie's politics, and required some convincing to do it. According to the star's memoirs, she agreed initially because Jean-Luc Godard was one of the few political filmmakers around; but when she found out about the content of the script, she wanted to leave. In the end, Fonda said she did the work, kept her head down, and tried not to cause any trouble with the Maestro.

You can see the thinking behind *All's Well:* to produce a more audience-friendly feature-length version of the political/ Dziga Vertov Group films, and whole political experiment and ideological explorations of the past five years. So, your story stages a strike – an event that creates a dramatic structure (the beginnings of the strike, the conflicting views of it, the escalation of political activity, and the return to work). A strike is a pretext for discussing all of the left-wing notions you fancy – the relation between workers and bosses, the role of capitalism in contemporary society, the relation between labour and living, how capitalism structures contemporary society, identity, psychology, etc, how socialist principles operate in a real, practical situation, and how the class struggle is unfolding in the wake of the civil and political debates of May, 1968.

Then you plonk two well-known stars into the middle of it. The initial scenario is simple: they get caught up in the strike. Doesn't matter how – they will be the audience's observer figures for what the film *really* wants to discuss: not the romantic relationship of the couple, but the situation of the workers at the factory.

❂

Jean-Luc Godard was ill at the time of making *Tout Va Bien*, recovering from his near-fatal motorcycle accident in June, 1971 (he was a passenger on the bike with Christine Marsollier). Godard was in a coma for nearly a month (some said a week); he suffered many internal injuries, a fractured skull and a broken pelvis. He was in and out of hospital for months afterwards. Jean-Pierre Gorin said he wrote most of the dialogue, and much of the structure, but Godard was on set all of the time. (*All's Well* is thus not 'a Jean-Luc Godard film' like many of his previous outings; not only was it a co-conceived and co-directed piece, Godard was also at a low point, recovering from being in a coma. Even so, *All's Well* is made in the shadow of Godard, so to speak, under the spell of Godard, and in a thoroughly Godardian manner).

There was tension on the set between the two Annes in Godard's life: Anne Wiazemsky and Anne-Marie Miéville, the Wife and the Future Girlfriend of the Director – Godard wanted Wiazemsky to appear in three parts in *Tout Va Bien* (presumably as one of the strikers,[3] and perhaps as one of the victims of the May, 1968 scenes), but Gorin and Miéville weren't keen; and when Wiazemsky suggested that she do the on-set photography, Miéville insisted that *she* could do it (B, 361). In the end, Wiazemsky appeared in the Carrefour hypermarket sequence (by the far the best in the movie, and the crowning achievement of the political films of the 1968-1973 era).

❂

3 Notice that among the strikers in the factory there is a woman who resembles Wiazamesky, complete with the trademark very long brown hair.

All's Well was a meditation on what May, 1968 meant, its influence, how to incorporate its impact into contemporary life; it was also a History of France between 1968 and 1972 (the opening captions flash up 'May, 1968' and 'May, 1972'); and like the other Dziga Vertov Group films, *All's Well* explored left-wing ideology and politics, and topics such as strikes, workers, bosses, capitalism, consumerism, the class struggle, Marxism, Leninism, and the dreaded, loathed and demonized bourgeoisie.

The first half of the 1972 film concentrated on a workers' strike at a factory, in which the boss (Vittorio Capprioli)[4] and two visitors (Jane Fonda and Yves Montand) are held hostage by the strikers. (The film orchestrated three social forces, according to Godard – the management and the factory boss, the Communist Party, and the left-wing).

The factory boss is a buffoon – of course – which automatically shifts our sympathies to the downtrodden workers (the manager is another of the little, Italian prima donnas that Godard liked to satirize – usually they're film producers of the Carlo Ponti/ Dino de Laurentiis type).

Prior to the strike (where the 'story' starts), *All's Well* set up the world of the narrative in a familiar Godardian fashion: take a man and a woman, a city, the working class, the bourgeoisie, the workers, a factory, and proceed to make a film. The Prologue, narrated by a man and a woman heard later on but never seen (the usual Inidentified Voices Off of the 1968-1973 political films), consisted of the filmmaking process being examined in a self-conscious, Brechtian manner (for Jean-Pierre Gorin, *All's Well* was a film of Brechtian realism, not bourgeois realism. Bertholt Brecht remarked that 'realism doesn't consist in reproducing reality, but in showing how things *really* are'. This was one of Godard's favourite Brecht quotes).

4 A Brechtian actor and film director.

Only a Jean-Luc Godard film would begin with the film director signing bank cheques in close-up for each of the departments and services a modern film requires: opticals, laboratories, crew, insurance, etc. Has any other film ever shown the director signing the cheques that pay for everything in a film? Completely outrageous, and totally Godard.

The star images of Jane Fonda and Yves Montand were discussed (films must have stars to obtain financing, runs the movie's commentary), as were other aspects of contemporary entertainment cinema (such as having a story, romantic interest, the 'Him' and the 'Her' of many Godard movies, etc. That's the addition of commercial cinema, a love story, with stars, because a film just about strikes and workers and left-wing politics wouldn't reach the intended audience. The picture acknowledges the necessity of banal elements such as a love story but really doesn't want to be bothered with them. We see vignettes which illustrate the voiceover).

The Prologue of *All's Well* is also an apology to the sections of the film's audience (the young militants) who were expecting a truly left-wing, politically incisive movie: *All's Well* apologizes that it has to use movie stars to raise money and attract an audience.

All's Well is thus yet another of Jean-Luc Godard's many films about films, films about how films are made – and with a romantic couple at the centre. (Godard had already delivered this theme in *Contempt* and others, and would go on to rehash the scenario in pictures such as *Passion*, one of his most elegant and convincing versions of the theme. Making a movie plus a love affair – cinema and love – that's enough to keep Godard going for centuries of filmmaking).

All's Well was meant to be a 'love story', but also a break-up (of course – a happy, affectionate couple wouldn't work in this picture. So it's yet another of Godard's stories of a relationship in crisis). It was about the relationship between the lovers,[5] but also between themselves and production, how they're defined by their work, and the lovers and the social realm. (Romantic love and labour is another of Godard's recurring themes, which he would return to many times after 1972).

Jane Fonda and Yves Montand appear in the exposition Prologue of *All's Well*; we see brief vignettes of them at work (Montand watching rushes of a Remington shaving ad in a screening room,[6] echoing the famous scene in *Contempt,* and Fonda as a foreign correspondent doing a V.O. for the American Broadcasting System at a mic in a recording studio), but they are only on the fringes of the strike sequence; so that most of the first thirty minutes of *All's Well* comprises political monologues and scenes of irate workers. The approach seems designed to alienate a general audience (beyond Brechtian alienation effects), to be anti-entertainment or 'anti-bourgoise'.

All's Well's Prologue includes a fleeting scene of Jane Fonda and Yves Montand walking together – the dialogue is self-consciously ultra-banal (along the lines of 'what do you love about me?'). Of course 'He' mentions 'Her' body, mouth, ass, etc. The duologue is a reprise of several moments in Godard's previous work, including of course *Contempt* (the 1963 movie is referenced several times in *All's Well*; it seems to slyly dig at having to hire famous stars, just as *Contempt* seemed to rebel against using stars like Brigitte Bardot, by subverting the way that a conventional movie would film said star).

---

5 Instead of showing the sexual side of the relationship, the film offers photographs (Susan holds up a photo of a penis). This might be influenced by *Persona* (*Persona*'s main titles featured an erection).

6 This sequence is distinctly Godardian, with its images of a men's shaver commercial where a guy tests different razors by rubbing his cheek on a woman's naked *cul.* A reference to women's asses also occurs in the banal dialogue introducing the couple.

The strike in *All's Well* was staged on a giant, cutaway set of two floors of the factory's administration building (the Chief Executive Offier's office, the outer administration office, and so on, with neon signs added), covered in slow, lateral tracking shots. It was an *hommage* to the films of Jerry Lewis (*The Ladies' Man*, 1961) – Godard was a big Lewis fan (Lewis is regarded as a titan for French *cinéastes*). As in *Weekend*, members of the cast performed lengthy monologues to camera (several are reading from idiot boards,[7] or holding the script; Godard can get away with that).

✪

By the end of the first half of *All's Well*, then, the viewer had been exposed to a rigorous exploration of left-wing politics and strike action, investigated in great detail in the monologues. Socialism, Marxism, Communism and other left-wing ideologies were analyzed in a generally solemn, semi-documentary fashion.

The factory was a Salumi sausage factory: the workers sport white coats with blood stains on the front (unsubtle commentary on exploitation – and the usual symbolic links between meat/ food, survival, killing and eating, pigs and capitalists, etc). There are images of people at work which Jean-Luc Godard favours, and once again an emphasis on the dehumanizing nature of manual labour, on labour as slavery. There's plenty of Godardian to-ing and fro-ing in the cutaway set as the strike continues (with many scenes of angry pushing and shoving, as people try to cross the lines).

We see/ hear several monologues to-camera in the strike section of *All's Well* – from the C.E.O., the shop steward, the workers, etc. Immediately you are struck by a notably different acting style – a much more conventional perform-ance style, a traditional, theatrical manner – which doesn't fit with the rest of Godard's political cinema of the period at all. It

7 Even a professional actor like Yves Montand does it (during his monologue).

presents a different kind of awkward behaviour, self-conscious in a different way. (Vittorio Capprioli's turn as the C.E.O. is completely out of place in *Tout Va Bien*).

More Godardian are the stylized cutaways to other members of the strike force, who're listening to the monologues (echoing the approach of *Weekend*, where one guy talked, but it was off-screen – we watched a different guy in close-up), and arranged in *tableaux*.

The problem with *Tout Va Bien* in its depiction of the strike is that it *is* bourgeois, despite its efforts to be non-bourgeois and pro-Brechtian: it's too straight, too conventional – well, 'conventional', that is, after we've seen what Jean-Luc Godard can do in cinema in the previous fourteen years! *All's Well* is too literal, too immature, too much like what a bunch of students *think* political cinema or political theatre might be.

I've seen *All's Well* several times, but watching it after going through nearly all of Godard's work up to 1972, and every single feature film, in chronological order, *All's Well* seems a mere footnote, a re-hash of material that Godard had already filmed better elsewhere. Instead of trying to make a version of the 1968-1973 political works and the Dziga Vertov Group films that would appeal to a wider audience, Godard and Gorin could've made the Dziga Vertov Group/ political films more appealing in the first place! (*All's Well* is a missed opportunity; its potential is not fulfilled; and the material is squandered and frittered away).

✪

In the second half, *Tout Va Bien* opened out, and followed Yves Montand's Jacques and Jane Fonda's Susan in their daily lives – arguing at home, Susan recording news reports for A.B.S. (American Broadcasting System)[8] and

8 The film plays with multiple languages, as in *Contempt*, with Susan speaking in English and being translated into French. In her to-camera monologue, Susan speaks in American and a female voice translates in voiceover.

Jacques (named 'Cineaste') shooting an ultra-banal TV commercial for Dim Tights in a film studio (with dancing girls).

Yves Montand's character Jacques, as he explains in a long to-camera speech (in a break during the filming of the television ad), in response to off-camera questions (Jean-Pierre Gorin said it was Montand's best performance on film), was once a *Nouvelle Vague* director, but is now firmly embedded in the capitalist system by making TV ads (a bitter swipe at some of Godard's contemporaries – Godard dubbed advertizing fascism.9 Hmmm, until the Master himself, the fervent former Maoist-Maxist, later directed TV commercials. And the Dziga Vertov Group had also produced a commercial – which was never shown, of course).

Some critics thought the speech was improvized. Eh? Don't they listen? It's not only clearly scripted, it's stuffed with Godardisms (refs. to Brecht, to the New Wave, to fellow French film directors, to May, 1968, etc). Actors *do not* make up their own dialogue in a Jean-Luc Godard movie!

All's Well played with Jane Fonda's star image as a political activist but also as a glamorous, Hollywood actress – *Barbarella, Klute,, Barefoot In the Park, The Chase, They Shoot Horses, Don't They?*, etc (Fonda was well-known for her outspoken critique of Imperialist Amerika, in which she exploited her fame as a platform for protesting against the Vietnam War; she was dubbed 'Hanoi Jane').

As well as Jane Fonda working at the American Broadcasting System service in Paris and Yves Montand in his film studio, the second half of *All's Well* also recreated some of the events of May, 1968 (specifically, the protests which turned ugly, involving riot police storming students).

The staging of these scenes was a little shoddy, reducing incendiary material to an amateur level (compare

9 Such as François Truffaut, who had sold out, according to Godard.

them with the footage of the real riots included in *A Film Like the Others*). Yet there are more extras, and more ingredients to these scenes than in many Godard films. Looking closer at how these scenes were mounted, they look like they were directed by Gorin or someone else, not the Maestro. Besides, Godard seldom includes fleshed-out flashbacks like this in any of his films. A Godard movie that raised the issue of the events of May, 1968 in France (or any historical event) would do so within dialogue, or at most with photographs (or with the newsreel in *A Film Like the Others*). For example, in *The Little Soldier*, the hero Bruno Forestier tells a long story about the French Resistance. Godard could've illustrated the story with an acted-out flashback, but he didn't, and he hardly ever does.

And, in another Godardian bid for padding out the running time, *All's Well* cleverly recycled material we'd already seen (couched under the guise of discussions of the strike at the sausage factory – which had by then *already* used the same shots twice).[10] Plus, the 1968 recreations used the same shots twice. And more recycling occurred during the domestic spat. And, in a somewhat desperate effort to find something for Jane Fonda to do, the film features a lengthy take or two of her, while we hear dialogue and/ or scenes offscreen (sometimes she turns to look at the camera). Well, I guess that's one way of featuring your (expensive) star– leave the camera on her while Voices Off tell the story or deliver the message. Then you sort justify to yourself that the star is featured in the movie.

❂

A mid-film section of *All's Well* explored the working conditions of the sausage factory, with scenes of delivering animal carcasses, preparing meat, packaging it, etc. The voiceover added explanations of what we're seeing. Godard

10 Part of this is justified as Marxist self-criticism.

has been fond of filming people at work throughout his career (even when it's not part of a burning ideological rant).

These scenes were inserted around the halfway point, when the bourgeois couple were released, the strike was over, and the workers went back to work. *All's Well* was keen to detail the working conditions at the factory – the number of breaks the workers had, for example, and the strict adherence to working hours. (In a crude send-up of this issue, the manager is desperate for the restroom, but the workers fill up the bathrooms or send him the wrong way. And while he's busting for relief, they inform him of the breaks they are allowed on the factory floor).

Along the way, *All's Well* featured the customary Godardian settings (a factory, a gas station, an enormous building site, roadsides), and the familiar Godardian techniques (live sound, sudden silences, multiple voices off, music suddenly stopping and starting, etc).

❂

The domestic scenes in *All's Well*, of 'Him' and 'Her', don't convince, are indifferently staged and performed, and aren't particularly interesting (there isn't much chemistry between Jane Fonda and Yves Montand – they don't convince as lovers). The film as political-ideological text doesn't want or need the pandering to stardom (casting stars), isn't interested in them, can't be bothered to write a decent erotic-psychological narrative for them, and winds up their 'story' or relationship with a sad, inconsequential meeting in a café. Jean-Luc Godard, for one, had been here many times before; and yet, as he admits, he kept coming back to stories or scenes of 'Her' and 'Him' many times after 1972 and *Tout Va Bien*.

The weary, bickering acting style of the relationship scenes in *All's Well* is too easy, and too much like what actors think that they should be doing in a Godard movie. This increasingly became the default performance style in a Godard movie (you see it in *Passion*, in *Slow Motion,* in *First Name: Carmen* and the later films). Or is it the influence of Anne-Marie Miélville?

We have Susan's bitter complaints about how Jacques views their relationship (played largely on close-ups of Jane Fonda); we have Susan finding recording her material frustrating; and we have Susan voicing quasi-feminist views (which would crop up many times in later Godard movies).

The domestic/ psychological/ quasi-romantic subplot of 'Him' and 'Her' in *All's Well* isn't integrated satisfyingly into the movie (the voiceover kind of admits that). *All's Well* stages a strike, recreations of May, 1968, discussions of left-wing/ socialist/ communist politics and ideology, and decon-structions of capitalism – and yet it wants to put a relationship-falling-apart subplot in there! With two film stars! (You can see how the script could be re-structured: you put the scenes of the relationship falling apart *before* the strike, so that when we visit the factory, we already know 'Him' and 'Her'. But then it becomes *their* story, how *they* react to the strike at the factory. It has more dramatic impact for the workers who're striking that we meet them *along with* the two film stars).

❂

Godard and Gorin saved the best 'til last in *All's Well*: it's a masterpiece sequence shot, a work of genius, one of the greatest shots in recent cinema, hitting social, economic, ideological, psychological, cultural and cinematic targets with absolute self-assurance and skill. If the rest of Godard's political films of 1968 to 1973 and the Dziga Vertov Group films were at this level, we would have one of the greatest series of political works in all cinema.

It's a wonderful scene staged in a Carrefour hype-rmarket, covered in a single 9.5 minute take. The camera drifts back and forth laterally behind a row of customers, cashiers and check-outs; Jane Fonda wanders up and down (the camera follows her for much of the shot), making notes and speaking a waspish commentary in voiceover (partly reacting to the events); the camera passes a man loudly recruiting for the French branch of the Communist Party, selling subscriptions and Communist Party books at a knock-down price (F 4.75, down from F 5.50!). He reads out passages from the book.[11] It's a great piece of comedy, carefully staged, ending in a Buster Keaton *melée*, as student protesters rush in, closely followed by the riot police.

Anne Wiazemsky leads the young radicals subverting capitalism's operation of consumption, bursting in from the back of the store; at first the militant youths hurry over to the Communist Party guy, and soon argue with him (thus, they might be Gauchists, but they don't align themselves automatically with Communism, or French Communism). Wiazemsky is incensed that the Communist Party book seller is unable to answer a question posed by one of her crew. This leads to a loud argument.

Anne Wiazmensky is foremost among those crying, 'it's free!' and 'help yourself!', and giving out goods to shoppers. The activists encourage customers to take their shopping carts from the check-outs towards the exit without paying. Food is thrown about. The range of reactions runs from people not sure what to do, some are bemused when the militants start to fling things off the shelves into their shopping carts, to others who head straight for the exits. The police enter the fray towards the end of the sequence, and attack some activists. It's glorious.

All of the critique of consumer capitalism is contained in the images of the camera drifting past endless check-outs

11 Anne Wiazemsky and her chums argue with the Communist Party guy. Wiazemsky demands that the guy explains what he's talking about. He sees them as trouble-makers (which they are).

and the consumers with their shopping carts of goods. The cash registers chime non-stop. Nothing more is required: the shot says it all. The mindless consumerism of capitalism and its endless bounty of consumer goods and the banality of it all and the moronic stupor of the people buying stuff and yet more stuff, has never been done better. (Susan remarks that the supermarket is just like a factory).[12] It's also extraordinary that even fifty years later supermarkets look *exactly the same*! The row of check-outs, the shelves of goods, the store layout, the interaction of the customers – it's all still the same!

This shot sums up all of Western consumerism in a single, brilliant image – more than the trash-but-hip films of Andy Warhol, or the polemical attacks on consumerism by Pier Paolo Pasolini (in *Salò, or 120 Days in Sodom*), or any number of radical, left-wing outings. (Even without the additional, performance art-style bits of business, the shot is dazzling, partly due to context within a film examining left-wing politics and ideology.)

But *Tout Va Bien* is a politicized piece of cinema, and the additions of the guy zealously selling Communism, or the descent into chaos, as the protestors clash with the police, with the consumers caught up in the middle, add narrative elements to the sequence, dramatizing the pro-leftist ideology.

But Godard and Gorin's tight formal control of this set-piece is also what makes it really work. There's something about the lateral tracking shot device here that gives the sequence its magical tension and comedy, the way that it contains at first the regimented lines of check-outs, cashiers, cash tills and consumers, and then the chaotic battle between police and protestors. That it's a sequence shot is vital: the scene could be covered in the conventional manner (breaking it down into short shots), but the long take gives the scene

12 True – but Godard relates lots of organizations and buildings to factories.

such energy and tension. While *All's Well* was apparently directed largely by Gorin, shots like this are totally Godard (it's full of numerous Godardian touches). If only all of the 1968-1973 political films and the Dziga Vertov Group works had been as good as this.

❂

Go to any industrialized part of the world and you'll soon find the environment which the filmmakers selected for the ending of *All's Well*: shabby waste ground, abandoned industrial buildings, and those in-between zones on the edge of every town on the planet.

All's Well might've ended more satisfyingly with the Carrefour supermarket shot, but it opted for a coda: a summing-up of the film (using the male and female narrators from the Prologue), indications of the continuation of the class struggle in La France, and snippets from earlier scenes (including soundbites).

All of this played over another lengthy tracking shot (this one seemingly taken from a slow-moving train. Oh no! A train! Wait — not *that* sort of train? Don't tell me that a modern, capitalist society leads to the cattle trucks!).

Meanwhile, the 'He' and 'She' theme, featuring Fonda and Montand, reached a non-conclusion, as they meet in a café, with nothing much to say.

LETTER TO JANE

You didn't contribute enough donations to the Communist Party, did you?

You didn't hand out those Marxist-Leninist leaflets as you promised, did you?

You didn't class-struggle enough, did you?

You didn't instigate mayhem and strikes at your workplace, did you?

This film (in 52 very long minutes) will remind you again what you have to do.

The companion piece to *All's Well* was *Letter To Jane* (1972), a vitriolic assault on Jane Fonda, comprising a commentary over a still image of Fonda in Vietnam during the Vietnam War which appeared in *L'Express*, taken by Joseph Kraft (as well as a slideshow from *The Grapes of Wrath, All's Well, Klute, The Magnificent Ambersons*, and others, including Vladimir Lenin and Mao Zedong, of course).

Was *Letter To Jane* serious? A joke? For some it would be a nasty and childish trick to play on the star of your latest film. According to Jean-Pierre Gorin, it wasn't a 'letter' to a film star (change the title, then!), but a disquisition on photography, on the media image, on how images relates to politics and to texts.

Letter To Jane is a lecture, or a rant, or a series of questions, in the manner of the Dziga Vertov Group films (remember those? – where the films insisted: keep asking questions, keep struggling, keep supplying us with cigarettes, etc).

Godard and Gorin take turns to read out aloud the sacred text they've prepared. If you've seen the Dziga Vertov Group films already, you won't find anything new here. If you don't know the political movies, this will seem a strange form of presentation – two men reading from an essay while we look at a picture of a film star, or at still frames taken from the movie in question, *Tout Va Bien* (and one or two other photos). Thus, *Letter To Jane* is hard-going, just like the Dziga Vertov Group works.

So it's hairshirt time, it's get on your knees on the cold, stone floor of your monk's cell time, it's ten hours in solitary confinement time.

✿

The Two G.s circle around the concept of the photograph of Jane Fonda many times: they return to it, they can't leave it alone. They change their mode of address – instead of talking to the audience, they send part of their diatribe towards Jane Fonda herself. (They also hope that she will respond. Did she? I very much doubt it!).

For variety in this over-long political rant, the filmmakers re-frame the photo several times; they also lamely add lots of black leader, the go-to padding for the political films of 1968-1973. (*What do we do now, Jean-Luc? Oh, cut in some more black leader, and I'll repeat a phrase, I'll repeat a phrase*).

✿

Letter To Jane is a continuation of the political films of the 1968-1973 period for Jean-Luc Godard and Jean-Pierre Gorin. And it also resembles a college essay for a politics course. Gorin went to university, but Godard didn't – is this film and the other political films of 68-73 a kind of stand-in or replacement for Godard's lost university years? Maybe this is a (guilt-ridden) equivalent for his post-graduate studies in *Left-Wing Ideology*? Or is it his course of 12 adult education classes in *Marxism And Maoism the Easy Way* (Wednesday nights, 19.00-21.00)?

Certainly, sections of *Letter To Jane* resemble the too-earnest scribblings of a keen but misguided politics student, the fruit of hours dedicated to intense political discussions in a Left Bank café (they can only afford one cup of coffee, so they nurse it for hours), in between visits to the cinema and ogling girls.

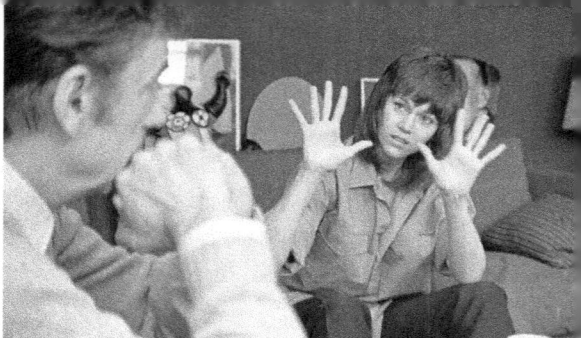

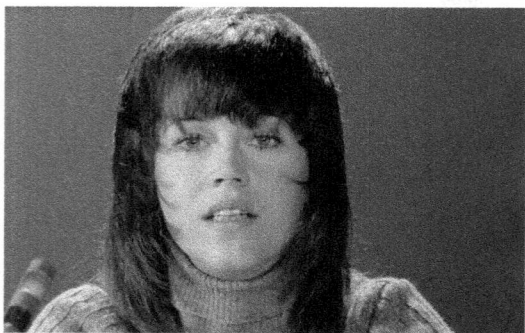

All's Well (1972)

TODO VA BIEN

Letter To Jane (1972).

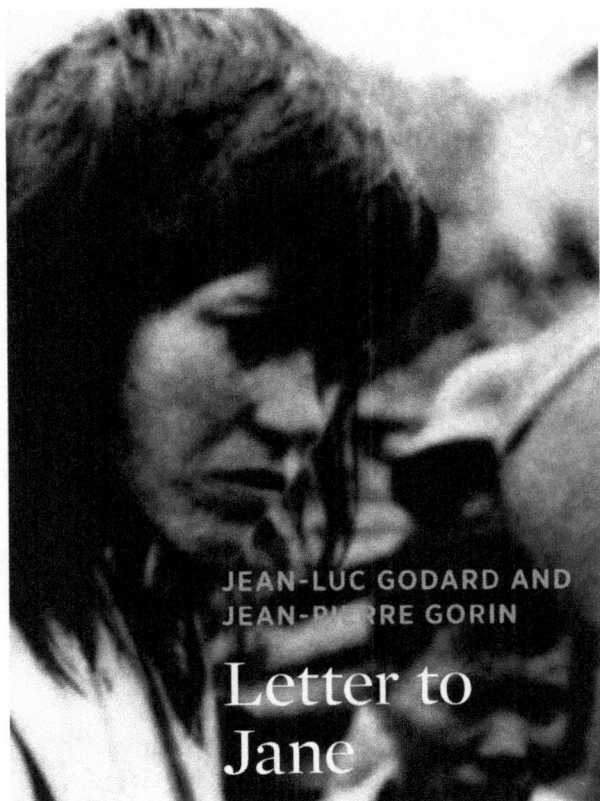

APPENDICES

FILM AVAILABILITY

Many of the key films directed by Jean-Luc Godard —
Breathless, Weekend, Passion, Pierrot Le Fou, etc — are
available on video and DVD (with some more recently coming
out on Blu-ray). But a large number of television and video
projects are not available in any of the usual places. Much of
Godard's work in TV and video in the 1970s remains largely
unknown (and there is a *lot* of it).

There are of course many differences in the editions, in
key areas such as dubbing and subtitles. In general, the
original language versions are always the ones to go for, or
any dub which Godard oversaw. (For instance, the *Contempt*
DVD contains a terrible English language dub).

I would recommend always watching a movie in the
original language, if possible. Some critics have noted that
subtitles don't do justice to works like *Histoire(s) du Cinéma.*
You just have to accept that. It doesn't matter if you don't
speak French, either: sit back and enjoy a genius at the height
of his powers creating a work unlike anything else in the
history of anything.

The following are the main distributors to try first:

In the U.S.A.: Criterion. Lionsgate. Wellspring Media.

In Britain and Europe: Studio Canal. Artificial Eye.
Optimum Home Entertainment. Nouveaux Pictures. Umbrella
Entertainment.

GODARDISMS

- 'This life is either nothing, or it has to be everything'.

- 'Everyone is searching. Everyone is in between'.

- 'Things are right in front of us. Why make them up?'

- 'It's necessary to struggle on two fronts at the same time'.

- 'You can only think of something if you think of something else'.

- 'Partout c'est beau' ('everywhere is beautiful').

- 'We're jesters. We out-live our problems'.

- 'Everyday you live moments that seem exceptional'.

- 'When one of my character says 'I love you', the 'I' is taken from one context, the 'love' from another and the 'you' from a third'.

- 'To show and to show myself showing'.

- 'I have no ideas'.

- 'There is nothing invented in the cinema. All one can do in the cinema is observe and put in order that which one has seen *if* one has been able to see well'.

- 'Cinema is life'.

- 'Instead of making films, we'll make cinema'.

- 'Everything can be put into a film. Everything should be put into a film'.

- 'No matter where or when, the classics always work'.

- 'We're in an old part of the universe, where nothing happens'.

- 'Every desire must meet its lassitude, its truth'.

- 'Orgasm is the only moment when you can't cheat life'.

- 'Advertizing is a form of fascism'.
- 'If I speak of time, it has gone already'.

THE BEST OF GODARD

Jean-Luc Godard produced his top ten lists in his film criticism for each year (i.e., the best of 1963: *Le Procès de Jeanne d'Arc, The Exterminating Angel, The Birds, The Nutty Professor*, etc), so here's two Godard lists:

SOME OF THE BEST GODARD MOMENTS

(20 best moments – in no particular order)

1. Joseph touching Mary's belly in *Hail Mary*.

2. Marianne and Ferdinand on the beach in *Pierrot le Fou*.

3. Marianne and Ferdinand dancing and singing in *Pierrot le Fou*.

4. The night of love poetry in *Alphaville*.

5. The Madison dance in *Bande à Part*.

6. The traffic jam in *Weekend*.

7. Nana in the cinema in *Vivre Sa Vie*.

8. Angéla and Emile communicating with book covers in *A Woman Is a Woman*.

9. Paul in the shopping mall in *Masculin Féminin*.

10. Michel and Patricia on the Champs-Élysées in *Breathless*.

11. The *tableaux* of paintings in *Passion*.

12. The cosmic coffee cup in *Two or Three Things I*

Know About Her.

13. The quoting from books scene in *Two or Three Things I Know About Her.*

14. The supermarket sequence in *Tout Va Bien.*

15. The Italian cinema montage in *Histoire(s) du Cinéma.*

16. The war montage in *Notre Musique.*

17. The porn and paperback bookstore scene in *One Plus One.*

18. The dance of hands in *A Married Woman.*

19. The projection room scene in *Contempt.*

20. Worshipping Brigitte Bardot in *Contempt.*

TEN BEST GODARD FILMS

(In no particular order)

1. *Hail Mary*
2. *Pierrot le Fou*
3. *Bande à Part*
4. *Weekend*
5. *Two or Three Things I Know About Her*
6. *Passion*
7. *Vivre Sa Vie*
8. *Contempt*
9. *Masculin Féminin*
10. *La Chinoise*

INGREDIENTS FOR
A GODARD MOVIE

To make a Jean-Luc Godard movie, you will need:

- scenes in cinemas, nightclubs, bars, cafés and hotels
- characters undressing
- nude women[1]
- characters discussing sex and love
- sudden alterations in sound, from local sound to silence
- very loud sounds
- the background sound - in cafés for example – almost drowning out dialogue
- music fading in abruptly then disappearing
- classical music; contemporary new music; cheesy pop songs
- poetic dialogue, including quotes from classic poets
- characters reading aloud from books
- attacks on North Amerika, capitalism, war, the Vietnam War, politics
- off-screen gunshots
- guns
- cars (big Yank cars, Alfa Romeos, 2CVs, a Mercedes)
- cameras (characters carrying cameras)
- tape recorders
- tins of red, blue and yellow paint
- coloured filters for the camera

---

1 Tell the actors that nudity is required *before* you ask them to undress on set.

- characters quoting from Hollywood movies

- snatches of pop songs (don't worry about copyright: just go ahead!)

- quotations from movies (again, don't let rights issues stop you!)

- characters suddenly looking into the camera

- characters breaking out into dances

- characters hunched over pinball machines or juke-boxes

- characters eternally smoking, lighting up cigarettes, asking people for cigarettes

- characters in bathrooms, looking in mirrors

- characters fiddling with their hair

- jump cuts

- tracking shots along walls, cafes or traffic jams

- the camera dollying in and out unmotivated, or panning slowly around a room

- actors being interviewed

- close-ups of money changing hands

- the camera panning over posters, billboards, post-cards, book covers, magazine covers

- philosophical, humorous and graphic intertitles, often edited musically

- shots of workers and factories

- a Métro scene

- tracking shots from the windows of cars around Paris

- handheld shots of characters walking Paris's streets.

- a variety of voiceovers, including by the director

- silly accents

- characters dressing up as figures from history and literature

FANS ON THE FILMS OF JEAN-LUC GODARD

Extracts from online reviews of Jean-Luc Godard's movies.

GODARD PAGE ON FACEBOOK

He is a poetic genius, I love all his work but esp his collabs w/ Anna Karina!

•

Said what I said.... JLG ...great influence on my thoughts & intellectual life...

•

All my admiration, appreciation, let's say LOVE, for your creative life, films, courage and perseverance... Long Live Godard

•

Sartre du Cinéma

•

GODARD... LE CINEMA!

•

Je vous salue Godardiens....

AMAZON.COM

Regardless of how the mystique is generated, *Breathless* provides a wonderful cinematic experience, as it is full of surprises and leaves the audience in a breathtaking, yet quirky visual journey.

•

My Life to Live is a truly remarkable film: a synthesis of artistic vision and moral tale, suffused with haunting melody, the ballad of a contemporary tragedy.

•

Band of Outsiders is playful, wondrous, hilarious, breezy, but at the same time melancholic, dark in its undertones.

•

Band of Outsiders is a really, really great movie. Simple, minimalist, and very expressive.

ON *PIERROT LE FOU*

PIERROT is one of the few examples of true mystical cinema that we have.

•

Pierrot le Fou is the most beautiful movie I have ever seen.

•

What I love about the two Godard/ Belmondo films (*Breathless* and *Pierrot le Fou*) is the marriage of the sacred and profane, the comic and the tragic, the high and the low. Only true masters achieve a world view that encompasses so much of life... It's a very funny film in parts and a very sad film in other parts and even a bit mystical toward the end. It's a poignant elegy for the brevity of all things.

•

As for Belmondo, the screen has never been visited by a cooler presence since the days of Bogart. Anna Karina, on the other hand, seems to have the ability to swallow the earth and all it contains through her magnificently large eyes.

•

Give *Pierrot le Fou* a shot, it defied everything I thought it would be. I don't think I'll ever see anything else like it.

•

Godard is wonderfully inventive in his use of language, situations, visuals, images. He inspires me. One of my favorite parts of *Pierrot le Fou* is the scene in which Jean-Paul and Anna romp through a forest, hand-in-hand, improvising lyrics (my own romantic fantasy).

•

It is fresh, it is exciting, it is dangerous, it is meaningful, and it is loud, abrasive and epic in every sense of the word. It is cinema; cut, paste and send.

•

Godard's *Pierrot le Fou* is one of the most successful comedy/ tragedy/ political/ crime-thriller/ musicals he ever made. It breaks all the rules, as all his movies do, but plays with such gusto and joie de vivre to keep any audience in their seat until the end.

ON *CONTEMPT*

Contempt is Jean-Luc Godard's masterpiece, and quite possibly the best film of the 60s. The film has so many layers and meanings, one viewing is not enough.

•

This is a superior film to *Breathless*, IMHO... the film is total eye candy, if not due to the awesome BB, then by the gorgeous locations...

•

A truly haunting movie. A must-see Godard classic.

•

What a great movie this is and I saw it 20 times.

ON *HAIL MARY*

Hail Mary is perhaps Godard's most spiritual film and it can be quite lyrical as it attempts to tell the story of the Annunciation in a modern setting... Godard uses the film to contrast pure love with love of the flesh and does quite a good job. So why only three stars? Godard's film moves at a glacial pace and his difficult philosophy is on display in its most brutal form. There are moments of complete confusion for the viewer as one tries to sort it all out.

•

To see this movie when it screened in Boston, I had to cross a picket line set up by the SLAVES OF THE IMMACULATE HEART OF MARY, the vestiges of a rabid right wing anti-semitic movement headed by the radio personality Father Coughlin (father of hate radio) in the 1930s.

It was worth it to see what was arguably Godard's most beautiful film. Like most really smart people, Godard is only about 20% right, but that beats the 2% average for the rest of us. Godard's musings on the Rubik cube as an argument for intelligent design are crap, but the tension between Mary's conflicted maternal sexuality and Joseph's subjugated male sexuality are as primordial as the blues and every bit as poetic. The gynecological exam (much more humane in France than the US) that validates her prepartum virginity throws arguments about physical purity into the pit of absurdity where they belong.

•

'Hail Mary' released in 1985 is quite likely the most controversial film of the 20th century. Banned by the Catholic Church for its raw and sometimes scathing modern day depiction of the Virgin Mary, I believe this is a movie whose time has finally come and will soon be recognized as the classic it truly is. After listening to all the ranting and raving condemning this film you will surely be surprised, and I hope delighted, by what you experience when you finally watch it.

AT THE INTERNET MOVIE DATABASE

ON *PASSION*

I found the film compelling and intriguing; I wanted to know more about the people and the universe that they populated. The lack of narrative structure was not a negative factor in my enjoyment of the film, for the anarchic content was, of itself, enough to keep my mind from wandering away from it. Godard's reflexive jibes at cinema convention were acerbic and witty, carrying with them a tremendous knowledge of the mechanics of filmmaking. The story of *Passion*, what story there is, is subservient to the process of filmmaking and Godard's desire to subvert it. For me, that is what makes this film so entertaining.

●

The characters' aggressive tussling, either through physical pulling and pushing or through their cars (reminiscent of Godard's masterpiece *Weekend*), also signify the difficulty and pain inherent in any kind of birth. The quiet moments call out to be examined and celebrated as much as the grand statements while others jostle for their money, their moment, or even a simple explanation as to what it all means.

●

Like most of Godard's late work, this mosaic approach will not appeal to all who cross its path (what film ever does?) but, even if it does ultimately fall short of answering any of the questions it asks, adherents will find much to ruminate on.

●

Godard's *Passion* is a puzzle, and Delacroix's *The Entry of the Crusaders into Constantinople* is a puzzle with historical information behind it. I'd have to say that watching Godard's *Passion* was like being spoon-fed personal beliefs; not a work, but his philosophy. But, I liked it.

●

Jean-Luc Godard makes me think clearer. After having read the other comments accusing *Passion* of being boring and pretentious crap, I can only say that I strongly disagree. Comments like those just make me angry. JLG's films are definitely not boring; unless you are completely unintellectual and don't have a clue of what is going on. *Passion* and JLG's other films are fresh and intellectual and philosophic. Godard is unique.

AT I.G.N. BOARDS

He made me love movies.

•

Pierret Le Fou and *Contempt* are my two favorites by a long shot.

•

Definitely, definitely give all his 60's films a shot. He had one of the most indisputably great directorial runs ever.

AT METACRITIC.COM

ON *NOTRE MUSIQUE*

No review necessary. He is the greatest French filmmaker since Bresson, and certainly the most profound and influential of the past 50 years. See this movie at all costs if it is playing anywhere within 50 miles of you.

•

Sublime, dense and illuminating. Godard's creates a symphonic fugue of parallels and associations, dualities and ironies, struggling towards the light.

•

I give Maestro Godard a 10-infinity for this masterpiece. Forever the experimentalist, he creates a symphonic fragment that also seems like a visual jaunt through Faulkner's *Sound and Fury*. It is a provocative examination of reality and something else.

•

Spectacular!! GODard is GOD of cinema!!

FILMOGRAPHY

The chief works of Jean-Luc Godard as film and TV director.

    Breathless (1960), a.k.a. *À Bout de souffle*
    The Little Soldier (1960/ 63), a.k.a. *Le Petit Soldat*
    A Woman Is a Woman (1961), a.k.a. *Une femme est une femme*
    My Life to Live 1962), a.k.a. *Vivre sa Vie*
    Contempt (1963), a.k.a. *Le Mépris*
    The Soldiers (1963), a.k.a. *Les Carabiniers*
    Band of Outsiders (1964), a.k.a. *Bande à part*
    A Married Woman (1964), a.k.a. *Une femme mariée*
    Crazy Pete (1965), a.k.a. *Pierrot le Fou*
    Alphaville: A Strange Adventure of Lemmy Caution (1965), a.k.a. *Alphaville, une étrange aventure de Lemmy Caution*
    Made in U.S.A. (1966)
    Masculine, Feminine (1966), a.k.a. *Masculin féminin: 15 faits précis*
    Two of Three Things I Know About Her (1967), a.k.a. *2 ou 3 choses que je sais d'elle*
    Weekend (1967), a.k.a. *Le Week-end*
    La Chinoise Or, More Actually, After the Fashion of the Chinese (1967), a.k.a. *La Chinoise, ou Plutôt à la Chinoise*
    One Plus One (1968), a.k.a. *Sympathy For the Devil*
    A Film Like Any Other (1968), a.k.a. *Un film comme les autres*
    Joy of Learning (1969), a.k.a. *Le gai savoir*
    The Wind From the East (1970), a.k.a. *Le vent d'est*
    British Sounds (1970), a.k.a. *See You at Mao*
    Pravda (1970)
    Vladimir and Rosa (1970), a.k.a. *Vladimir et Rosa*
    Struggle in Italy (1971), a.k.a. *Lotte in Italia*
    All's Well (1972), a.k.a. *Tout va bien*
    Number Two (1975), *Numéro deux*
    Here and Elsewhere (1976), a.k.a. *Ici et ailleurs*
    France/ Tour/ Detour/ Two Children (1977), *France/ tour/*

detour/ deux enfants

How's It Going? (1978), a.k.a. Comment ça va?

Scenario For Sauve Qui Peut La Vie (1980), a.k.a. Scénario de 'Sauve qui peut la vie'

Slow Motion (1980), a.k.a. Sauve qui peut (la vie)

Passion (1982)

First Name: Carmen (1983), a.k.a. Prénom Carmen

Detective (1985), a.k.a. Détective

Hail Mary (1985), a.k.a. Je vous salue, Marie

Soft and Hard (1986), a.k.a. A Soft Conversation Between Two Friends On a Hard Subject

Grandeur and Decadence (1986), a.k.a. Grandeur et décadence d'un petit commerce de cinéma (part of Série noire TV series)

Keep Your Right Up (1987), a.k.a. Soigne ta droite

King Lear (1987)

The Darty Report (1989), a.k.a. Le rapport Darty

New Wave (1990), a.k.a. Nouvelle vague

Germany Year 90 Nine Zero (1991), a.k.a. Allemagne 90 neuf zéro

Woe Is Me (1993), a.k.a. Hélas pour moi

The Children Plan Russian (1993), a.k.a. Les enfants jouent à la Russie

Hail, Sarajevo (1993), a.k.a. Je vous salue, Sarajevo

JLG By JLG (1995), a.k.a. JLG/ JLG – autoportrait de décembre

For Ever Mozart (1996)

Histor(ies) of Cinema (1998), a.k.a. Histoire(s) du cinéma

Origins of the 21st Century (2000), a.k.a. De l'origine du XXIe siècle

In Praise of Love (2001), a.k.a. Éloge de l'amour

Liberty and Homeland (2002), a.k.a. Liberté et patrie

Chosen Moments of Histoire(s) of Cinema (2004), a.k.a. Moments choisis des histoire(s) du cinéma

Our Music (2004), a.k.a. Notre musique

The True False Passport (2006), a.k.a. Vrai faux passeport

Socialism (2010), a.k.a. Film socialisme

Goodbye To Language (2014), a.k.a. Adieu au Langage

Bridges of Sarajevo (2014), a.k.a. Les Ponts de Sarajevo

The Image Book (2018), a.k.a. Le Livre d'Image

BIBLIOGRAPHY

BY JEAN-LUC GODARD

Vivre Sa Vie, in *L'Avant-Scène Cinéma*, 19, Oct, 1962

Jean-Luc Godard, ed. T. Mussman, Dutton, New York, NY, 1968

Alphaville, tr. P. Whitehead, Lorrimer, London, 1969

Introduction à une véritable histoire du cinéma, Editions Albatros, Paris, 1977

Godard On Godard, ed. A. Bergala, Cahiers du Cinéma, Paris, 1985

Revolution, 1, February, 1985

Godard On Godard, eds. J. Narobi & T. Milne, Da Capo, New York, NY, 1986

Interview, in R. Bellour, 1992

Interview, "Godard in His 'Fifth Period'", by K. Dieckmann, in M. Locke, 1993

Interview, Montréal Film Festival, 1995

Interviews, ed. D. Sterritt, University of Mississippi Press, Jackson, 1998

Godard On Godard 2, ed. A. Bergala, Cahiers du Cinéma, Paris, 1998

Histoire(s) du cinéma, Galimard-Gaumont, Paris, 1998

"An Audience With Uncle Jean-Luc", *The Guardian*, Feb 11, 2000

"The Godard Interview: I, A Man of the Image", with M. Witt, in M. Temple, 2004

OTHERS

R. Alder. *New York Times*, January 9, 1969

R. Altman, ed. *Sound Theory, Sound Practice*, Routledge, London, 1992

—. *Film/ Genre*, British Film Institute, London, 1999

D. Andrew. *The Major Film Theories*, Oxford University Press, Oxford, 1976

—. *Concepts In Film Theory*, Oxford University Press, Oxford,

1984

—. ed. *Breathless*, Rutgers University Press, New Brunswick, NJ, 1987

G. Andrew. *The Film Handbook*, Longman, London, 1989

R. Armes. *French Cinema,* Oxford University Press, Oxford, 1985

J. Aumont. "The Fall of the Gods: Jean-Luc Godard's *Le Mépris"*, in S. Hayward, 1990

—. *Amnésies: fictions de cinéma d'après Jean-Luc Godard*, P.O.L., Paris, 1999

G. Austin. *Contemporary French Cinema,* Manchester University Press, Manchester, 1996

M. Barker, ed. *The Video Nasties: Freedom and Censorship In the Media*, Pluto Press, London, 1984

—. & J. Petley, eds. *Ill Effects: The Media/ Violence Debate*, Routledge, London, 1997

S. Barrowclough. "Godard's Marie", *Sight & Sound*, 52, 2, Spring, 1985

R. Barthes. *The Pleasure of the Text*, Hill and Wang, New York, NY, 1975

—. *S/Z*, Hill and Wang, New York, NY, 1974

—. *Image, Music, Text*, tr. S. Heath, Fontana, London, 1984

G. Bataille. *Literature and Evil*, Calder & Boyars, London, 1973

—. *The Story of the Eye,* Penguin, London, 1982

L. Bawden, ed. *The Oxford Companion To Film*, Oxford University Press, Oxford, 1976

A. Bazin. *What Is Cinema?,* University of California Press, Berkeley, CA, 1960, 2 vols

—. "Cinema and Theology", *South Atlantic Quarterly*, 91, 2, 1992

M. Beja. *Film and Literature: An Introduction,* Longman, London, 1979

R. Bellour & M. Bandy, eds. *Jean-Luc Godard,* M.O.M.A., N.Y., 1992

A. Bergala. *Nul mieux que Godard*, Cahiers du Cinéma, Paris, 1999

R. Bergan & R. Karney. *Bloomsbury Foreign Film Guide*, Bloomsbury, London, 1988

I. Bergman. *Bergman On Bergman, Interviews With Ingmar Bergman*, eds. S. Björkman, *et al,* tr. P. B. Austin, Touch-stone, New York, NY, 1986

—. *The Magic Lantern: An Autobiography*, London, 1988

—. *Images: My Life In Film,* Faber, London, 1994

P. Biskind. *Easy Riders, Raging Bulls: How the Sex 'n' Drugs 'n' Rock 'n' Roll Generation Saved Hollywood*, Blooms-bury, London, 1998

P. Bogdanovitch. *This Is Orson Welles*, Da Capo, New York, 1998

D. Bordwell & K. Thompson. *Film Art: An Introduction*, McGraw-Hill Publishing Company, New York, NY, 1979

—. *The Films of Carl-Theodor Dreyer*, University of California, Berkeley, 1981

—. *et al. The Classical Hollywood Cinema: Film Style and Mode of Production To 1960*, Routledge, London, 1985

—. *Narration In the Fiction Film*, Routledge, London, 1988

—. *Ozu and the Poetics of Cinema*, British Film Institute, London, 1988

—. *Making Meaning*, Harvard University Press, Cambridge, MA, 1989

—. & N. Caroll, eds. *Post-Theory: Reconstructing Film Studies*, University of Wisconsin Press, Madison, WI, 1996

—. *The Way Hollywood Tells It*, University of California Press, Berkeley, CA, 2006

F. Brady. *Citizen Welles*, Scribner's, New York, 1989

P. Braunberger. *Pierre Braunberger*, Centre National de la Cinématographie, Paris, 1987

D. Breskin. *Inner Voices: Filmmakers In Conversation*, Da Capo, New York, 1997

R. Bresson. *Notes On the Cinematographer*, Quartet, London, 1986

R. Brody. *Everything Is Cinema: The Working Life of Jean-Luc Godard*, Faber, London, 2008

R. Brown, ed. *Focus On Godard*, Prentice-Hall, N.J., 1972

Z. Bruneau. *En Attendant Godard*, Maurice Nadeau, Paris, 2014

S. Bukatman. *Terminal Identity: The Virtual Subject In Postmodern Science Fiction*, Duke University Press, Durham, NC, 1993

P.J. Burgard, ed. *Nietzsche and the Feminine*, University Press of Virginia, Charlottesville, 1994

I. Butler. *Religion In the Cinema,* A.S. Barnes, New York, NY, 1969

J. Butler. *Gender Trouble: Feminism and the Subversion of Identity*, Routledge, London, 1990

M. Caen. "Eye of the Cyclone", *Cahiers du Cinéma*, 2, British Film Institute, London, 1966

I. Cameron, ed. *The Films of Jean-Luc Godard*, Praeger, N.Y., 1969

V. Canby. "*Vladimir and Rosa", New York Times*, April 30, 1971

N. Carroll. *Mystifying Movies: Fads and Fallacies of Contemporary Film Theory,* Columbia University Press, New York, NY, 1988

J. Caughie, ed. *Theories of Authorship: A Reader*, Routledge, London, 1988

—. & A. Kuhn, eds. *The Sexual Subject: A* Screen *Reader In Sexuality*, Routledge, London, 1992

M. Cerisuelo. *Jean-Luc Godard*, Lherminier, Paris, 1989

G. Chester & J. Dickey, eds. *Feminism and Censorship: The Current Debate*, Prism Press, Bridport, Dorset, 1988

J. Chown. *Hollywood Auteur: Francis Coppola*, Praeger, New York, NY, 1988

M. Ciment. *Projections 9: French Filmmakers On Filmmaking*, Faber, London, 1999

H. Cixous. *The Newly Born Woman*, tr. B. Wing, Minnesota University Press, Minneapolis, 1986

—. *The Hélène Cixous Reader*, ed. Susan Sellers, Blackwell, Oxford, 1994

J. Collet: *Jean-Luc Godard*, Crown, 1968

T. Conley. "Language Gone Mad", in D. Wills, 2000

D.A. Cook. *A History of Narrative Film*, W.W. Norton, New York, NY, 1981, 1990, 1996

—. *Lost Illusions: American Cinema In the Shadow of Watergate and Vietnam*, Scribners, New York, NY, 2000

P. Cook, ed. *The Cinema Book*, British Film Institute, London, 1985

—. & M. Bernink, eds. *The Cinema Book*, 2nd ed., British Film Institute, London, 1999

T. Corrigan. *A Cinema Without Walls: Movies and Culture After Vietnam*, Rutgers University Press, NJ, 1991

—. *New German Cinema*, Indiana University Press, Bloomington, IN, 1994

J. Cott. *Rolling Stone*, June, 1969.

P. Cowie. *The Cinema of Orson Welles*, Da Capo, New York, NY, 1973

—. *Ingmar Bergman*, Secker & Warburg, London, 1982

—. *Coppola: A Biography*, Da Capo Press, 1994

A. Croce. "*Breathless*", *Film Quarterly*, 14, Spring, 1961, in D. Andrew,1987

S. Cunningham & R. Harley. "The Logic of the Virgin Mother: A Discussion of *Hail Mary*", *Screen,* 28, 1, Winter, 1987

C. Desbarats & J.P. Gorce, eds. *L'Effet-Godard*, Milan, Toulouse, 1989

G. Day & C. Bloch, eds. *Perspectives On Pornography: Sexuality In Film and Literature*, Macmillan, London, 1988

J. de Baroncelli. *Le Monde*, Nov 9, 1965

M. Deeley. *Blade Runners, Deer Hunters and Blowing the Bloody Doors Off*, Faber, London, 2008

T. de Lauretis & S. Heath, eds. *The Cinematic Apparatus*, St Martin's Press, New York, NY, 1980

—. *Alice Doesn't: Feminism, Semiotics, Cinema,* Indiana University Press, Bloomington, IN, 1984

—. *Technologies of Gender*, Macmillan, London, 1987

G. Deleuze & F. Guattari. *Cinema 1: The Movement Image*, Athlone Press, London, 1989

—. *Cinema 2: The Time Image*, Athlone Press, London, 1989

—. *What Is Philosophy?*, Verso, London, 1994

J. Derrida. *Of Grammatology*, Johns Hopkins University Press, Baltimore, MD, 1976

—. *Spurs: Nietzsche's Styles,* University of Chicago Press, Chicago, IL, 1979

—. *Writing and Difference,* University of Chicago Press, Chicago, IL, 1987

—. *Archive Fever,* University of Chicago Press, Chicago, IL, 1999

R. Dienst. "The Imaginary Element", in D. Willis, 2000

W.W. Dixon. *The Films of Jean-Luc Godard*, State University of New York Press, Albany, NY, 1997

L. Doan, ed. *The Lesbian Postmodern*, Columbia University Press, New York, NY, 1994

M. Doane *et al*, eds. *Re-Visions: Essays In Feminist Film Criticism*, University Publications of America, Frederick, MD, 1983

—. *Femmes Fatales: Feminism, Film Theory*, Routledge, London, 1991

J. Douin. *Jean-Luc Godard*, Rivages, Paris, 1994

Steven C. Dubin. *Arresting Images: Impolitic Art and Uncivil Actions*, Routledge, London, 1992

R. Durgnat. *Films and Feelings*, Faber, London, 1967

—. *A Mirror For England: British Movies From Austerity To Affluence,* Faber, London, 1970

A. Dworkin. *Pornography: Men Possessing Women,* Women's Press, London, 1984

—. *Intercourse*, Arrow, London, 1988

—. *Letters From a War Zone: Writings, 1976-1987*, Secker & Warburg, London, 1988

A. Easthope, ed. *Contemporary Film Theory*, Longman, London, 1993

M. Eliade. *Ordeal By Labyrinth*, University of Chicago Press, Chicago, IL, 1984

—. *Symbolism, the Sacred and the Arts*, Crossroad, New York, NY, 1985

T. Elsaesser. *New German Cinema: A History*, Macmillan, London, 1989

—. *The B.F.I. Companion To German Cinema*, British Film Institute, London, 1999

—. *European Cinema*, Amsterdam University Press, Amsterdam, 2005

R. Evans. *The Kid Stays In the Picture,* New York, NY, 1994

D. Fairservice. *Film Editing*, Manchester University Press, Manchester, 2001

M. Farber. *Negative Space*, Studio Vista, London, 1971

A. Farassino. *Jean-Luc Godard*, Il Castoro, Milan, 1996

J.L. Fell, ed. *Film Before Griffith*, University of California

Press, Berkeley, CA, 1983

F. Fellini. *Fellini On Fellini*, Delacorte, New York, NY, 1976

J. Finler. *The Movie Directors Story*, Octopus Books, London, 1985

—. *The Hollywood Story*, Wallflower Press, London, 2003

C. Fleming. *High Concept: Don Simpson and the Hollywood Culture of Excess*, Bloomsbury, London, 1998

G.E. Forshey. *American Religious and Biblical Spectaculars*, Praeger, Westport, CT, 1992

M. Foucault. *The History of Sexuality*, Penguin, London, 1981

—. *The Use of Pleasure: The History of Sexuality*, vol. 2, Penguin, London, 1987

—. *Politics, Philosophy, Culture: Interviews and Other Writings, 1977-1984*, ed. L.D. Kritzmon, Routledge, New York, NY, 1990

J. Franklin. *New German Cinema*, Columbus Books, 1986

K. French, ed. *Screen Violence*, Bloomsbury, London, 1996

P. French *et al. The Films of Jean-Luc Godard,* Blue Star House, 1967

F. Gado. *The Passion of Ingmar Bergman*, Durham, NC, 1986

J. Gallagher. *Film Directors On Directing*, Praeger, New York, NY, 1989

H. Geduld, ed. *Filmmakers On Filmmaking*, Indiana University Press, Bloomington, IN, 1967

J. Geiger & R. Rutsky, eds. *Film Analysis*, Norton & Company, New York, NY, 2005

J. Gelmis. *The Film Director As Superstar*, Penguin, London, 1974

D. Georgakas & L. Rubenstein, eds. *Art, Politics, Cinema: The Cineaste Interviews*, Pluto Press, London, 1985

J. Gerber. *Anatole Dauman: Pictures of a Producer*, British Film Institute, London, 1992

L. Gianetti: *Godard and Others*, Tantivy, 1975

—. *Understanding Movies*, Prentice-Hall, NJ, 1982

P.C. Gibson & R. Gibson, eds. *Dirty Looks: Women, Pornography, Power*, British Film Institute, London, 1993

J. Gomez. *Ken Russell*, Muller, 1976

M. Goodwin & G. Marcus. *Double Feature,* Outerbridge & Lazard, New York, 1972

R. Gottesman, ed. *Focus On Citizen Kane,* Prentice-Hall, Englewood Cliffs, NJ, 1971

— ed. *Focus On Orson Welles,* Prentice-Hall, Englewood Cliffs, NJ, 1976

P. Grace. *The Religious Film: Christianity and the Hagiopic*, Wiley-Blackwell, Sussex, 2009

D. Graham, ed. *Film and Religion*, St Mungo Press, 1997

B.K. Grant, ed. *Film Genre*, Scarecrow Press, Metuchen, NJ, 1977

—. ed. *Crisis Cinema: The Apocalyptic Idea In Postmodern Narrative Film,* Maisonneuve Press, 1993

—. *Film Genre Reader II*, University of Texas Press, Austin, TX, 1995

J. Green. *The Encyclopedia of Censorship*, Facts on File, New York, NY, 1990

N. Greene. *Pier Paolo Pasolini*, Princeton University Press, Princeton, NJ, 1990

N. Griffin & K. Masters. *Hit & Run: How Jon Peters and Peter Guber Took Sony For a Ride In Hollywood*, Simon & Schuster, New York, NY, 1996

E. Grosz. *Sexual Subversions*, Allen & Unwin, London, 1989

—. *Volatile Bodies,* Indiana University Press, Bloomington, IN, 1994

—. *Space, Time and Perversion*, Routledge, London, 1995

I. Halberstadt. *Pix*, 2, British Film Institute, 1997

L. Hanlon. *Fragments: Bresson's Film Style*, Farleigh Dickinson University Press, Rutherford, 1986

S. Harwood. *French National Cinema,* Routledge, London, 1993

M. Haskell. "Immaculate Deception", *Vogue*, Oct, 1985

S. Hayward & G. Vincendeau, eds. *French Film*, Routledge, London, 1990

S. Heath. *Questions of Cinema*, Macmillan, London, 1981

—. *Cinema and Language*, University Presses of America, 1983

J. Hellmann. *American Myth and the Legacy of Vietman*, Columbia, 1986

W. Herzog. *Herzog On Herzog*, ed. P. Cronin, Faber & Faber, London, 2002

G. Hickenlooper. *Reel Conversations: Candid Interviews With Film's Foremost Directors and Critics*, Citadel, New York, NY, 1991

C. Higham. *Orson Welles,* St Martin's Press, New York, NY, 1985

J. Hill & P.C. Gibson, eds. *The Oxford Guide To Film Studies*, Oxford University Press, Oxford, 1998

J. Hillier, ed. *Cahiers du Cinéma: The 1950s, New-Realism, Hollywood, New Wave*, Harvard University Press, Cambridge, MA, 1985

—. ed. *Cahiers du Cinéma: The 1960s*, Harvard University Press, Cambridge, MA, 1986

—. *The New Hollywood*, Studio Vista, London, 1992

—. *American Independent Cinema: A Sight & Sound Reader*, British Film Institute, London, 2001

L.C. Hillstrom, ed. *International Dictionary of Films and Filmmakers: Directors*, St James Press, London, 1997

F. Hölderlin. *Poems and Fragments*, tr. M. Hamburger, Anvil, London, 1994

D. Holmes & A. Smith, eds. *100 Years of European Cinema*,

Manchester University Press, Manchester, 2000

A. Horton & J. Maretta, eds. *Modern European Filmmakers*, Ungar, New York, NY, 1981

A. Insdorf. *Indelible Shadows: Film and the Holocaust*, Cambridge University Press, Cambridge, 1989

L. Irigaray. *The Irigaray Reader,* ed. M. Whitford, Blackwell, Oxford, 1991

H. Jacobson. "*Hail Mary*", *Film Comment*, 21, Nov, 1985

F. Jameson. *Signatures of the Visible*, Routledge, New York, NY, 1990

—. *Postmodernism, or the Cultural Logic of Late Capitalism*, Verso, London, 1991

P. Kael. *Kiss Kiss Bang Bang*, Bantam, New York, NY, 1969

—. *Going Steady*, Bantam, New York, 1971

—. *Taking It All In*, Marion Boyars, London, 1986

—. *State of the Art*, Marion Boyars, London, 1987

—. *Movie Love*, Marion Boyars, London, 1992

A. Kaes. *From Hitler To Heimat: The Return of History As Film*, Harvard University Press, Cambridge, MA, 1989

N. Kagan. *The Cinema of Oliver Stone*, Roundhouse, 1995

E. Ann Kaplan, ed. *Psychoanalysis and Cinema*, Routledge, London, 1990

—. ed. *Women In Film Noir*, British Film Institute, London, 1998

B.F. Kawin. *Mindscreen: Bergman, Godard and First-Person Film*, Princeton University Press, Princeton, NJ, 1978

—. *How Movies Work*, Macmillan, New York, NY, 1987

P. Keough, ed. *Flesh and Blood: The National Society of Film Critics On Sex, Violence, and Censorship*, Mercury House, San Francisco, CA, 1995

M. Kermode. *Hatchet Job*, Picador, London, 2013

M. Kinder. "A Thrice-Told Tale: Godard's *Le Mépris*", in A. Horton, 1981

G. Kindem. *The International Movie Industry*, Southern Illinois University Press, Carbondale, IL, 2000

R. Kinnard & T. Davis. *Divine Images: A History of Jesus On the Screen,* Citadel Press, New York, NY, 1992

M. Klein. *Film Quarterly*, 19, 3, 1966

T. Jefferson Kline. *Bertolucci's Dream Loom: A Psychoanalytic Study of Cinema*, University of Massachusetts Press, Amherst, 1987

P. Kolker. *The Altering Eye: Contemporary International Cinema*, Oxford University Press, New York, NY, 1983

—. *Bernardo Bertolucci*, British Film Institute, London, 1985

—. *A Cinema of Loneliness: Penn, Kubrick, Coppola, Scorsese, Altman*, Oxford University Press, New York, NY, 1988

—. *A Cinema of Loneliness: Penn, Stone, Kubrick, Scorsese, Spielberg, Altman*, Oxford University Press, New York, NY,

2000

S. Kracauer. *Theory of Film*, Princeton University Press, Princeton, NJ, 1997

J. Kreidl. *Jean-Luc Godard*, Twayne, Boston, 1980

L. Kreitzer. *The New Testament In Fiction and Film*, J.S.O.T., 1993

—. *The Old Testament In Fiction and Film*, Sheffield Academic Press, Sheffield, 1994

J. Kristeva. article in *Art Press*, 4, 1984-85

—. *Powers of Horror: An Essay On Abjection*, tr. Leon S. Roudiez, Columbia University Press, New York, 1982

—. *The Kristeva Reader*, ed. T. Moi, Blackwell, Oxford, 1986

—. *Tales of Love*, tr. Leon S. Roudiez, Columbia University Press, New York, 1987

—. *Black Sun: Depression and Melancholy*, tr. L.S. Roudiez, Columbia University Press, New York, NY, 1989

—. *Strangers To Ourselves*, tr. L. Roudiez, Harvester Wheatsheaf, Hemel Hempstead, 1991

B. Krohn. *Hitchcock At Work*, Phaidon, London, 2000

A. Kuhn. *Women's Pictures: Feminism and the Cinema*, Routledge & Kegan Paul, London, 1982

J. Lacan. *Écrits: A Selection*, tr. Alan Sheridan, Tavistock, 1977

—. and the École Freudienne. *Feminine Sexuality*, ed. J. Mitchell and J. Rose, Macmillan, London, 1988

M. Landy. "Godard: Thinking Media", *Film-Philosophy*, 6, 30, Sept, 2002

M. Lanning. *Vietnam At the Movies*, Fawcett Columbine, New York, NY, 1994

R. Lapsley & M. Westlake, eds. *Film Theory: An Introduction*, Manchester University Press, Manchester, 1988

A. Lawton. *Kinoglasnost: Soviet Cinema In Our Time*, Cambridge University Press, Cambridge, 1992

—. *The Red Screen: Politics, Society, Art In Soviet Cinema*, Routledge, London, 1992

J. Leach. *A Possible Cinema: The Films of Alain Tanner*, Scarecrow Press, Metuchen, NJ, 1984

B. Leaming. *Orson Welles*, Viking, New York, 1985

V. Lebeau. *Psychoanalysis and Cinema*, Wallflower, London, 2001

R. Lefèvre. *Ingmar Bergman*, Paris, 1983

P. Leprohan. *The Italian Cinema*, tr. R. Greaves & O. Stallybrass, Secker & Warburg, London, 1972

Julia Lesage. "Godard-Gorin's *Wind From the East*: Looking at a film politically," *Jump Cut*, no. 4, 1974

—. *Jean-Luc Godard: A Guide To References and Resources*, G.K. Hall, Boston, 1979

J. Leutrat. *Des traces qui nous ressemblent: Passion de Jean-Luc Godard*, Comp' Act, Seyssel, 1990

—. *Jean-Luc Godard*, Schena-Didier, Paris, 1998
—. "Godard's Tricolor", in D. Wills, 2000
P. Lev. *The Euro-American Cinema*, University of Texas Press, Austin, 1993
E. Levy. *Cinema of Outsiders: The Rise of American Independent Film,* New York University Press, New York, NY, 1999
J. Lewis. *The Road To Romance and Ruin: Teen Films and Youth Culture*, Routledge, London, 1992
—. *Whom God Wishes To Destroy: Francis Coppola and the New Hollywood*, Duke University Press, Durham, NC, 1995
—. ed. *New American Cinema*, Duke University Press, Durham, NC, 1998
—. *Hollywood v. Hard Core: How the Struggle Over Censorship Created the Modern Film Industry,* New York University Press, New York, NY, 2000
—. ed. *The End of Cinema As We Know It: American Film In the Nineties*, New York University Press, New York, NY, 2002
J. Leyda, ed *Filmmakers Speak*, Da Capo, New York, 1977/ 84
—. *Kino: A History of the Russian and Soviet Cinema*, 3rd edition, Allen & Unwin, London, 1983
M. Litch. *Philosophy Through Film*, Routledge, London, 2002
P. Livington. *Ingmar Bergman and the Rituals of Art*, Cornell University Press, Ithaca, NY, 1982
V. LoBrutto. *Sound-On-Film*, Praeger, New York, NY, 1994
M. Locke & C. Warren, eds. *Hail Mary: Women and the Sacred In Film*, Southern Illinois University Press, Carbondale, 1993
R. Long. *Ingmar Bergman*, Abrams, New York, NY, 1994
Y. Loshitzky. *The Radical Faces of Godard and Bertolucci*, Wayne State University Press, Detroit, MI, 1995
—. ed. *Spielberg's Holocaust: Critical Interpretation On 'Schindler's List'*, Indiana University Press, Bloomington, IN, 1997
L. Lourdeaux. *Italian and Irish Filmmakers In America: Ford, Capra, Coppola and Scorsese*, Temple University Press, Philadelphia, PA, 1990
J. MacBean. "Godard and the Dziga Vertov Group", *Film Quarterly*, 26, 1, Autumn, 1972
—. *Film and Revolution*, Indiana University Press, Bloomington, IN, 1975
C. MacCabe. "Principles of realism and pleasure", *Screen*, 17, 3, Autumn, 1976
—. *Godard, Images, Sound, Politics*, Macmillan/ British Film Institute, London, 1980
—. *Godard: A Portrait of the Artist At 70*, Faber, London, 2003
P. Malone. *Movie Christs and Antichrists*, Crossroad, 1990

R. Maltby. *Harmless Entertainment: Hollywood and the Ideology of Consensus*, Scarecrow Press, Metuchen, NJ, 1983

—. & I. Craven. *Hollywood Cinema: An Introduction*, Blackwell, Oxford, 1995

—. *Hollywood Cinema*, 2nd ed., Blackwell, Oxford, 2003

M. Mancini & G. Perella. *Pier Paolo Pasolini: corpi e luoghi*, Theorema, Bologna, 1982

Mao Tse-tung. *The Little Red Book (Quotations From Chairman Mao Tse-tung)*, Foreign Language Press, Peking, 1967

M. Marie. *The French New Wave*, Blackwell, Oxfrord, 2003

E. Marks & I. de Courtivron, eds. *New French Feminisms: an anthology*, Harvester Wheatsheaf, Hemel Hempstead, 1981

A. Martin. "Recital: Three Lyrical Interludes In Godard", in M. Temple, 2000

T. Martin. *Images and the Imageless: a Study In Religious Consciousness and Film,* Bucknell University Press, 1981

G. Mast *et al,* eds. *Film Theory and Criticism: Introductory Readings*, Oxford University Press, New York, NY, 1992a

—. & B Kawin, *A Short History of the Movies*, Macmillan, New York, NY, 1992b

E. Mathijs, ed. *The Cinema of the Low Countries*, Wallflower Press, London, 2004

T.D. Matthews. *Censored*, Chatto & Windus, London, 1994

J.R. May & M. Bird, eds. *Religion In Film*, University of Tennessee Press, Knoxville, 1982

—. *Image and Likeness: Religious Vision In American Film Classics*, Paulist, 1992

—. *New Image of Religious Film*, Sheed & Ward, London, 1996

J. Mayne. *The Woman At the Keyhole: Feminism and Women's Cinema*, Indiana University Press, Bloomington, IN, 1990

L. Mazdon. *Encore Hollywood: Remaking French Cinema,* British Film Institute, London, 2000

M. Medved. *Hollywood vs. America*, HarperCollins, London, 1992

P. Mellencamp & P. Rosen, eds. *Cinema Histories, Cinema Practices*, University Publications of America, Frederick, MD, 1984

—. *A Fine Romance: Five Ages of Film Feminism*, Temple University Press, Philadelphia, PA, 1995

X. Mendik & S. Schneider, eds. *Underground U.S.A.: Film-making Beyond the Hollywood Canon*, Wallflower Press, London, 2002

J. Mellen. "*Vladimir and Rosa*", *Cinéaste,* 4, 3, Winter, 1971

M. Merrill. "Black Panthers In the New Wave", *Film Culture*, 53, 54, 55, Spring, 1972

C. Metz. *Film Language: A Semiotics of the Cinema*, tr. M.

Taylor, Oxford University Press, New York, NY, 1974

M. Miles. *Seeing and Believing: Religion and Values In the Movies*, Beacon, Boston, MA, 1996

F. Miller. *Censored Hollywood: Sex, Sin and Violence On Screen,* Turner Publishing, Atlanta, 1994

M.C. Miller. ed. *Seeing Through Movies*, Pantheon, New York, NY, 1990

T. Miller *et al*, eds. *Global Hollywood*, British Film Institute, London, 2001

T. Milne. *Sight & Sound*, 34, 1, 1966

T. Modleski, ed. *Studies In Entertainment*, Indiana University Press, Bloomington, IN, 1987

—. *The Women Who Knew Too Much: Hitchcock and Feminist Theory*, Methuen, London, 1988

—. *Feminism Without Women: Culture and Criticism In a 'Postfeminist' Age*, Routledge, London, 1991

T. Moi. *Sexual/ Textual Politics: Feminist Literary Theory*, Methuen, London, 1983

J. Monaco. *The Films of Stanley Kubrick*, New York, NY, 1974

—. *The New Wave: Truffaut, Godard, Chabrol, Rohmer, Rivette*, Oxford University Press, New York, NY, 1977a

—. *How To Read a Film*, Oxford University Press, New York, NY, 1977b

G. Moore, ed. *Conrad On Film*, Oxford University Press, Oxford, 1997

K. Moore. "Reincarnating the Radical: Godard's *Je vous salue, Marie*", *Cinema Journal*, 34, 1, Fall, 1994

P. Mosley. *Ingmar Bergman*, Marion Boyars, London, 1981

G. Mulholland. *Popcorn: Fifty Years of Rock 'n' Roll Movies*, Orion Books, London, 2011

R. Murphy. *Sixties British Cinema*, British Film Institute, London, 1992

—. ed. *British Cinema of the 90s*, British Film Institute, London, 2000

—. ed. *The British Cinema Book*, Palgrave/ Macmillan, London, 2nd edition, 2009

R. Murray. *Images In the Dark: An Encyclopedia of Gay and Lesbian Film and Video*, Titan Books, London, 1998

J. Naremore. *The Magic World of Orson Welles,* Southern Methodist University Press, Dallas, TX, 1989

—. ed. *Orson Welles's Citizen Kane: A Casebook*, Oxford University Press, New York, NY, 2004

J. Natoli. *Hauntings: Popular Film and American Culture 1990-92*, State University of New York Press, Albany, NY, 1994

—. *Speeding To the Millennium: Film and Culture 1993-1995*, State University of New York Press, Albany, NY, 1998

—. *Postmodern Journeys: Film and Culture, 1996-1998*, State University of New York Press, Albany, NY, 2001

S. Neale. *Cinema and Technology*, Macmillan, London, 1985

—. & B. Neve. *Film and Politics In America*, Routledge, London, 1992

—. & M. Smith, eds. *Contemporary Hollywood Cinema*, Routledge, London, 1998

—. *Genre and Hollywood*, Routledge, London, 2000

—. *Genre and Contemporary Hollywood*, Routledge, London, 2002

J. Nelmes, ed. *An Introduction To Film Studies*, Routledge, London, 1996

T. Nelson. *Kubrick: Inside a Film Artist's Maze*, Indiana University Press, Bloomington, IN, 1982

R. Neupert. "*Je vous salue, Marie:* Godard the Father", *Film Criticism*, 10, 1, Autumn, 1985

—. *The End: Narration and Closure In the Cinema*, Wayne State University Press, Detroit, MI, 1995

—. *A History of the French New Wave*, University of Wisconsin Press, Maidson, 2003

P. Norman. *The Stones*, Elm Tree, 1972

—. *Sympathy For the Devil: The Rolling Stones Story*, Linden Press, New York, NY, 1984

—. *Mick Jagger,* HarperCollins, 2012

G. Nowell-Smith. *Visconti*, British Film Institute, London, 1973

—. ed. *The Oxford History of World Cinema*, Oxford University Press, Oxford, 1996

—. & S. Ricci, eds. *Hollywood and Europe*, British Film Institute, London, 1998

Michael O'Pray. *Avant-Garde Film*, Wallflower Press, London, 2003

J. Orr & C. Nicholson, eds. *Cinema and Fiction*, Edinburgh University Press, Edinburgh, 1992

—. *Cinema and Modernity*, Polity Press, Cambridge, 1993

—. *Contemporary Cinema*, Edinburgh University Press, Edinburgh, 1998

—. & O. Taxidou, eds. *Postwar Cinema and Modernity: A Film Reader*, Edinburgh University Press, Edinburgh, 2000

C. Ostwalt. "Religion & Popular Movies", *Journal of Religion and Film,* 2, 3, 1998

R. Palmer, ed. *The Cinematic Text*, A.M.S., New York, NY, 1989

—. *Hollywood's Dark Cinema: The American Film Noir*, Twayne, New York, NY, 1994

—. ed. *Perspectives On Film Noir*, G.K. Hall, Boston, 1996

J. Park. *Learning To Dream: The New British Cinema*, Faber, London, 1984

—. *British Cinema*, B.T. Batsford, London, 1990

P.P. Pasolini. *Il Vangelo Secondo Matteo*, Garzanti, Milan, 1964

—. *Oedipus Rex*, Lorrimer Publishing, 1984

—. *Pasolini On Pasolini*, ed. O. Stack, Thames & Hudson,

London, 1969

A. Pavelin. *Fifty Religious Films,* A.P. Pavelin, Chiselhurst, Kent, 1990

R. Peck, ed. "Myth, Religious Typology and Recent Cinema", *Christianity and Literature,* 42, 1993

C. Penley, ed. *Feminism and Film Theory,* Routledge, London, 1988

—. *et al,* eds. *Close Encounters: Film, Feminism and Science Fiction,* University of Minnesota Press, Minneapolis, 1991

—. & A. Ross, eds. *Technoculture,* University of Minnesota Press, Minneapolis, MN, 1991

V.F. Perkins. *Film As Film: Understanding and Judging Movies,* Penguin, London, 1972

D. Petrie. *Creativity and Constraint In the British Film Industry,* Macmillan, London, 1991

—. ed. *New Questions of British Cinema,* British Film Institute, London, 1992

—. *Screening Europe: Image and Identity In Contemporary European Cinema,* British Film Institute, London, 1992

—. *Inside Stories: Diaries of Filmmakers At Work,* British Film Institute, London, 1996

G. Phelps. *Film Censorship,* Gollancz, London, 1975

J. Phillips. *You'll Never Eat Lunch In This Town Again,* Heinemann, London, 1991

K. Phillips. *New German Filmmakers,* Ungar, New York, NY, 1984

Pierrot le Fou, tr. P. Whitehead, Lorrimer, London, 1969

C. Potter. *Image, Sound and Story: The Art of Telling In Film,* Secker & Warburg, London, 1990

P. Powrie, ed. *French Cinema In the 1990s,* Oxford University Press, Oxford, 1999

—. *Jean-Jacques Beineix,* Manchester University Press, Manchester, 2001

M. Praz. *The Romantic Agony,* tr. Davidson, Oxford University Press, Oxford, 1933

R. Prendergast. *Film Music,* W.W. Norton, New York, NY, 1992

S. Prince. *Savage Cinema: Sam Peckinpah and the Rise of Ultraviolent Movies,* University of Texas Press, Austin, TX, 1998

—. ed. *Screening Violence,* Athlone Press, London, 2000

—. *A New Pot of Gold: Hollywood Under the Electronic Rainbow,* Scribners, New York, NY, 2000

S. Projansky. *Watching Rape: Film and Television In Postfeminism Culture,* New York University Press, New York, NY, 2001

M. Pye & Lynda Myles. *The Movie Brats: How the Film Generation Took Over Hollywood,* Faber, London, 1979

E. Rabkin & G. Slusser, eds. *Shadows of the Magic Lamp:*

Fantasy and Science Fiction In Film, Southern Illinois University Press, Carbondale, IL, 1985

T. Rayns, ed. *Fassbinder*, British Film Institute, London, 1979

K. Reader. *Robert Bresson,* Manchester University Press, Mancheser, 2000

A. Reinhartz. "Jesus in Film: Hollywood Perspectives on the Jewishness of Jesus", *Journal of Religion and Film,* 2, 2, 1998

E. Rentschler. *West German Film*, Redgrave, New York, NY, 1984

—. ed. *German Film and Literature*, Methuen, London, 1986

—. ed. *West German Filmmakers On Film: Visions and Voices*, Holmes & Meier, New York, NY, 1988

P. Rice & P. Waugh, eds. *Modern Literary Theory: A Reader*, Arnold, London, 1992

J. Richards, ed. *Films and British National Identity*, Manchester University Press, Manchester, 1997

K. Richards. *Life,* Weidenfeld & Nicholson, London, 2010

M. Richardson. *Surrealism and Cinema*, Berg, New York, NY, 2006

D. Richie. *The Films of Akira Kurosawa*, University of California Press, Berkeley, CA, 1965

S. Richmond. *The Rough Guide To Anime*, Rough Guides, 2009

A. Riding. "What's In a Name If the Name Is Godard?", *New York Times*, Oct 25, 1992

R. Rinaldi. *Pier Paolo Pasolini*, Mursia, Milan, 1982

J. Riordan. *Stone*, Aurum, London, 1996

G. Ritzer. *The McDonaldization of Society*, Sage, London, 1995

—. *The McDonaldization Thesis*, Sage, London, 1997

J. Robertson. *The British Board of Film Censors*, Croom Helm, 1985

—. *The Hidden Cinema*, Routledge, London, 1989

D. Robinson. *World Cinema*, Methuen, London, 1981

G. Rodgerson & E. Wilson, eds. *Pornography and Censorship*, Lawrence & Wishart, London, 1991

S. Rohdie. *Antonioni*, British Film Institute, London, 1990

—. *The Passion of Pier Paolo Pasolini*, British Film Institute, London, 1995

G. Roheim, ed. *Psychoanalysis and the Social Sciences*, III, International University Press, New York, NY, 1951

V. Roloff & S. Winter, eds. *Godard Intermedial*, Stauffenburg, Tübinigen, 1997

P. Rosen, ed. *Narrative, Apparatus, Ideology: A Film Theory Reader*, Columbia University Press, New York, NY, 1986

J. Rosenbaum. "Eight Obstacles To the Appreciation of Godard In the United States", in R. Bellour, 1992

—. *Placing Movies*, University of California Press, Berkeley, CA, 1995

A. Rosenstone, ed. *Revisioning History: Film and the Construction of a New Past*, Princeton University Press, Princeton, NJ, 1995

R. Roud. *Jean-Luc Godard*, Thames & Hudson, London, 1970

M. Roussel. *France-Soir*, Jan 23, 1985

M Rubenstein. *Postcards From Alphaville: Jean-Luc Godard In Contemporary Art*, Institute for Contemporary Art, Long Island City, 1992

R. Ruiz. *The Poetics of Cinema*, Dis Voir, Paris, 1995

K. Russell. *A British Picture: An Autobiography*, Heinemann, London, 1989

M. Russell & J. Young. *Film Music,* RotoVision, 2000

V. Russo. *The Celluloid Closet: Homosexuality In the Movies*, Harper & Row, New York, NY, 1981

T. Ryall. *Alfred Hitchcock and the British Cinema*, Croom Helm, 1986

C. Salewicz. *Oliver Stone*, Orion, London, 1999

J. Sanford. *The New German Cinema*, Da Capo Press, New York, NY, 1982

A. Sarris. "Jean-Luc Godard Now", *Interview*, 24, 7, July, 1994

T. Schatz. *Hollywood Genres,* Random House, New York, NY, 1981

—. *Old Hollywood/ New Hollywood*, U.M.I. Research Press, Ann Arbor, MI, 1983

—. *The Genius of the System: Hollywood Filmmaking In the Studio Era*, Pantheon, New York, NY 1988

P. Schrader. *Transcendental Style In Film: Ozu, Bresson, Dreyer*, Da Capo Press, 1972

M. Schumacher. *Francis Ford Coppola*, Bloomsbury, London, 2000

M. Scorsese. *Scorsese On Scorsese*, ed. D. Thompson & I. Christie, Faber, London, 1989, 1995

Screen Reader I: Cinema/ Ideology/ Politics, Society for Education in Film & TV, 1977

Screen Reader II: Cinema and Semiotics, British Film Institute, London, 1982

C. Sharrett, ed. *Crisis Cinema*, Maisonneuve Press, Washington, DC, 1993

T. Shaw. *British Cinema and the Cold War*, I.B. Tauris, London, 2001

D. Shipman. *The Story of Cinema*, Hodder & Stoughton, London, 1984

—. *Caught In the Act: Sex and Eroticism In the Movies*, Hamish Hamilton, London, 1986

T. Shone. *Blockbuster: How the Jaws and Jedi Generation Turned Hollywood Into a Boom-Town*, Scribner, London, 2005

E. Showalter, ed. *The New Feminist Criticism,* Virago, London,

1986

R. Shuker. *Understanding Popular Music*, Routledge, London, 1994

—. *Key Concepts In Popular Music,* Routledge, London, 1998

E. Siciliano. *Pasolini: A Biography*, Bloomsbury, London, 1987

L. Sider *et al*, eds. *Soundscapes: The School of Sound Lectures 1998-2001*, Wallflower Press, London, 2003

M. Silberman. *German Cinema,* Wayne State University Press, Detroit, MI, 1995

K. Silverman. *The Subject of Semiotics*, Oxford University Press, New York, NY, 1983

—. *The Acoustic Mirror: The Female Voice In Psychoanalysis and Cinema*, Indiana University Press, Bloomington, IN, 1988

—. *Male Subjectivity At the Margins*, Routledge, London, 1992

—. & H. Farocki. *Speaking About Godard*, New York University Press, New York, NY, 1998

P. Adams Sitney, ed. *The Film Culture Reader*, Praeger, New York, NY, 1970

—. ed. *The Avant-Garde Film: A Reader of Theory and Criticism*, New York University Press, New York, NY, 1978

—. *Visionary Film: The American Avant-Garde, 1943-1978,* 2nd ed., Oxford University Press, New York, NY, 1979

—. *Vital Crises In Italian Cinema*, University of Texas Press, Austin, TX, 1995

D. Smith. *American Filmmakers Today*, Blandford Press, Poole, 1984

J. Smith. *Looking Away: Hollywood and Vietnam*, Scribner's, New York, NY, 1975

M. Smith. *Engaging Characters*, Oxford University Press, 1995

V. Sobchack. *The Limits of Infinity: The American Science Fiction Film*, A.S. Barnes, New York, NY, 1980

—. *Screening Space: The American Science Fiction Film*, Ungar, New York, NY, 1987/1993

—. *The Address of the Eye: A Phenomenology of Film Experience*, Princeton University Press, Princeton, NJ, 1992

—. ed. *The Persistence of History: Cinema, Television, and the Modern Event*, Routledge, London, 1995

A. Solomon. *20th Century-Fox: A Corporate and Financial History*, Scarcrow Press, Metuchen, NJ, 1988

J. Solomon. *The Ancient World In the Cinema*, London, 1978

—. *The Ancient World In the Cinema*, Yale University Press, New Haven, CT, 2001

S. Sontag. *Styles of Radical Will*, Farrar, Straus & Giroux, New York, 1966

P. Sorlin. *The Film In History: Restaging the Past*, Blackwell, Oxford, 1980

S. Spignesi. *The Woody Allen Companion*, Plexus, London, 1994

D. Spoto. *The Life of Alfred Hitchcock*, Collins, London, 1983

J. Stacey. *Hollywood Cinema and Female Spectatorship*, Routledge, London, 1994

J. Staiger. *Interpreting Films*, Princeton University Press, Princeton, NJ, 1992

—. *Perverse Spectators: The Practices of Film Reception*, New York University Press, New York, NY, 2000

R. Stam *et al. New Vocabularies In Film Semiotics*, Routledge, London, 1992

B. Steene. *Ingmar Bergman*, Twayne, Boston, MA, 1968

—. ed. *Focus On The Seventh Seal*, Prentice-Hall, Englewood Cliffs, NJ, 1972

—. *Ingmar Bergman: A Guide To References and Resources*, Boston, MA, 1987

N. Steimatsky. "Pasolini on Terra Sancta: Towards a Theology of Film", *Yale Journal of Criticism*, 11, 1, 1998

E. Stein. *"Hail Mary"*, *Film Comment*, 21, Nov, 1985

L. Stern. *The Scorsese Connection*, British Film Institute, London, 1995

D. Sterritt. *The Films of Jean-Luc Godard*, Cambridge University Press, Cambridge, 1999

—. "Godardiana: A Reply to Marcia Landy", *Film-Philosophy*, 6, 31, Sept, 2002

P. Steven, ed. *Jump Cut: Hollywood, Politics and Counter Cinema*, Between the Lines, Toronto, 1985

G. Stewart. *Between Film and Screen: Modernism's Photo Synthesis*, University of Chicago Press, Chicago, IL, 1999

J. Still & M. Worton, eds. *Textuality and Sexuality: Reading Theories and Practices*, Manchester University Press, Manchester, 1993

S. Street. *British National Cinema*, Routledge, London, 1997/ 2009

C. Sylvester, ed. *The Penguin Book of Hollywood*, Penguin, London, 1999

Y. Tasker. *Spectacular Bodies: Gender, Genre and the Action Cinema*, Routledge, London, 1993

—. *Working Girls: Gender and Sexuality In Popular Cinema*, Routledge, London, 1998

—. ed. *Fifty Contemporary Filmmakers*, Routledge, London, 2002

R. Taylor & I. Christie, eds. *The Film Factory: Russian and Soviet Cinema In Documents*, Routledge, London, 1988

—. *Inside the Film Factory: New Approaches To Russian and Soviet Cinema*, Routledge, London, 1991

—. & D. Spring, eds. *Stalinism and Soviet Cinema*, Routledge, London, 1993

—. *et al*, eds. *The B.F.I. Companion To Eastern European and*

Russian Cinema, British Film Institute, London, 2000

M. Temple & J. Williams, eds. *The Cinema Alone: Essays On the Work of Jean-Luc Godard, 1985-2000*, Amsterdam University Press, Amsterdam, 2000

——. *et al*, eds. *Godard For Ever*, Black Dog Publishing, London, 2004

S. Teo. *Hong Kong Cinema*, British Film Institute, London, 1997

D. Thomas. *Reading Hollywood: Spaces and Meanings In American Film*, Wallflower, London, 2001

N. Thomas, ed. *International Dictionary of Films and Filmmakers: Films*, St James Press, London, 1990

K. Thompson. *Exporting Entertainment: America In the World Film Market, 1907-1934*, British Film Institute, London, 1985

——. *Breaking the Glass Armor: Neoformalist Film Analysis*, Princeton University Press, Princeton, NJ, 1988

——. & D. Bordwell. *Film History: An Introduction*, McGraw-Hill, New York, NY, 1994

——. *Storytelling In the New Hollywood*, Harvard University Press, Cambridge, MA, 1999

D. Thomson. "That Breathless Moment", *Sight & Sound*, 7, 1994

——. *A Biographical Dictionary of Film*, Deutsch, London, 1995

——. *Rosebud: The Story of Orson Welles*, Little, Brown, Boston, MA, 1996

——. *The Big Screen*, Allen Lane 2012

C. Tohill & P. Tombs. *Immoral Tales: Sex and Horror Cinema In Europe 1956-1984*, Titan Books, London, 1995

C. Tonetti. *Luchino Visconti*, Columbus Books, 1985

——. *Bernardo Bertolucci*, Twayne, Boston, MA, 1994

R.B. Toplin, ed. *Oliver Stone's USA*, University of Kansas Press, Lawrence, KS, 2000

——. *Reel History: In Defense of Hollywood*, University of Kansas Press, Lawrence, KS, 2002

E. Törnqvist. *Between Stage and Screen: Ingmar Bergman Directs*, Amsterdam University Press, Amsterdam, 1995

J. Trevelyan. *What the Censor Saw*, Michael Joseph, London, 1973

H. Trosman. *Contemporary Psychoanalysis and Masterworks of Art and Film*, New York University Press, New York, NY, 2000

F. Truffaut. *The Films In My Life*, tr. L. Mayhew, Penguin, London, 1982

——. *Hitchcock*, Simon & Schuster, New York, NY, 1984

K. Turan & S.F. Zito: *Sinema: American Pornographic Films and the People Who Make Them*, Praeger, New York, NY, 1974

P. Tyler. *Sex Psyche Etcetera In the Film*, Horizon, New York, NY, 1969

——. *Screening the Sexes: Homosexuality In the Movies,*

Doubleday, New York, NY, 1973

M. Valck & M. Hagener, eds. *Cinephilia: Movies, Love and Memory*, Amsterdam University Press, Amsterdam, 2005

K. Van Gunden. *Fantasy Films*, McFarland, Jefferson, NC 1989

—. *Postmodern Auteurs: Coppola, Lucas, De Palma, Spielberg and Scorsese*, McFarland, Jefferson, NC 1991

R. van Scheers. *Paul Verhoeven*, Faber, London, 1997

G. Vincendeau, ed. *Encyclopedia of European Cinema*, British Film Institute, London, 1995

—. ed. *Film/ Literature/ Heritage: A Sight & Sound Reader*, British Film Institute, London, 2001

P. Virilio & S. Lotringer. *The Aesthetics of Disappearance*, tr. P. Beitchman, Semiotext(e), New York, NY, 1991

—. *War and Cinema*, Verso, London, 1992

—. *The Vision Machine*, tr. J. Rose, Indiana University Press, Bloomington, IN, 1994

—. *The Art of the Motor*, tr. J. Rose, Minnesota University Press, Minneapolis, 1995

J. Vizzard. *See No Evil: Life Inside a Hollywood Censor*, Simon & Schuster, New York, NY, 1970

A. Vogel. *Film As a Subversive Art*, Weidenfeld & Nicolson, London, 1974

J. Vronskaya. *Young Soviet Film Makers*, Allen & Unwin, London, 1972

A. Walker. *Sex In the Movies*, Penguin, London, 1968

—. *National Heroes: British Cinema In the Seventies and Eighties*, Harrap, London, 1985

—. *Hollywood, England: The British Film Industry In the Sixties*, Harrap, London, 1986

—. *et al. Stanley Kubrick, Director*, Weidenfeld & Nicolson, London, 1999

J. Walker. *The Once and Future Film: British Cinema In the 1970s and 1980s*, Methuen, London, 1985

—. *Art and Artists On Screen*, Manchester University Press, Manchester, 1993

M. Walsh. "Godard and Me: Jean-Pierre Gorin Talks", *Take One*, 5, 1, Feb, 1976

J. Wasko. *Movies and Money*, Ablex, NJ, 1982

—. *Hollywood In the Information Age*, Polity Press, Cambridge, 1994

J. Waters. "*Hail Mary*", *American Film*, 11, Jan, 1986

P. Webb. *The Erotic Arts*, Secker & Warburg, London, 1975

A. Weiss. *Vampires and Violets: Lesbians In Film*, Penguin, London, 1993

E. Weiss. & J. Belton, eds. *Film Sound: Theory and Practice*, Columbia University Press, New York, NY, 1989

O. Welles. *This Is Orson Welles*, HarperCollins, London, 1992

—. *Orson Welles: Interviews*, ed. M. Estrin, University of

Mississippi Press, Jackson, 2002

A. White. "Double Helix: Jean-Luc Godard", *Film Comment*, 32, 2, Mch, 1996

L. White. *Obsession*, T.V. Boardman, London, 1962

V. Wright Wexman. *Roman Polanski*, Columbus Books, 1987

P. Willemen, ed. *Pier Paolo Pasolini*, British Film Institute, London, 1977

J. Williams & M. Temple, eds. *The Cinema Alone: Essays On the Work of Jean-Luc Godard*, Amsterdam University Press, Amsterdam, 2000

L. Williams, ed. *Viewing Positions: Ways of Seeing Film*, Rutgers University Press, New Brunswick, NJ, 1995

L.R. Williams. *Critical Desire: Psychoanalysis and the Literary Subject*, Arnold, London, 1995

—. *Sex In the Head*, Harvester Wheatsheaf, Hemel Hempstead, 1995

S. Willis. *High Contrast: Race and Gender In Contemporary Hollywood Film*, Duke University Press, Durham, NC, 1997

D. Wills, ed. *Jean-Luc Godard's Pierrot le Fou*, Cambridge University Press, 2000

R. Wilson & W. Dissanayake, eds. *Global/ Local: Cultural Production and the Transnational Imaginary*, Duke University Press, Durham, NC, 1996

E. Wistrich. *'I Don't Mind the Sex It's the Violence': Film Censorship Explored*, Marion Boyars, London, 1978

M. Wolf. *The Entertainment Economy,* Penguin, London, 1999

P. Wollen: *Signs and Meaning In the Cinema*, Secker & Warburg, London, 1972

—. *Readings and Writings: Semiotic Counter-Strategies*, Verso, London, 1982

B. Wood. *Orson Welles*, Greenwood Press, Westport, CT, 1990

M. Wood. *America In the Movies*, London, 1974

P. Wood, ed. *Scorsese: A Journey Through the American Psyche*, Plexus, London, 2005

R. Wood. *Ingmar Bergman*, Praeger, New York, NY, 1969

—. *Hollywood From Vietnam To Reagan... and Beyond*, Columbia University Press, New York, NY, 2003

T. Woods. *Beginning Postmodernism,* Manchester University Press, Manchester, 1999

J. Wyatt. *High Concept: Movies and Marketing In Hollywood*, University of Texas Press, Austin, TX, 1994

E.C.M. Yau, ed. *At Full Speed: Hong Kong Cinema In a Borderless World,* University of Minnesota Press, Minneapolis, MN, 1998

J. Young, ed. *The Art of Memory: Holocaust Memorials In History*, Prestel, New York, NY, 1994

V. Young. *Cinema Borealis: Ingmar Bergman and the Swedish Ethos*, Avon, New York, NY, 1971

J. Zipes, ed. *The Oxford Companion To Fairy Tales*, Oxford University Press, 2000

—. *The Enchanted Screen: The Unknown History of Fairy-tale Films*, Routledge, New York, NY, 2011

S. Zizek. *Looking Awry*, Verso, London, 1991

—. *Enjoy Your Symptom Jacques Lacan In Hollywood and Out*, Routledge, New York, NY, 1992

—. *The Metastases of Enjoyment*, Verso, London, 1994

—. *The Indivisible Remainder*, Verso, London, 1996

—. *The Fright of Real Tears: The Uses and Misuses of Lacan In Film Theory*, British Film Institute, London, 1999

J. Zuker. *Francis Ford Coppola: A Guide To References and Resources*, G.K. Hall, Boston, MA, 1984

JEREMY ROBINSON has published poetry, fiction, and studies of J.R.R. Tolkien, Samuel Beckett, Thomas Hardy, André Gide and D.H. Lawrence. Robinson has edited poetry books by Novalis, Ursula Le Guin, Friedrich Hölderlin, Francesco Petrarch, Dante Alighieri, Arseny Tarkovsky, and Rainer Maria Rilke.

Books on film and animation include: *The Akira Book* • *The Art of Katsuhiro Otomo* • *The Art of Masamune Shirow* • *The Ghost In the Shell Book* • *Fullmetal Alchemist* • *Cowboy Bebop: The Anime and Movie* • *The Cinema of Hayao Miyazaki* • *Hayao Miyazaki: Pocket Guide* • *Princess Mononoke: Pocket Movie Guide* • *Spirited Away: Pocket Movie Guide* • *Blade Runner and the Cinema of Philip K. Dick* • *Blade Runner: Pocket Movie Guide* • *The Cinema of Donald Cammell* • *Performance: Donald Cammell: Nic Roeg: Pocket Movie Guide* • *Pasolini: Il Cinema di Poesia/ The Cinema of Poetry* • *Salo: Pocket Movie Guide* • *The Trilogy of Life Movies: Pocket Movie Guide* • *The Gospel According To Matthew: Pocket Movie Guide* • *The Ecstatic Cinema of Tony Ching Siu-tung* • *Tsui Hark: The Dragon Master of Chinese Cinema* • *The Swordsman: Pocket Movie Guide* • *A Chinese Ghost Story: Pocket Movie Guide* • *Ken Russell: England's Great Visionary Film Director and Music Lover* • *Tommy: Ken Russell: The Who: Pocket Movie Guide* • *Women In Love: Ken Russell: D.H. Lawrence: Pocket Movie Guide* • *The Devils: Ken Russell: Pocket Movie Guide* • *Walerian Borowczyk: Cinema of Erotic Dreams* • *The Beast: Pocket Movie Guide* • *The Lord of the Rings Movies* • *The Fellowship of the Ring: Pocket Movie Guide* • *The Two Towers: Pocket Movie Guide* • *The Return of the King: Pocket Movie Guide* • *Jean-Luc Godard: The Passion of Cinema* • *The Sacred Cinema of Andrei Tarkovsky* • *Andrei Tarkovsky: Pocket Guide.*

'It's amazing for me to see my work treated with such passion and respect. There is nothing resembling it in the U.S. in relation to my work.'
(Andrea Dworkin)

'This model monograph – it is an exemplary job, and I'm very proud that he has accorded me a couple of mentions... The subject matter of his book is beautifully organised and dead on beam.'
(Lawrence Durrell, on *The Light Eternal: A Study of J.M.W. Turner*)

'Jeremy Robinson's poetry is certainly jammed with ideas, and I find it very interesting for that reason. It's certainly a strong imprint of his personality.'
(Colin Wilson)

'*Sex-Magic-Poetry-Cornwall* is a very rich essay... It is a very good piece... vastly stimulating and insightful.'
(Peter Redgrove)

ARTS, PAINTING, SCULPTURE

web: www.crmoon.com • e-mail: cresmopub@yahoo.co.uk

The Art of Andy Goldsworthy
Andy Goldsworthy: Touching Nature
Andy Goldsworthy in Close-Up
Andy Goldsworthy: Pocket Guide
Andy Goldsworthy In America
Land Art: A Complete Guide
The Art of Richard Long
Richard Long: Pocket Guide
Land Art In Great Britain
Land Art in Close-Up
Land Art In the U.S.A.
Land Art: Pocket Guide
Installation Art in Close-Up
Minimal Art and Artists In the 1960s and After
Colourfield Painting
Land Art DVD, TV documentary
Andy Goldsworthy DVD, TV documentary
The Erotic Object: Sexuality in Sculpture From Prehistory to the Present Day
Sex in Art: Pornography and Pleasure in Painting and Sculpture
Postwar Art
Sacred Gardens: The Garden in Myth, Religion and Art
Glorification: Religious Abstraction in Renaissance and 20th Century Art
Early Netherlandish Painting
Jasper Johns
Brice MardenLeonardo da Vinci
Piero della Francesca
Giovanni Bellini
Fra Angelico: Art and Religion in the Renaissance
Mark Rothko: The Art of Transcendence
Frank Stella: American Abstract Artist
Alison Wilding: The Embrace of Sculpture
Vincent van Gogh: Visionary Landscapes
Eric Gill: Nuptials of God
Constantin Brancusi: Sculpting the Essence of Things
Max Beckmann
Gustave Moreau
Caravaggio
Egon Schiele: Sex and Death In Purple Stockings
Delizioso Fotografico Fervore: Works In Process 1
Sacro Cuore: Works In Process 2
The Light Eternal: J.M.W. Turner
The Madonna Glorified: Karen Arthurs

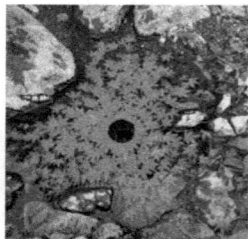

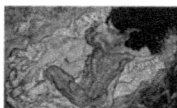

LITERATURE

J.R.R. Tolkien: The Books, The Films, The Whole Cultural Phenomenon
J.R.R. Tolkien: Pocket Guide
Beauties, Beasts and Enchantment: Classic French Fairy Tales
Tolkien's Heroic Quest
Brothers Grimm: German Popular Stories
Sexing Hardy: Thomas Hardy and Feminism
Thomas Hardy's *Tess of the d'Urbervilles*
Thomas Hardy's *Jude the Obscure*
Thomas Hardy: The Tragic Novels
Love and Tragedy: Thomas Hardy
The Poetry of Landscape in Hardy
Wessex Revisited: Thomas Hardy and John Cowper Powys
Wolfgang Iser: Essays and Interviews
Petrarch, Dante and the Troubadours
Maurice Sendak and the Art of Children's Book Illustration
Andrea Dworkin
Cixous, Irigaray, Kristeva: The *Jouissance* of French Feminism
Julia Kristeva: Art, Love, Melancholy, Philosophy, Semiotics and Psychoanalysis
Hélene Cixous I Love You: The *Jouissance* of Writing
Luce Irigaray: Lips, Kissing, and the Politics of Sexual Difference
Peter Redgrove: Here Comes the Flood
Peter Redgrove: Sex-Magic-Poetry-Cornwall
Lawrence Durrell: Between Love and Death, East and West
Love, Culture & Poetry: Lawrence Durrell
Cavafy: Anatomy of a Soul
German Romantic Poetry: Goethe, Novalis, Heine, Hölderlin
Novalis: *Hymns To the Night*
Feminism and Shakespeare
Shakespeare: *The Sonnets*
Shakespeare: Love, Poetry & Magic
The Passion of D.H. Lawrence
D.H. Lawrence: Symbolic Landscapes
D.H. Lawrence: Infinite Sensual Violence
The Ecstasies of John Cowper Powys
Sensualism and Mythology: The Wessex Novels of John Cowper Powys
Amorous Life: John Cowper Powys (H.W. Fawkner)
Postmodern Powys: New Essays on John Cowper Powys (Joe Boulter)
Rethinking Powys: Critical Essays on John Cowper Powys
Paul Bowles & Bernardo Bertolucci
Rainer Maria Rilke
Joseph Conrad: *Heart of Darkness*
In the Dim Void: Samuel Beckett
Samuel Beckett Goes into the Silence
André Gide: Fiction and Fervour
Jackie Collins and the Blockbuster Novel
Blinded By Her Light: The Love-Poetry of Robert Graves

POETRY

Ursula Le Guin: *Walking In Cornwall*
Peter Redgrove: Here Comes The Flood
Peter Redgrove: Sex-Magic-Poetry-Cornwall
Dante: Selections From the *Vita Nuova*
Petrarch, Dante and the Troubadours
William Shakespeare: *The Sonnets*
William Shakespeare: Complete Poems
Blinded By Her Light: The Love-Poetry of Robert Graves
Emily Dickinson: Selected Poems
Emily Brontë: Poems
Thomas Hardy: Selected Poems
Percy Bysshe Shelley: Poems
John Keats: Selected Poems
John Keats: Poems of 1820
D.H. Lawrence: Selected Poems
Edmund Spenser: Poems
Edmund Spenser: *Amoretti*
John Donne: Poems
Henry Vaughan: Poems
Sir Thomas Wyatt: Poems
Robert Herrick: Selected Poems
Rilke: Space, Essence and Angels in the Poetry of Rainer Maria Rilke
Rainer Maria Rilke: Selected Poems
Friedrich Hölderlin: Selected Poems
Arseny Tarkovsky: Selected Poems
Paul Verlaine: Selected Poems
Novalis: *Hymns To the Night*
Arthur Rimbaud: Selected Poems
Arthur Rimbaud: *A Season in Hell*
Arthur Rimbaud and the Magic of Poetry
D.J. Enright: By-Blows
Jeremy Reed: *Brigitte's Blue Heart*
Jeremy Reed: *Claudia Schiffer's Red Shoes*
Gorgeous Little Orpheus
Radiance: New Poems
Crescent Moon Book of Nature Poetry
Crescent Moon Book of Love Poetry
Crescent Moon Book of Mystical Poetry
Crescent Moon Book of Elizabethan Love Poetry
Crescent Moon Book of Metaphysical Poetry
Crescent Moon Book of Romantic Poetry
Pagan America: New American Poetry

MEDIA, CINEMA, FEMINISM and CULTURAL STUDIES

J.R.R. Tolkien: The Books, The Films, The Whole Cultural Phenomenon
J.R.R. Tolkien: Pocket Guide
The *Lord of the Rings* Movies: Pocket Guide
The Ghost Dance: The Origins of Religion
The Cinema of Hayao Miyazaki
Hayao Miyazaki: *Princess Mononoke*: Pocket Movie Guide
Hayao Miyazaki: *Spirited Away*: Pocket Movie Guide
The Peyote Cult
HomeGround: The Kate Bush Anthology
Tim Burton : Hallowe'en For Hollywood
Ken Russell
Cixous, Irigaray, Kristeva: The *Jouissance* of French Feminism
Julia Kristeva: Art, Love, Melancholy, Philosophy, Semiotics and Psychoanalysis
Luce Irigaray: Lips, Kissing, and the Politics of Sexual Difference
Hélene Cixous I Love You: The *Jouissance* of Writing
Andrea Dworkin
'Cosmo Woman': The World of Women's Magazines
Women in Pop Music
Discovering the Goddess (Geoffrey Ashe)
The Poetry of Cinema
The Sacred Cinema of Andrei Tarkovsky
Andrei Tarkovsky: Pocket Guide
Andrei Tarkovsky: *Mirror*: Pocket Movie Guide
Walerian Borowczyk: Cinema of Erotic Dreams
Jean-Luc Godard: The Passion of Cinema
Jean-Luc Godard: Pocket Guide
John Hughes and Eighties Cinema
Ferris Buller's Day Off: Pocket Movie Guide
The Cinema of Richard Linklater
Liv Tyler: Star In Ascendance
Blade Runner and the Films of Philip K. Dick
Paul Bowles and Bernardo Bertolucci
Media Hell: Radio, TV and the Press
Detonation Britain: Nuclear War in the UK
Feminism and Shakespeare
Wild Zones: Pornography, Art and Feminism
Sex in Art: Pornography and Pleasure in Painting and Sculpture
Sexing Hardy: Thomas Hardy and Feminism

*The Light Eternal is a model monograph, an exemplary job. The subject matter of the book is
beautifully organised and dead on beam.* (Lawrence Durrell)
It is amazing for me to see my work treated with such passion and respect. (Andrea Dworkin)
Sex-Magic-Poetry-Cornwall is a very rich essay... It is like a brightly-lighted box. (Peter Redgrove)

CRESCENT MOON PUBLISHING P.O. Box 1312, Maidstone, Kent, ME14 5XU, Great Britain
0044-1622-729593 cresmopub@yahoo.co.uk www.crmoon.com

www.ingramcontent.com/pod-product-compliance
Lightning Source LLC
Chambersburg PA
CBHW062359090426
42740CB00010B/1332